How Vocabulary is Learned

Published in this series
Oxford Handbooks for Language Teachers

How Vocabulary is Learned

Stuart Webb and Paul Nation

OXFORD
UNIVERSITY PRESS

OXFORD
UNIVERSITY PRESS

ACKNOWLEDGEMENTS

The authors and publisher are grateful to those who have given permission to reproduce the following extracts and adaptations of copyright material: p.17 excerpts from A New Academic Wordlist by Averil Coxhead, *TESOL Quarterly*, Vol. 34, No. 2, Appendix A, Summer 2000, John Wiley & Sons Inc. © TESOL International Association, reprinted by permission. p.18 excerpt from 'Animals, values and tourism – structural shifts in UK dolphin tourism provision' by Peter Hughes, *Tourism Management*, Vol. 22, Issue 4, August 2001, pp.321–329, Copyright (2001), reprinted by permission of Elsevier. p.23 from 'A Phrasal Expressions List' by Martinez, R. and Schmitt, N. from *Applied Linguistics*, 2012, Vol. 33 (3): 299–320, reprinted by permission of Oxford University Press and the authors. p.46 table from 'How Large Can a Receptive Vocabulary Be?' by Robin Goulden, Paul Nation and John Read, from *Applied Linguistics*, 1990, Vol. 11 (4): 341–363, reprinted by permission of Oxford University Press, John Read and Paul Nation. p.50 excerpt from 'Learning Words from Context' by William E. Nagy, Patricia A. Herman, Richard C. Anderson, p. David Pearson, reprinted by permission of John Wiley & Sons Inc., from *Reading Research Quarterly*, Vol. 20 (2), 1985, permission conveyed through Copyright Clearance Center, Inc. p.91 Table 5.1 'Amount of reading input and time needed to learn each of the most frequent 9,000 word families' adapted from 'How much input do you need to learn the most frequent 9,000 words?' by Paul Nation, Victoria University of Wellington, in *Reading in a Foreign Language*, October 2014, Vol. 26, (2), reprinted by permission. p.106 adapted from Cambridge Applied Linguistics: *Learning Vocabulary in Another Language* by I. S. P. Nation, © Cambridge University Press 2001. p.146 adapted from the Project Gutenberg version of Sir Arthur Conan Doyle's *The Adventures of Sherlock Holmes*, by Sonia Millett, reprinted by permission of Sonia Millett. p.156 excerpt 'Extensive reading' adapted from 'Top Ten Principles for Teaching Extensive Reading' by Richard Day and Julian Bamford, in *Reading in a Foreign Language*, Vol. 14, (2), October 2002, reprinted by permission. p.168 adapted from Wei, Z. 'Does teaching mnemonics for vocabulary learning make a difference? Putting the keyword method and the word part technique to the test' from *Language Teaching Research*, Vol. 19 (1), pp.43–69, Copyright © 2014 by the Author, reprinted by permission of SAGE Publications, Ltd. p.170 excerpt from Johannsen, Milner, and Chase, *World English 3* with Student CD-ROM (US), 1E. © 2010 Heinle/ELT, a part of Cengage Learning, Inc., reprinted by permission, www.cengage.com/permissions. p.172 screenshot from *Oxford Advanced Learner's Dictionary*, http://www.oxfordlearnersdictionaries.com/definition/english/, reproduced by permission of Oxford University Press. p.204 screenshot from the *Picture Vocabulary Size Test*, reproduced by permission of Paul Nation and Laurence Anthony. pp.205–7 excerpts from 'Diagnostic tests of English vocabulary learning proficiency: guessing from context and knowledge of word parts' by Yosuke Sasao, 2013, Victoria University of Wellington, reprinted by permission. pp.212–13 screenshots of concordances for the keywords 'effect' and 'affect' in a one million word written section of the British National Corpus using the online concordance at Compleat Lexical Tutor (www.lextutor.ca), reproduced by permission of the Compleat Lexical Tutor. pp.214–15 excerpt from L. C. Smith and N. N. Mare, *Reading for Today 3: Issues for Today* (4th ed.), © 2011, 2004, 1995 Heinle/ELT, a part of Cengage Learning, Inc., reprinted by permission, www.cengage.com/permissions. p.236 table adapted from *Researching and Analyzing Vocabulary* by I. S. P. Nation and Stuart Webb, 2011, reprinted by permission of Cengage Learning SO, permission conveyed through Copyright Clearance Center, Inc. pp.245–50 Appendix 1: 'The Essential Word List' by T. N. Y. Dang and S. Webb from *Making and Using Word Lists for Language Learning and Testing* by I. S. P. Nation (2016), © John Benjamins, reprinted by permission of John Benjamins Publishing Co. pp.251–62 Appendix 2 from 'The updated Vocabulary Levels Test: Developing and validating two new forms of the VLT.' by Webb, S., Sasao, Y., & Ballance, O., reprinted by permission. pp.263–6 Appendix 3 adapted from 'The word part technique: A very useful vocabulary teaching technique' by Wei Zheng and Paul Nation, *Modern English Teacher*, Vol. 22, (1) reprinted by permission. pp.267–74 Appendix 4 adapted from 'The Word Part Levels Test' by Sasao, Y., and Webb, S., *Language Teaching Research*, Vol. 21 (1), SAGE Journals, reprinted by permission of SAGE Publications, Ltd.

For Liam, Owen, and Machiko – S.W.

CONTENTS

Contents

ACKNOWLEDGEMENTS

We have been fortunate to have witnessed first-hand how vocabulary is learned in a variety of places. These opportunities have provided the inspiration for this book. In particular, we are grateful to our colleagues and students at Victoria University of Wellington, Temple University Japan, Koran Women's Junior College, and the University of Western Ontario who have helped to motivate and improve our studies of vocabulary.

There is a large community of researchers who investigate vocabulary that have also had an impact on what we have written. We are grateful for the work of Michael West and Earl Stevick, who were pioneers in the field, and Batia Laufer, Paul Meara, John Read, Jan Hulstijn, William Nagy, Michael Graves, Frank Boers, Norbert Schmitt, and Tom Cobb, whose research has helped to shape the way we think about teaching and learning vocabulary. We are also grateful to Thi Ngoc Yen Dang, Yosuke Sasao, Oliver Ballance, and Zheng Wei for allowing us to include some of their work in the appendices.

At Oxford University Press, we wish to thank Nick Ellis for his early encouragement, Kate Chomacki for her careful editing, and Sophie Rogers, Julia Bell, Andrew Dilger, and Sarah Finch for their work in guiding us through this project.

INTRODUCTION

There is a long history of research on teaching and learning vocabulary, with a large proportion of this research conducted in recent years. According to one estimate, about 30% of research on vocabulary in the last 100 years has been carried out since 2001 (Nation, 2013). With so much research on vocabulary learning, we might expect widespread agreement on how vocabulary should be taught and learned. Research findings have certainly influenced vocabulary learning. However, there are many approaches to learning words, a great deal of variation in how vocabulary is presented in materials, and large differences in the lexical development of learners. This suggests a lack of clarity on how vocabulary might best be learned.

Although language teachers and learners often place considerable emphasis on vocabulary learning, there is relatively little published material available to guide them towards designing an effective vocabulary learning programme. This may be due in part to the fact that there is still research to be done. However, we have also found that the answers to some important questions at the heart of this topic have not made their way from research to the classroom. This book aims to address some of these key questions.

ACTIVITY   **Some key questions**

Can you answer these questions about vocabulary learning? Write brief responses for each question.

1   What is the teacher's role?

2   What is the student's role?

3   Why do some students make greater progress than others?

4   How much classroom time should be spent teaching vocabulary?

5   How many words should students learn at a time, and how often?

6   How much vocabulary should students learn per year?

7   What is the best way to group vocabulary for learning?

8   How should teachers select vocabulary activities?

9   When is meaning-focused input appropriate inside the classroom?

10   Is there value in language-focused learning?

11   Is it useful to provide students with the L1 translations of unknown words?

12   To what extent are words which are taught by teachers ever really known by students?

Each of these questions will be discussed within this book, and revisited and answered in detail in Chapter 10.

The central aim of this book is to introduce readers to the major ideas behind the teaching and learning of vocabulary, with a practical focus on using vocabulary learning techniques and designing a programme. The information in the book is strongly research-based. It does not promote any particular language teaching approach; rather, it stresses the need to balance the learning opportunities in a programme. We describe the conditions that are needed for vocabulary learning to occur, suggest how various activities can best be used and adapted to optimize vocabulary learning, and highlight a range of useful resources. After reading the book, teachers should be familiar with the major ideas and principles that relate to the teaching and learning of vocabulary, be able to evaluate a range of vocabulary-focused activities, and be ready to design a balanced vocabulary learning programme.

The book begins with a chapter looking at the value of different words for learning. This is central to answering the question of which words should be learned. Chapter 2 focuses on what is involved in learning words. This is usually a gradual process whereby information about a word's form, meaning, and use is gained through encountering it again and again. We highlight the fact that there is much to learn about each word.

Chapters 3 to 5 examine the different ways in which vocabulary tends to be learned. In Chapter 3, we look at how many words are generally learned by first language (L1) and second language (L2) learners, and consider the difference between **incidental learning**, which is how words are typically learned in the L1, and **deliberate learning**. In Chapter 4, we turn our attention to the complex conditions that contribute to vocabulary development. Building on the two preceding chapters, Chapter 5 provides an overview of a wide range of important and popular vocabulary activities, covering the four skills of listening, speaking, reading, and writing.

Chapters 6 to 10 examine practical aspects of teaching and learning vocabulary. In Chapter 6, we look at how vocabulary learning might be affected by the context in which it is learned. We examine how learning vocabulary may be different in the second and foreign language learning contexts, and how the proficiency or age of students affects teaching and learning. We also discuss how the number of students might influence how words are learned in the classroom. In Chapter 7, we outline the need for students to learn vocabulary on their own outside the classroom, and provide suggestions on how teachers can guide students towards becoming effective and efficient learners of vocabulary. The main focus of this chapter is on key strategies that should be taught to help learners maximize their lexical development.

Chapter 8 draws on much that has been discussed earlier in the book and applies it to the development of a vocabulary learning programme. At the heart of this chapter is the concept of creating a balanced programme for learning words on the basis of the **principle of the four strands**: **meaning-focused input**, **meaning-focused output**, **language-focused learning**, and **fluency development**. In Chapter 9, we look at some of the different resources that can be used for vocabulary learning; we highlight the research that supports their use, and provide guidelines on how different types of resource might be selected and used. The final chapter recaps the main topics addressed in the book by answering questions that are often asked about how vocabulary is learned.

Each chapter includes a number of activities to help readers evaluate their understanding of the discussion, and keys to these activities are provided at the end of the chapter where appropriate. We also round off the discussion in each chapter with several questions for reflection, followed by a list of suggestions for further reading for those who are interested in exploring the topic further.

At the back of the book, we have included four appendices of useful resources for teaching and learning vocabulary that have been developed in recent research. Appendix 1 presents a list of essential words for beginner-level students; Appendix 2 is a recent version of a widely used vocabulary test; Appendix 3 consists of a list of useful word stems; and Appendix 4 is the intermediate level of a test designed to measure knowledge of affixes. These are followed by a Glossary for any terms (in bold) which may be unfamiliar or have a specific meaning or significance in the field of vocabulary acquisition. The Website references section includes links to online resources mentioned in the book, and the Bibliography provides full details of referenced works.

There is also a companion website with additional resources you can use to engage further with the topics covered in this book. The website can be accessed at www.oup.com/elt/teacher/hvil.

1 WHICH WORDS SHOULD BE LEARNED?

Introduction

Words are the building blocks of language. They are central to listening, speaking, reading, and writing, and are therefore an essential component of almost every aspect of our lives. If we cannot produce the words that are needed to convey our intended meaning, we may not be able to make ourselves understood. Similarly, if we do not know some of the words that we encounter, then we may be unable to understand what we hear or read. Moreover, developing lexical knowledge—that is, the number of different words that we know and how well we know these words—provides the necessary foundation for learning other aspects of language, such as **pragmatics**, **syntax**, **morphology**, and **phonology** (Biber & Conrad, 2001). All of these play an important role in first language (L1) and second language (L2) learning, and the extent to which students know words is highly correlated with their grades (Laufer & Goldstein, 2004). Therefore, when teaching and learning vocabulary in a second language, a key question is: which words should be learned? In this chapter, we look at the importance of vocabulary, how frequency affects the value of words, how different types of words have been classified, and how we might measure knowledge of these different categories of words. By focusing on learning the words with the greatest value, both vocabulary and language learning may become more efficient.

Importance of learning vocabulary

The importance of learning vocabulary is revealed in many ways. Soon after we are born, we begin to distinguish between the words spoken around us, and eventually develop the ability to produce these words ourselves. The books we read as children are typically designed to promote vocabulary learning; pictures are provided to illustrate the meaning of key **content words**; and the forms of words are emphasized to help us learn their spellings. Dictionaries are considered to be an essential resource that can be used to increase knowledge of vocabulary that we encounter, in both our first and other languages. In situations where another language may be needed, there are books with lists of essential words and phrases, or travel guidebooks that include lists of key words. This focus on developing vocabulary knowledge emphasizes the fact that words are viewed as being key to communication.

In all stages of our education, vocabulary is central to learning content. Useful words are purposefully introduced by teachers, and unknown words are often taught as they are encountered. As each new topic is introduced, key vocabulary is carefully explained to facilitate comprehension of content. The spelling and pronunciation of words might be modelled, their meaning explained with definitions, diagrams, and translations, and examples given to illustrate the ways in which they can be used. Common exercises such as word searches and crossword puzzles help to familiarize learners with the forms of words. Multiple-choice and matching exercises are often used to strengthen knowledge of the meanings of words, and writing and speaking tasks are used to develop the ability to use words correctly. The value that learners place on vocabulary can be seen in their notes, with new words often being copied down as they are taught and encountered.

Perhaps no aspect of language learning is as satisfying as vocabulary learning. Over a short period of time, it can be difficult for learners to see the degree to which they have improved in their use of different language skills, or the extent to which their knowledge of grammar has increased. However, the quantifiable nature of vocabulary learning can make the progress of lexical development relatively clear. Learners may be able to list and count the words that they have recently learned, and this can motivate further learning.

Relative value of words

Different words have different values for learners; these values are typically indicated by their frequency in the language. For example, it is much more useful to know 'find', 'flower', and 'food' than it is to know 'fluctuate', 'foam', and 'fragrant'; and all of these words have greater value to learners than 'filch', 'flume', and 'frump'. More frequent words tend to have greater value than less frequent words, because they are more likely to be needed for communication.

Words have been classified according to their frequency in different types of discourse. The most commonly used vocabulary categories are **high-frequency** and **low-frequency**. The terms **technical vocabulary** and **academic vocabulary** refer to words that are more frequent within specific discourse types. These categories are useful because they provide some indication of which words are important to learn. High-frequency words are encountered regularly in all forms of speech and writing, so not knowing these words can lead to a lack of understanding and difficulty in communicating. For example, 'horse' – 'steed' and 'house' – 'dwelling' are synonymous word pairs made up of one high-frequency word and one low-frequency word. Although the words in each pair convey similar meanings, the high-frequency words 'horse' and 'house' are of much greater value, because these words will be encountered and needed for communication much more often than the lower-frequency words 'steed' and 'dwelling'.

If we look at words according to their frequency in English, it is easy to see how the relative value of words changes. When assessing frequency, we often use the concept of **word families**. A word family consists of a **headword** (for example, 'assume'), its **inflections** ('assumes', 'assumed', 'assuming'), and its **derivations** ('unassuming', 'unassumingly'). Table 1.1 shows words at five different levels of frequency. The words in the first column are from the 1,000 most frequent word families in English, and the words in the last column are from the 20th 1,000 most frequent word families (that is, the 19,001–20,000 most frequent words). We can see that the words in the first column, at the highest frequency level, are extremely familiar. Words at this level occur with such high frequency that a lack of knowledge of them is likely to inhibit comprehension and the ability to communicate effectively. In contrast, words in the last two columns, from the tenth and 20th frequency levels, are encountered and used less often, and are less likely to be known even to native speakers of English.

1st 1,000	2nd 1,000	5th 1,000	10th 1,000	20th 1,000
a	accent	abbey	abet	abaya
baby	background	badge	baboon	binnacle
cake	cable	calf	cacophony	chiastic
dad	damage	dairy	dandelion	dactyl

Table 1.1 Words at different frequency levels in Nation's British National Corpus/ Corpus of Contemporary American English (BNC/COCA) word lists (Nation, 2012a)

Just how important it is to learn high-frequency words is underlined here by the use of **corpora**. The **corpus** in this case represents the spoken language that is found in US and British television programmes. Table 1.2 shows the percentage of vocabulary that is found at each of five BNC/COCA word frequency levels in a corpus of 88 television programmes. The differences between the percentages indicate the relative value of knowing vocabulary at each level.

Frequency level	Percentage of words %
1st 1,000	85.35
2nd 1,000	4.12
5th 1,000	0.59
10th 1,000	0.11
20th 1,000	0.01

Table 1.2 The percentage of words at different frequency levels in a corpus of television programmes

What is clearly evident here is the importance of learning the 1,000 most frequent words. Knowing these words would allow learners to understand just over 85% of the vocabulary in these television programmes. This is why researchers have long advocated learning words according to their frequency (West, 1953; Nation, 1990, 2001, 2013a). In contrast, knowing the second 1,000 most frequent words would allow learners to know just over a further 4% of the words in the television programmes. Learning the second 1,000 most frequent words is still important, because knowing 4% more of the vocabulary that is encountered will have a positive impact on comprehension. However, in this particular comparison, there is clearly far greater value for learners in knowing the 1,000 highest-frequency words.

The change in the frequency of words is explained by **Zipf's law** (1949), named after the psycholinguist George Kingsley Zipf, which reveals in statistical terms that, if we rank words according to their use, there is a patterned decline in the frequency of items. Zipf found that there are a small number of very frequent words and a very large number of infrequent words. This means that if we look at the vocabulary in any text, the majority of words will occur only once or twice. There will be a few words that occur many times in a text, but most of these will be function words such as articles, conjunctions, auxiliary words, etc. Table 1.2 shows the diminishing value of knowing words at the first, second, fifth, tenth, and 20th 1,000 word frequency levels. At the fifth 1,000 word frequency level, the words represent less than 1% of the words in the television programmes; and knowing the 20th 1,000 most frequent words represents only 0.01% of the vocabulary. Because the relative value of words diminishes quickly, there is not a great deal of difference between the values of words at the lower-frequency levels. For example, the difference in the proportion of words found in the television programmes from the fifth and tenth 1,000 word frequency levels was only 0.48%. All words from 4,001 up to 9,000 are important, because they are encountered with sufficient frequency that they can support comprehension. Nevertheless, it is worth recognizing that within these levels—after the third 1,000 word frequency level, perhaps—there may be little practical value in prioritizing words from one level over those in another, as the difference in value between them will be so insignificant.

In terms of L2 learning, research shows that L2 words tend to be learned according to their frequency (Schmitt, Schmitt, & Clapham, 2001; Webb & Chang, 2012a). So learners of **English as a Second Language** (ESL) tend to know a greater proportion of words at the first 1,000 word frequency level than those at the second 1,000 word frequency level; and they know more words at the second 1,000 word frequency level than those at the third 1,000 word frequency level, and so on. This is intuitively logical, because we are more likely to learn the words that we encounter most often. However, the effects of frequency are less clear in the **English as a Foreign Language** (EFL) context, because L2 input is often limited. This highlights the need to carefully consider the context of learning when examining the relative value of words. (See Chapter 6 for an in-depth discussion of this point.)

ACTIVITY 1.1   Assessing word frequency

Look at the list of 15 words from five frequency levels in the BNC/COCA word lists (2012a). Rank the words according to their frequency in English by putting them in the correct column of the chart. Then check your answers at the end of the chapter.

| abate   abyss   accept   achieve   adamant   adore   affable   age |
| airline   allergy   almost   ambiance   ample   anoint   appropriate |

Word frequency levels				
1st 1,000	3rd 1,000	5th 1,000	7th 1,000	9th 1,000

Word frequency lists

As we mentioned earlier in this chapter, the categories 'high-frequency', 'low-frequency', 'technical', and 'academic' have been used to label words in different discourse types (Nation, 1990, 2001, 2008) and are now widely accepted in the literature on vocabulary. We will now look at each of the categories in more detail.

High-frequency words

There is a long history of research aimed at identifying the most frequent English words (Carroll, Davies, & Richman, 1971; Francis & Kučera, 1982; Leech, Rayson, & Wilson, 2001; Swenson & West, 1934; Thorndike & Lorge, 1944; West, 1953). Although frequency is not the only criterion for identifying the words that are most valuable to learn (the needs and motivation of the learner are also significant), it is perhaps the most important, for the reasons outlined so far in this chapter.

The best-known study of high-frequency words is Michael West's **General Service List** (GSL) (1953). West developed a **word list** of approximately 2,000 word families, primarily by counting the occurrences of each word in a five-million-word corpus of written texts. Although West was not the first to make a **frequency list** in this manner, his was the most detailed and enduring. His achievement is also particularly noteworthy, since it was done without the aid of computers. Making lists before the advent of computer technology involved listing every word in the corpus and counting how many times each word was found, then ranking the words according to their frequency. His aim as an English language teacher and researcher was to make a list of the words that would be most useful to learners, so various other criteria such as 'ease of learning' and 'necessity' were also used to select items. Studies have since shown that these 2,000 word families account for 71.5–89.6% of the vocabulary in a wide range of discourse types (Brezina & Gablasova, 2015; Coxhead & Hirsh, 2007; Hyland & Tse, 2007; Nation & Hwang, 1995; Nation, 2004a). Because of the high degree of **lexical coverage** that the GSL provides, it has been widely viewed as a starting point for vocabulary learning. However, its relevance has inevitably declined with age. Based on vocabulary found in texts from the 1930s, it includes words like 'carriage', 'shilling', and 'telegraph', which are far less frequent today, and omits words that have become more frequent, such as 'computer', 'internet', and 'television'.

Three notable lists (or sets of lists) of high-frequency vocabulary have been developed in recent years. The first is the **British National Corpus** (BNC) lists (Nation, 2006), which might best be described as being representative of vocabulary used primarily in formal written texts in the UK. The second is the British National Corpus/Corpus of Contemporary American English (BNC/COCA) lists (Nation, 2012a), which are representative of the vocabulary used in both spoken and written English in the UK and the USA. The third is the **new-General Service List** (new-GSL) (Brezina and Gablasova, 2015). This list was designed to include all of the most frequent English words, although it is perhaps more representative of written English than spoken English due to the corpora from which it was derived.

Each of these lists accounts for a greater proportion of the English language than the GSL, not least because they include vocabulary that is more relevant to the 21st century and are therefore of greater value to learners today (Dang & Webb, 2016a). Although there is a considerable degree of overlap between the three lists, there is also a reasonable amount of variation. Of these lists, Thi Ngoc Yen Dang and Stuart Webb (2016a) found that the 2,000 most frequent words from the BNC/COCA lists (Nation, 2012a) appeared to account for the greatest proportion of the English language. This suggests that if one of the three were to be used as a whole, that one would provide the greatest value to learners. However, they also found that each of the lists included items that perhaps did not deserve to be considered high frequency. Moreover, when the items in the lists were ranked according to their frequency in nine corpora of spoken English and nine corpora of written English, it was found that the new-GSL included the greatest number of very frequent items. Thus, if only a portion of a list were to be used, then the new-GSL might have the greatest value.

How many items should be included in a list of high-frequency words?

There has been some debate about the appropriate number of words to include in a high-frequency word list (Dang & Webb, 2016a, 2016b; Engels, 1968; Nation, 2001; Schmitt & Schmitt, 2014). Because the GSL was made up of 2,000 word families, subsequent lists have tended to include a similar number. The argument for this figure is based on the high degree of lexical coverage that 2,000 word families provides. Table 1.3 shows the percentage of lexical coverage provided by the 2,000 most frequent word families from the BNC lists in different types of discourse and text.

	novels	newspapers	conversation	television	films	lectures
% of 2,000 words	86.95–91.71	81.54–84.33	89.35	89.53	90.67	89.61

Table 1.3 Lexical coverage provided by the 2,000 most frequent word families in different types of discourse/text (adapted from Dang & Webb, 2014; Nation, 2006; Webb & Rodgers, 2009a, 2009b)

Norbert Schmitt and Diane Schmitt (2014) suggest that a more appropriate threshold for high-frequency vocabulary is 3,000 word families. They argue that knowing 3,000 word families would allow learners to understand 98% of the words in most graded reading materials, as well as 95% of the vocabulary used in spoken discourse. Importantly, on this point, research indicates that learners are likely to understand speech when 95% of the words used are known (van Zeeland & Schmitt, 2013). Similarly, they are likely to be able to comprehend written discourse when 98% of the words in a text are known (Hu & Nation, 2000; Schmitt, Jiang, & Grabe, 2011). Learning the 3,000 most frequent word families would therefore seem to have some very important pedagogical implications.

In contrast, L. K. Engels (1968) and Thi Ngoc Yen Dang and Stuart Webb (2016a) suggest that high-frequency vocabulary should be set at around 1,000 word families. Their argument for classifying a smaller number of words as high frequency is that beyond 1,000 word families, the relative value of knowing each additional set of 1,000 word families drops substantially; knowing the 1,000 most frequent word families allows you to understand approximately 65–85% of the vocabulary in spoken and written discourse, whereas knowing the second 1,000 most frequent word families typically allows you to understand 3–10% more of the words that you encounter. Dang and Webb also indicate that language learners often failed to learn all the word families in the GSL, suggesting therefore that the 2,000 word families target is perhaps not achievable for most learners.

Dang and Webb (2016b) examined the coverage provided by items in the four word lists discussed above, taking an approach that was somewhat different from that taken by earlier studies, in that they used **lemmas** and lemma headwords as the units of counting words, rather than word families. Lemmas are made up of a headword (for example, 'accept') and just its inflections ('accepts', 'accepted', 'accepting'), not its derivations ('acceptable', 'unacceptable', 'acceptance'). They suggested that lemma headwords are the most commonly used unit of counting both inside and outside the classroom, and that a word list aimed at beginners should focus on the practical significance of the unit of counting. They found that, by ranking the headwords from the four source lists according to their lexical coverage, they could create a list that accounted for a greater proportion of spoken and written language than any of the original lists. Dang and Webb found that the 800 most frequent lemmas was an appropriate cut-off point for a beginner-level word list; if learners knew only the 800 lemma headwords, they were likely to know 60% of the words they encountered, and this would increase to 75% if they also knew the inflections of these words.

Dang and Webb's research culminated in the **Essential Word List** (EWL)— see Appendix 1. This represents a practical vocabulary learning target that may be attained within two years of study. One of the key features of the EWL is that it differentiates between content words (for example, 'know', 'like', 'well', 'just'), of which there are 624 in the list, and function words (for example, 'the', 'and', 'of', 'to'), of which there are 176. The reason for differentiating between these two types of words is because they tend to be learned in different ways. Moreover, the content words are grouped into 50-word sets according to their frequency of occurrence so that teachers can more easily introduce them into their curriculum. After this stage, learning the 3,000 most frequent word families would be the next step in lexical development, because as Schmitt and Schmitt (2014) suggest, these items are key to comprehension of spoken and written discourse.

While there may be disagreement about how many words should be considered 'high frequency', there is no reason why teachers could not begin by using one word list with a more narrow focus, such as the EWL, then move on to using word lists which are broader in scope if students are ready for the challenge.

Multi-word combinations

All of the high-frequency lists mentioned above are made up of individual words. However, a large proportion of the English language consists of **multi-word combinations**. For example, Britt Erman and Beatrice Warren (2000) report that they constitute 52.3% of writing and 58.6% of speech. Similarly, Jimmie Hill (2001) suggests that as much as 70% of English is made up of **formulaic language**, with the number of multi-word combinations surpassing that of individual words. Because the frequency of a sequence of words can only be as high as the most frequent word in that sequence (in the COCA, for example, 'take place' is encountered 6,755 times, while 'take' and 'place' are encountered 383,046 and 250,949 times respectively), there are relatively few multi-word combinations that can be considered high frequency.

ACTIVITY 1.2   **Identifying the most frequent multi-word combinations**

Using your intuition, make a list of what you believe to be the 20 most frequent multi-word combinations. Then compare your ideas with the notes at the end of the chapter.

Two studies have examined the frequency of multi-word combinations. Ron Martinez and Norbert Schmitt (2012) found that 505 **phrasal expressions** had sufficient frequency to be included in the 5,000 most frequent word families in the BNC. Of these, 85 (including 'have got to', 'based on', 'each other', 'take place') fell within the 2,000 word frequency level, and another 32 (including 'have to', 'of course', 'at least', 'rather than') fell within the 1,000 word frequency level. Dongkwang Shin and Paul Nation (2008) examined the frequency of multi-word combinations in both the spoken and written sections of the BNC. They found that 84 items (including 'you know', 'a bit', 'come on') had sufficient frequency to be included within the 1,000 word frequency level, and 224 items met the frequency threshold to be included within the second 1,000 word frequency level. They also reported that the frequency of the multi-word combinations varied between spoken and written text; multi-word combinations were 50–100% more frequent in speech than in writing.

We typically learn high-frequency words in our first language incidentally, as we encounter them repeatedly in speech and writing. However, when we learn another language, we may need to deliberately learn most of these words. High-frequency words have the greatest value for language learning, so they deserve attention in the classroom. Knowledge of high-frequency words should then be expanded and strengthened during the language learning process, because they will be repeatedly encountered in input.

Low-frequency words

Any words that are not high-frequency are considered to be low-frequency. There are tens of thousands of low-frequency words in English, which means there is a considerable range in the levels of frequency within this category, with items such as 'alternate', 'ankle', and 'antique' (fourth 1,000 word frequency level) occurring far more often and consequently having much greater value than others which are very infrequent, such as 'anaerobe', 'anagnorisis', and 'anagogic' (24th 1,000 word frequency level). Native speakers of English typically learn between 15–20,000 word families (d'Anna, Zechmeister, & Hall, 1991; Goulden, Nation, & Read, 1990), so they would probably only recognize the latter examples as being low in frequency, because they tend to learn the former early on in their lexical development (while they may never learn the latter). The high frequency/ low frequency distinction is most appropriate for foreign language learners, who often make very little progress in lexical development, primarily due to their limited exposure to the L2. It should be noted that, although words tend to be learned according to their frequency of occurrence in the language, we do not focus exclusively on words from one category, so both high- and low-frequency words will be learned during the language learning process. Nevertheless, a relatively large proportion of high-frequency words are learned compared to low-frequency words.

Schmitt and Schmitt (2014) suggest breaking the low-frequency grouping into two categories: **mid-frequency** and low-frequency words:

- high-frequency = 1st 3,000 word families
- mid-frequency = 4th–9th 1,000 word families
- low-frequency = less frequent than the 9,000 most frequent word families.

The rationale behind this is that knowing the 9,000 most frequent word families (high- and mid-frequency) equates to sufficient vocabulary knowledge to understand speech and writing (Nation, 2006), so differentiating between the words before and after this point is useful. This again highlights the relative value of words; knowing the 9,000 most frequent word families tends to be more important for comprehension than knowing the tens of thousands of less frequent words. It also demonstrates the lexical challenges of learning a second language; a learning target of 9,000 word families requires an effective and efficient vocabulary learning programme and a great deal of contact with the target language.

Technical words

Low-frequency words may be relatively infrequent in the language as a whole, but they can be frequent within a specialized area. Words that are very frequent within a particular topic or discipline but less frequent outside that area are considered to be technical. For example, 'puck', 'rink', and 'arena' are much higher in frequency in discussions about ice hockey than they are in discussions about other topics. Similarly, 'adagio', 'allegro', and 'tremolo' are more common to discourse concerning classical music; and 'découpage', 'fresco', and 'palette' are more frequent in discussions of art. Technical words represent specialized knowledge that is essential to learning a particular topic; if you want to learn about psychology, engineering, or cooking, then you will need to learn the specialized vocabulary that is frequent within the literature on those subjects. We usually learn technical vocabulary as we learn about a topic. One reason for this is that language teachers often do not have the knowledge required to teach technical vocabulary. Many technical terms represent new meanings that are often unknown outside the specialist topic; language teachers might know a few of these terms, but there are likely to be many important words that are unknown, and looking at dictionary definitions is unlikely to provide sufficient background to adequately teach these words.

Most people recognize only low-frequency words as being technical in nature. However, research on technical vocabulary tends to include both high- and low-frequency technical words (Chung & Nation, 2003). For example, 'blood', 'bone', and 'skin' are high-frequency technical terms relating to medicine, and 'thorax', 'trachea', and 'vertebrae' are low-frequency technical terms from that discipline. All six of these words are considered important for studying medicine, but the higher-frequency items are more likely to be known in the initial stages of study.

The amount of technical vocabulary required can represent a considerable challenge to learning a subject. Betsy Quero (2015) analysed the vocabulary in a collection of introductory medical texts and found over 27,000 words that were technical in nature. Teresa Chung and Paul Nation (2003) classified 31.2% of the words in an anatomy text and 20.6% of the words in an applied linguistics text as technical terms. If there are 400 words on a page of a text, then this would represent 125 technical words per page in the former text and 82 per page in the latter. Although many of these words would be repeated within and between pages, if a student did not know any of the words, and needed to read 40 pages of a text, the lexical challenge of reading and understanding the text would be insurmountable.

Several lists of technical vocabulary have been developed in recent years. There are lists available for agriculture (Martinez, Beck, & Panza, 2009), applied linguistics (Vongpumivitch, Huang, & Chang, 2009), business (Konstantakis, 2007), chemistry (Valipouri & Nassaji, 2013), engineering (Hsu, 2014; Ward, 2009), medicine (Hsu, 2013; Quero, 2015; Wang, Liang, & Ge, 2008), nursing (Yang, 2015), pharmacology (Fraser, 2007), and science (Coxhead & Hirsh, 2007). Such lists are valuable resources for learning subjects because they provide a means of reducing the lexical burden of study. For example, if students can learn some of the medical vocabulary ahead of studying medicine, they may be able to focus more effort on learning other aspects of content.

Academic words

Words that are frequent across a wide range of academic disciplines and are infrequent in non-academic texts have been classified as academic vocabulary. We also call this **sub-technical** vocabulary. Technical words usually convey meanings that are central to understanding a topic, whereas academic words tend to be used to support the use of technical vocabulary (hence the term 'sub-technical'). Academic words pose challenges to learners because they are not well known, are typically not taught in content-based courses, and are less noticeable than technical vocabulary (Coxhead, 2000). Several lists of academic vocabulary have been created, and in most cases newer lists have improved on earlier lists (Campion & Elley, 1971; Coxhead, 2000; Gardner & Davies, 2014; Praninskas, 1972; Xue & Nation, 1984). Lists of academic words should not be learned before high-frequency words, because the larger proportion of language that the high-frequency words represent means that a lack of knowledge of these words will cause the most problems for language learners.

Academic word lists are a valuable resource for **English for Academic Purposes** (EAP) programmes, because they reveal the words that are useful for all those who plan to study in English-medium universities. Learning a list of frequent academic words may have a positive impact on the comprehension of academic discourse (lectures and academic texts) because, although many factors affect comprehension, vocabulary knowledge has been shown to have the greatest effect on whether or not a text will be understood (Laufer & Sim, 1985). Clearly, academic books and speech will be difficult to understand if many of the words that are used are unknown.

The best-known list of academic vocabulary is the **Academic Word List** (AWL) (Coxhead, 2000). This list is made up of 570 word families that were found to occur frequently over a range of academic disciplines. It is underpinned by the principle that the vocabulary included should be useful specifically for students preparing to study in English-medium universities, so the words in the GSL that were expected to be known by these students were not included in the AWL. Averil Coxhead found that the AWL accounted for about 10% of the words in academic written text and 1.4% of the words in non-academic text. Although 10% may seem an insignificant figure, it represents about 40 words on a page of academic text, which is substantial for a learner reading a text in L2. The word families in the AWL are ranked according to their range and frequency and put into ten alphabetical sub-lists, with the most frequent words included in the first sub-list and the least frequent words included in the tenth. This provides a useful order for learning the items: words in sub-list 1 should be focused on before those in sub-list 2, and so on. Table 1.4 shows the 60 headwords that make up the first sub-list of the AWL.

Sub-list 1					
analyse	constitute	establish	indicate	occur	role
approach	context	estimate	individual	percent	section
area	contract	evident	interpret	period	sector
assess	create	export	involve	policy	significant
assume	data	factor	issue	principle	similar
authority	define	finance	labour	proceed	source
available	derive	formula	legal	process	specific
benefit	distribute	function	legislate	require	structure
concept	economy	identify	major	research	theory
consist	environment	income	method	respond	vary

Table 1.4 The Academic Word List (AWL): sub-list 1: the 60 most frequent headwords (Coxhead, 2000)

The AWL has three limitations. First, it was developed around the GSL, which was published in 1953 and is, as noted above, now out of date. Tom Cobb (2010) found that a proportion of the words in the AWL would be classified as higher-frequency words using more recently developed word lists. This suggests that it would be useful to develop a newer list of academic vocabulary that excludes the latest high-frequency words. Second, there is some debate about whether the AWL adequately represents the academic vocabulary of a wide range of disciplines (Hyland & Tse, 2007). Third, Dang and Webb (2014) found that the AWL accounts for only 4% of the words used in academic spoken discourse. This suggests that it may also be useful to develop a word list that is specific to academic spoken discourse.

The **Academic Vocabulary List** (AVL) (Gardner & Davies, 2014) was developed as a possible successor to the AWL. It provides a comprehensive database of over 3,000 academic words that are ranked according to their frequency in academic discourse, making it a valuable resource of academic vocabulary. However, because it includes high-frequency words that are likely to be known to students preparing for academic study (for example, 'study', 'use', 'group', 'level', 'however') and is too big to be incorporated into a language course, its value might be as a resource for researchers rather than for teachers.

ACTIVITY 1.3   **Identifying academic and technical vocabulary**

Read the extract from a paper on tourism management. Circle any academic words and underline those that might be considered to be technical words in the field. Then check your answers at the end of the chapter.

> General concern for the environment within tourism practices does not guarantee that the rights and welfare of individual animals will be considered. Indeed, different philosophical positions: environmental ethics, animal welfare and animal rights would each have different implications if incorporated into tourism development. This paper reports on one case where the deliberate promotion of an animal rights perspective has brought about a structural transformation in tourism provision. In the UK, over the past ten years, there has been a complete shift away from viewing dolphins in captivity to viewing dolphins in the wild. This shift is illustrated with reference to the Morecambe Dolphin Campaign of 1989–1991, where animal rights activists brought about the closure of a dolphinarium through a combination of direct communication with tourists and through lobbying the licensing local authority. The different ethical issues associated with the UK's new wild dolphin watching infrastructure are illustrated with particular reference to the Moray Firth, Scotland. The importance of the tourism industry and tourism researchers recognising the significance of animals as individual actors is highlighted.

Materials extract 1.1 Hughes, P. (2001). Animals, values and tourism – structural shifts in UK dolphin tourism provision. Tourism Management, 22(4), 321–329.

Academic multi-word combinations

There are several lists of multi-word combinations that are more frequent in academic discourse than in other discourse types. When sequences of words do not conform to typical language patterns, there can be comprehension problems for readers and listeners, and this in turn can potentially lead to lower grades. Knowledge of the items in these should therefore improve comprehension, and may also help to reduce the number of unnatural expressions that might be used by language learners in their academic essays and presentations. Multi-word combinations is an umbrella term covering collocations and formulas.

Collocations

Kirsten Ackermann and Yu-Hua Chen (2013) developed the **Academic Collocations List** (ACL), which is made up of 2,468 adjective/noun, noun/noun, verb/noun, verb/adjective, verb/adverb, and adverb/verb **collocations** that are high in frequency across a range of academic disciplines (for example, 'brief overview', 'economic conditions', 'cast doubt', 'make explicit', 'differ significantly', 'adversely affect').

Formulas

Rita Simpson-Vlach and Nick Ellis (2010) created lists of three- to five-word formulas that are very frequent in academic written and spoken discourse. Examples of formulas found in academic speech are 'how many of you', 'nothing to do with', and 'one of these'. Examples of formulas commonly found in academic writing include 'it has been', 'none of these', and 'that is not'; and formulas common in both academic spoken and written discourse include 'is the case', 'is to be', and 'it can be'. Dilin Liu (2012) also developed a list of 228 multi-word combinations that are frequent across a range of academic disciplines and listed them according to their frequencies. Among those included in the highest-frequency band are 'such as', 'as well as', and 'suggest that'.

Measuring knowledge of words according to their frequency

At present, there are no standardized tests of technical vocabulary. However, there are tests that measure knowledge of high-frequency and academic words. The **Vocabulary Levels Test** (VLT) (Nation, 1983; Schmitt, Schmitt, & Clapham, 2001; Webb, Sasao, & Ballance, 2017) is perhaps the best-known and most widely used measure of vocabulary knowledge (Read, 2000). It measures knowledge of words at different frequency levels. The test was originally designed to measure knowledge of the 2,000, 3,000, 5,000, and 10,000 most frequent words, and academic words. The earlier versions of the tests were based on rather old frequency lists that are unlikely to reflect current language, and they did not measure the most important frequency level (the 1,000 most frequent words). In Stuart Webb, Yosuke Sasao, and Oliver Ballance's (2017) updated version of the test (see Appendix 2), there are five levels that measure knowledge of the 5,000 most frequent words (i.e. 1,000 words per level). In Norbert Schmitt, Diane Schmitt, and Caroline Clapham's version (2001), there is a level that allows teachers to measure knowledge of academic vocabulary included in the AWL.

How does the Vocabulary Levels Test work?

Questions
There are 30 questions for each level of the test. Students choose the correct word for each of the 30 definitions. It is not necessary to use all the levels with students. Instead, teachers can select the level or levels that are most appropriate. The most important level to measure is that of the 1,000 most frequent words, due to the relative importance of these words for language learning. Because learners often fail to master the high-frequency words (Webb & Chang, 2012a), in many contexts teachers may only need to administer the 1,000 and 2,000 word levels tests to their students.

Scoring
A score of 26 or higher out of 30 indicates that the vocabulary of a given level is relatively well known (Schmitt, Schmitt, & Clapham, 2001). It is useful to tell students their score for each level, rather than providing an overall score with the number of correct responses for the levels added together. The overall score is less useful because it may suggest that the high-frequency words are known, when in fact they are not. For example, consider the scores in Table 1.5.

	Level 1	Level 2	Level 3	Level 4	Level 5	TOTAL
Score	23/30	20/30	17/30	10/30	5/30	75/150

Table 1.5 Example scores in the Vocabulary Levels Test

Adding the scores for each level together may create the incorrect assumption that students know the high-frequency words because they have knowledge of 75/150 or approximately 2,500 out of the 5,000 most frequent words. However, the scores for each of the five levels indicate that none of these levels have been mastered and that teachers should focus on developing their students' knowledge of the 1,000 word frequency level because of its relative importance.

Teachers can also raise awareness of what the test scores represent, in order to provide learning targets and motivate progress. For example:

- if students achieve a score of 15/30 on the 1,000 word frequency level, this would indicate that they know about half of the 1,000 most frequent words. Explaining that knowing the 2,000 highest-frequency words should allow them to recognize 70–90% of English might motivate further study.
- knowing the 3,000 most frequent word families can enable students to recognize 95% of the words in most spoken discourse types and therefore have reasonable comprehension of conversations (van Zeeland & Schmitt, 2013), television programmes (Rodgers & Webb, 2011; Webb & Rodgers, 2009a), and films (Webb & Rodgers, 2009b).
- the 4,000 most frequent word families account for 95% of the words in academic lectures (Dang & Webb, 2014), so knowing these words can enable students to understand academic speech.
- the 8–9,000 most frequent word families account for 98% of the words in newspapers and novels, and reaching this level of vocabulary knowledge can enable students to understand written discourse (Nation, 2006).

A final note that the Vocabulary Levels Test should not be considered a test of vocabulary size. We will discuss tests of vocabulary size in more detail in Chapter 9.

Summary

Developing lexical knowledge is essential for improving language skills. Frequency information provides a useful indication of the relative value of words and the vocabulary that deserves attention in the classroom. As this chapter has highlighted, learning high-frequency vocabulary can contribute more to a learner's progress than learning lower-frequency vocabulary, because the most frequent words represent such a large proportion of the vocabulary that is encountered in both spoken and written discourse. Examining the frequency of words within a particular discourse type also helps us to identify the words that are most useful to learn if we intend to work within a specific area. There are lists of general, academic, and technical words, as well as lists of multi-word combinations, that are freely available as resources to support learning. Two particularly useful lists discussed in this chapter are the Essential Word List (Dang & Webb, 2016b), which represents 75% of English if the inflections are also known, and the Academic Word List (Coxhead, 2000), which represents 10% of the words used in academic discourse. It is also possible to measure students' knowledge of the 5,000 most frequent words using the Vocabulary Levels Test (Webb, Sasao, & Ballance, 2017).

Questions for reflection

1 Think about a specific class you teach or have taught. How do you choose the words that you teach to your students?

2 To what extent do you think the 2,000 most frequent word families are known by your students?

3 Which category of words (high-frequency, low-frequency, technical, academic) causes the most problems for your students?

Keys to activities

ACTIVITY 1.1   Assessing word frequency

It is relatively easy to differentiate between words that are very frequent and those that are less frequent. However, it can be quite challenging to differentiate between words in frequency levels which are not too far apart (Alderson, 2007). Here are the 15 words from the BNC/COCA lists (Nation, 2012a), grouped according to their five frequency levels.

Word frequency levels				
1st 1,000	3rd 1,000	5th 1,000	7th 1,000	9th 1,000
accept	achieve	adore	abate	abyss
age	appropriate	allergy	adamant	affable
almost	airline	ample	ambiance	anoint

ACTIVITY 1.2   Identifying the most frequent multi-word combinations

Teachers, native speakers of English, and advanced learners may be able to compile short lists of useful vocabulary based on their knowledge of the language. However, creating comprehensive word lists based on intuition is difficult. Here are the 50 most frequent phrasal expressions from Martinez and Schmitt's Phrasal Expressions List (Martinez & Schmitt, 2012).

1	have to	11	rather than	21	at all	31	in order to	41	due to
2	there is/are	12	so that	22	as if	32	have got (+ np)	42	fail to
3	such as	13	a little	23	used to (past)	33	have got to	43	each other
4	going to (future)	14	a bit (of)	24	was to	34	set up	44	in terms of
5	of course	15	as well as	25	not only	35	as to	45	no one
6	a few	16	in fact	26	those who	36	as well	46	pick up
7	at least	17	(be) likely to	27	deal with	37	based on	47	up to (maximum)
8	such a(n)	18	go on	28	lead to ('cause')	38	carry out	48	a single ('any')
9	I mean	19	is to	29	sort of	39	take place	49	no longer
10	a lot	20	a number of	30	the following	40	tend to	50	look for

Supplementary data adapted from Martinez & Schmitt (2012)

ACTIVITY 1.3   Identifying academic and technical vocabulary

Words from the Academic Word List (Coxhead, 2000) are in bold. The academic words are those that might occur in many different fields. Technical words for tourism management are underlined. These are more likely to occur within the specific field of tourism management, though it is important to remember that technical vocabulary can include high-frequency words as well as lower-frequency words; for example, 'closure', 'development', and 'practices' are common in English. There is currently no word list available for tourism management; if you disagree with any of our choices, think about the rationale for your different choice. Note that some words fall into both categories.

General concern for the **environment** within tourism practices does not guarantee that the rights and **welfare** of individual animals will be considered. Indeed, different **philosophical** positions: environmental **ethics**, animal **welfare** and animal rights would each have different **implications** if **incorporated** into tourism development. This paper reports on one case where the deliberate **promotion** of an animal rights **perspective** has brought about a **structural transformation** in tourism provision. In the UK, over the past ten years, there has been a complete **shift** away from viewing dolphins in captivity to viewing dolphins in the wild. This **shift** is **illustrated** with reference to the Morecambe Dolphin Campaign of 1989–1991, where animal rights activists brought about the <u>closure</u> of a dolphinarium through a combination of direct **communication** with <u>tourists</u> and through lobbying the **licensing** local **authority**. The different <u>ethical</u> **issues** associated with the UK's new <u>wild</u> dolphin-<u>watching</u> **infrastructure** are **illustrated** with particular reference to the Moray Firth, Scotland. The importance of the <u>tourism</u> <u>industry</u> and <u>tourism</u> **researchers** recognising the **significance** of animals as **individual** actors is **highlighted**.

Suggestions for further reading

Chung, T. M., & **Nation, I. S. P.** (2003). Technical vocabulary in specialized texts. *Reading in a Foreign Language, 15(2)*, 103–116.

This study shows how we might identify technical vocabulary in a text. Chung and Nation create a scale to help classify technical words. They also compare the proportion of technical words that are found in texts from different academic disciplines.

Coxhead, A. (2000). A new academic word list. *TESOL Quarterly, 34(2)*, 213–238.

This seminal study of academic vocabulary provides a useful approach to word list creation and introduces the Academic Word List, featuring 570 word families, which has become an important tool for preparing learners for study in English-medium universities.

Dang, T. N. Y., & **Webb, S.** (2016b) Making an essential word list for beginners. In I. S. P. Nation, *Making and using word lists for language learning and testing* (pp. 153–167, 188–195). Amsterdam: John Benjamins.

This study examines the relative value of items in four different high-frequency word lists. Dang and Webb challenge the assumption that lists of high-frequency vocabulary should include around 2,000 words. They introduce a list of 800 lemmas that accounts for 60% of the English language if only the headwords (for example, 'study') are known, and up to as much as 75% of spoken and written discourse if the inflections (for example, 'studies', 'studied', 'studying') are also known.

Schmitt, N., **Schmitt, D.**, & **Clapham, C.** (2001). Developing and exploring the behaviour of two new versions of the Vocabulary Levels Test. *Language Testing, 18(1)*, 55–88.

This important paper describes the process for updating the Vocabulary Levels Test (Nation, 1983). This Test has been one of the most important resources for language teachers, because it highlights the relative importance of learning high-frequency words.

2 LEARNING BURDEN

Introduction

The difficulty of learning a word in a foreign language can come from a variety of sources: the linguistic systems of the second language, the linguistic systems of the first language, the similarities between the learner's L1 and L2, the way in which the word is taught, and the learner's experience of the world. In this chapter, we look at what is involved in knowing a word and the difficulties faced in learning it. We consider what contributes the most weight to the **learning burden** of words, and how the burden can be reduced. We explain that, by understanding the various aspects of word knowledge and how to deal with them, teachers can make vocabulary learning much more efficient.

Defining the learning burden

The learning burden of a word is the amount of effort required to learn it (Swenson & West, 1934). In other words, measuring the learning burden of a word involves measuring the difficulty that learners will have in learning it. Research using **contrastive analysis**, which reached its peak in the 1960s, was in effect the study of the learning burden of words, though its focus was largely on comparing L1 and L2 grammatical features. The major goal of contrastive analysis was to work out which aspects of the L2 were likely to cause difficulty and would therefore need to be focused on in the learning process. In a classic article on the learning burden, Masanori Higa (1965) considered five categories of difficulty:

1 intrinsic difficulty
2 the interaction between previously learned words and new words
3 the interaction between words learned at the same time
4 the interaction between groups of words to be learned in sequence
5 the effect of repeated presentation.

In this chapter we touch on categories 1–3 from Higa's list, exploring categories 4 and 5 in Chapter 4.

Factors affecting difficulty

L1 versus L2

The learning burden of an L2 word depends primarily on how well it fits into the learner's existing systems of knowledge. In at least the early stages of learning another language, the dominant systems are those of the L1, and the ease or difficulty of learning a particular L2 word will largely depend on the similarities it shares with the roughly equivalent L1 word. It will also depend on the similarities between the various L1 and L2 linguistic systems, such as the phonological system, the writing and spelling systems, the morphological system, the lexical system, and the grammatical system. As learners' proficiency develops, the systems of the L2 will play an increasingly important role in determining the degree of learning burden. For example, native speakers of Spanish may find some English words easy to learn, but the same words may have a heavy learning burden for native speakers of Japanese, and vice versa. As learners gain control of the L2 systems, words which fit into these systems should become easier to learn.

Individual items versus linguistic systems

It is important to note that there are two levels of focus when dealing with the learning burden: on individual items, and on systems. For example, we can focus on the spelling of a particular word, or we can focus on a spelling rule that can be applied to a large number of words. In most cases, these two levels of focus complement each other: focusing on individual words provides examples that help to develop knowledge of systems, while focusing on a system can make individual words easier to learn.

Sources of learning burden

Because there are many aspects of word knowledge, ranging across form, meaning, and use, there are many sources of learning burden which correspond to these aspects. A word can be difficult for one or more of the following reasons:

- it has an irregular spelling
- it is difficult to pronounce
- it contains unfamiliar word parts
- there is no obvious connection between its form and its meaning
- understanding its meaning requires specialist knowledge
- it has unpredictable grammatical patterns
- it requires specific collocations
- there are constraints on its use, such as being used in only a particular dialect of the language.

ACTIVITY 2.1   **Learning difficult words**

How do you learn difficult words? Rank the following words from the easiest to learn (= 1) to the most difficult (= 8).

> abhor   boulder   crave   lick   mourn   pawn   reef   sob

Now answer the questions.

1 What information do you know, or can you work out, about each word?

2 How easy is it to use each word in a sentence?

Then read the notes on this activity at the end of the chapter.

Analysing the learning burden

In the context of Higa's categories, let us consider five aspects of word knowledge: **form–meaning connection**, word form (sounds and spelling), collocation, receptive and productive use, and **interference**. We will look at what most affects the learning burden in each case, and also what may help to reduce it.

Aspect 1: Form–meaning connection

Similar/borrowed words

The easiest L2 words to learn are **cognates** which are identical in form and meaning to L1 words. Although these are very uncommon, there are many cases where the L2 and L1 words share similarities. A native English speaker learning the French word 'table', for example, initially has little new to learn besides how to pronounce the word in French. In fact, around 60% of English words derive from French, Latin, or Greek, so speakers of French, Italian, Greek, and related languages find it relatively easy to learn the form–meaning connection of a large number of English words. Moreover, because of the very strong influence of English as the language of international communication, there is now a great deal of borrowing of English words into local languages. Frank Daulton (2008) estimates that around half of the 3,000 most frequent word families in English have been borrowed into Japanese in some form or other. Once these words have been assimilated, they often take on a life of their own, with their form and meaning adapted to suit local circumstances. For example, the loanword 'mansion' (マンション pronounced 'manshon') is used in Japanese to refer to apartments, which are very common in Japan, rather than large houses, which are uncommon there. Nonetheless, such borrowings into the L1 can have the effect of reducing the learning burden of borrowed words when they are learned as part of an L2 (Rogers, Webb, & Nakata, 2015).

Word parts

There is another advantage that comes from having words borrowed from other languages. Many French, Latin, and Greek words contain **word parts**, namely stems and affixes, many of which clearly contribute to the meaning of the words. So knowing what these word parts mean can make it easier to learn the meanings of words that contain them. For example, knowing that the prefix *com-* means 'together' or 'with' can make 'committee' and 'communicate' easier to learn.

Knowing common word parts can help to reduce the learning burden in the long run by giving learners the ability to analyse unknown words and work out what they might mean based on characteristics they share with words they do know. There are around 2,000 words from the third 1,000 to the tenth 1,000 word frequency level that share stems of a similar meaning with the 2,000 most frequent words in English. For example, the stem *-dict-*, meaning 'say', occurs in the high-frequency word 'indicate' (to say something indirectly). It also occurs with the meaning of 'say' in lower-frequency words such as 'dictate', 'dedicate', 'abdicate', 'predicate', 'vindicate', 'predict', 'contradict', 'verdict', 'indict', 'diction', and, less recognizably but with a similar meaning, in 'ditto' and 'index' (Wei & Nation, 2013). (See Appendix 3 for a list of useful word stems.)

Word senses

Another way in which the form–meaning connection of words can contribute to the learning burden concerns the different **referents** that words have. By listing different senses for a word, dictionaries encourage us to think that each word has several different meanings that we need to learn and store. For example, the entry for 'guilt' may have at least three senses:

1 the fact that you have done something wrong
2 the responsibility for doing something wrong
3 the feeling you have done something wrong.

It is good for dictionaries to provide detail about the different senses of words, and this information can be very helpful when encountering a word in context. However, we should not see these senses as necessarily having psychological reality; they are distinctions created by the dictionary-makers. It is no accident that the three senses are all signalled by the same word form 'guilt', since they all share the same **core meaning**: 'having done wrong'. When native speakers use the language either receptively or productively, they simply adapt the understanding or use of this word to the current communicative context. To put it another way, dealing with different word senses is usually an issue not of semantics but of pragmatics. Ruhl (1989) calls this the **monosemic bias**—that is, the assumption that a word has one inherent meaning (semantic), with the different senses in which it is used being determined by context (pragmatic). So if two words have the same or similar forms, we should assume they have the same meaning.

There are clearly exceptions to this, namely **homonyms**, **homographs**, and **homophones**, which are words that have the same spoken or written form (or both) but are unrelated in meaning. A commonly cited example is 'bank' (for money/by the river), but there are many other examples. Kevin Parent (2012) found that the 2,000 word families in the General Service List (1953) include 75 homonyms (words with the same spoken and written forms but unrelated meanings, for example 'bowl', 'rest', 'yard', 'miss') and ten homographs (words with the same written forms but different pronunciation and meanings, for example 'bow', 'wind', and 'lead'). Wang and Nation (2004) found that around 10% of the 570 words in the Academic Word List (Coxhead, 2000) are homonyms and homographs. There are also exceptions, where a sense of a word has deviated so far from the core meaning that it is on its way to becoming a homonym. Although most homonyms are not etymologically related, a few are; for example, 'second' (after 'first'/part of a minute). The connection between these previously related meanings became lost to users of the language, and they effectively became different words which need to be learned separately.

The L1 also encourages learners to see the various senses of the same word form as different words if those senses are represented by two or more different word forms in the L1. For example, in Thai and French, 'to know a person' and 'to know some facts' are expressed by two different words. Similarly, the fork you eat with and a fork in the road are two different words in Indonesian and many other languages. In contrast, when an L2 word form has a single meaning in the L1, then learners may be less likely to recognize different senses as different words.

The learning burden of word senses can be greatly reduced if both teachers and learners focus on the core meaning of words and deal with different senses largely as a matter of strategy and process rather than as a matter of learning additional meanings. There are very practical ways of doing this. First, and most importantly, the **guessing from context** strategy needs to be applied when a word is encountered which is used in an unfamiliar sense. Look at the following sentence from a reading text:

> A couple were smoking pipes, shoving the black tobacco down into the cups with wrinkled fingers.

The use of the word 'cups' is unusual here (we would normally expect 'bowls'), but the reader should have no trouble understanding it, because it is clearly consistent with the core meaning of 'cup', which refers to a particular shape.

Similarly, the use of 'cup' as a verb in 'he cupped her face in his hands' is comprehensible from the core meaning.

A second useful method of reducing the learning burden of word senses is to look at all the senses of a word given in a dictionary entry to work out the core meaning. It would be extremely helpful if dictionaries provided core meanings as well as senses, but at present this happens more by accident than by design. There is also value in learners being made consciously aware of the idea of core meanings and how a word which expresses a single core meaning in one language may express two separate meanings in another language. The goal should be to learn the core meaning of words in the L2 so that when a word is used in a strikingly new sense, it can be dealt with not as an unfamiliar word but as representing something related to what is already known about that word. Besides, seeing how different languages classify the world is part of the educational value of learning another language.

Aspect 2: Word form: sounds and spelling

Some L2 words are easy to learn because they have the same or a very similar form in the L1. It is usually easier to learn a language which belongs to the same language family as one you already know than it is to learn a language from a different language family. For example, it is easier for a speaker of French to learn Italian than Japanese.

Phonological systems

The learning burden of the sounds of an L2 depends on how close they are to the sounds of the L1; and the degree of closeness depends not only on the individual sounds of the L1 and L2, but also on the phonological systems. Learning the phonological system of a tone language like Mandarin can be an enormous hurdle for someone whose L1 is not a tone language. Similarly, a speaker of a syllable-timed language like Spanish, French, or Japanese will struggle to learn a stress-timed language like English, Arabic, or Russian. Within a language, sounds are combined in certain ways to create syllables, consonant clusters, and vowel clusters. Part of learning the phonological system of an L2 is becoming familiar with the permitted sound combinations. As familiarity with these combinations increases, the ease of learning the spoken forms of words will also increase.

This is important, because research has shown that the more pronounceable words are, the easier they are to learn (Ellis & Beaton, 1993; Rodgers, 1969). A crucial step that native speakers of an alphabetic language like English or Indonesian need to make in learning to read involves developing **phonological awareness**; that is, the awareness that words can be broken down into separate sounds, and that these sounds can be combined to form words. Many children need to reach the age of six before they can readily develop phonological awareness, although some do develop it earlier.

Phonological awareness is not just important for learning to read in the L1; it is equally important in the L2. Chieh-Fang Hu (2008) has shown, for example, that developing phonological awareness in the L2 can make learning L2 words easier and therefore more efficient. Indeed, it is not difficult to see why phonological awareness is so important for learning to read in an alphabetic language. Whether the language is being learned as the L1 or the L2, it serves as the basis for developing 'word attack' skills which help to decode the pronunciation and meanings of words, such as sounding out the letters of a word to access the spoken form.

A very effective way of developing phonological awareness with young learners is to play a game which involves identifying words that have been sounded out. For example, 'What word is this: /d/–/o/–/g/?' This game requires the learners to combine separate sounds in order to work out what word is being said. After a few weeks, when they have become good at identifying the words, the roles can be reversed, with the learners sounding out words for the teacher to identify.

Writing systems

The learning burden of the written forms of L2 words is heavily dependent on whether the L2 uses the same writing system as the L1, as do English and Spanish—albeit with minor variations such as the use of accents (for example, *n* and *ñ*). It will also depend on whether the L2 has an alphabetic or a syllabic writing system, as with Thai or Korean; or a logographic writing system, as with Mandarin, which involves learning a very large number of characters.

The learning burden of an alphabetic or a syllabic writing system depends in part on the degree of regularity within the system, even for native speakers of the language (Moseley, 1994). The alphabetic writing system of English is notorious for its irregularities. Even though they make up only a small (but frequent) part of the system, these irregularities increase the learning burden and make the English writing system more challenging than those of regularly spelled languages such as Malay or Māori.

Alphabet and spelling

After developing phonological awareness, the second major conceptual step that a native speaker of an alphabetic language must make when learning to read is master the 'alphabetic principle'—that is, the use of letters to represent the sounds of a language. The principle clearly builds on phonological awareness, because it involves relating separate sounds to individual letters. Learning the alphabetic principle also involves learning to recognize and produce the individual letters of the language.

There are several complementary approaches to learning the spelling system of a language:

- Opportunities to learn by doing lots of reading, i.e. learning through input. This is an **incidental learning** approach to spelling.
- Opportunities to learn by doing lots of writing, i.e. learning through output.
- Opportunities to learn through the deliberate study of rules and words, involving the **rote-learning** of difficult words and classification/analysis activities with regularly spelled words.
- Opportunities for learners to become fluent in their recognition of high-frequency words through **speed-reading** activities and through rapid identification of words on **flashcards**.

Aspect 3: Collocation

This chapter has so far considered two major factors concerning the learning burden of L2 vocabulary: the influence of the L1 and the characteristics of the L2. The learning burden of a word is also affected by a learner's knowledge of the wider world and by features that make certain words and multi-word combinations memorable. These two factors are particularly pertinent with regard to collocation. In essence, collocation refers to the use of certain words together. The meanings of the words, the grammar of the language, and our communicative intentions largely determine what these combinations will be. As Liu (2010) has shown, most combinations are not arbitrary but follow the rules of grammar and the semantic requirements of the words involved. However, there is also some degree of convention underlying certain combinations. All of these various factors mean that the learning burden of some collocations can be considerable.

Grammar rules
As Andrew Pawley and Frances Syder (1983) note, skill in using collocations underlies native-like selection of words and native-like fluency in language use. It is likely that high-frequency collocations are stored in memory as whole units (Wray, 2002), though this is largely out of convenience, not due to any arbitrariness in the collocation. Except for a few core idioms (such as 'as well' and 'by and large'), collocations tend to follow grammatical rules and are consistent with the meanings of the words involved in the collocation; 'strong tea', for example, involves the normal meanings of 'strong' and 'tea', which are consistent with their uses in other collocations, such as 'strong medicine' and 'green tea'.

Knowledge of the wider world

Knowledge of the wider world also plays a role in determining collocations. There are only certain things that we can say about tea, and this restricts the kinds of words that are likely to collocate with it. This knowledge guides learners in their use of collocation.

Memorability

Frank Boers and Seth Lindstromberg (2009) estimate that almost 20% of figurative expressions in English have **alliteration**, as in 'few and far between', and 'singing the same song'. A much smaller percentage of such expressions have poetic features such as rhyme, **slant rhyme**, word repetition, **assonance**, and **consonance**. These form-based features serve to make the multi-word combinations memorable, making them easier to retrieve when they are needed for productive use. This memorability seems to work for both deliberate and incidental learning (Boers, Lindstromberg, & Webb, 2014), thus serving to reduce the learning burden.

Overall meaning

The learning burden of collocations can also be reduced if learners are encouraged to see how the meanings of the parts relate to the meaning of the whole. For example, understanding that 'jump the gun' derives from an expression used to describe runners starting too early in a race (before the starting pistol has been fired) may help learners to better retain that collocation (Boers, Eyckmans, & Stengers, 2007). In English, there is a surprisingly small number of core idioms—around 100—where the relationship between the meanings of the parts and the meaning of the whole has been lost (Grant & Nation, 2006); for example, 'as well', 'out of hand', 'red herring', 'raining cats and dogs'. In these cases, rote-learning is required, otherwise a deliberately false **etymology** could be created. As learners' proficiency develops, their knowledge of the grammatical and semantic systems of the language will make the learning burden of collocations lighter.

Aspect 4: Receptive and productive use

Learning the form and meaning is only one step towards truly knowing a word or phrase. Words need to be used both receptively in listening and reading, and productively in speaking and writing. At least in terms of vocabulary, it is usually easier to learn to listen to and read a language than it is to learn to speak or write it. The knowledge required to listen or read is called **receptive knowledge**, and the knowledge required to speak and write is called **productive knowledge**. Research shows very clearly that it is easier to recall the meaning of a word passively than it is to learn and recall the form of a word in order to actively produce it (Griffin & Harley, 1996;

Laufer, Elder, Hill, & Congdon, 2004; Laufer & Goldstein, 2004; Mondria & Wiersma, 2004; Stoddard, 1929; Waring, 1997a; Webb, 2009a).

The learning burden of a word is affected by its use (receptive or productive). Research comparing the **receptive learning** and **productive learning** of vocabulary (Griffin & Harley, 1996; Mondria & Wiersma, 2004; Webb, 2009a, 2009b) has concluded that productive learning involves the knowledge needed for receptive use, whereas receptive learning may not involve the knowledge needed for productive use. This is not surprising, because when we read or listen (receptive use), we do not need to give attention to the details of knowledge needed for speaking and writing (productive use), such as what preposition typically follows this word, or whether that word is spelled with an *i* before the *e* or after it.

ACTIVITY 2.2   **Analysing the learning burden of words**

Think about what you have read in relation to aspects 1–4 of the learning burden of words and make notes about the four words/phrases in the table below. Then check your ideas at the end of the chapter.

	'meet'	'yacht'	'transportation'	'run the company'
Form–meaning connection				
Word form: sounds and spelling				
Collocation				
Receptive and productive use				

Aspect 5: Presentation and interference

So far in this chapter, we have touched on what Higa (1965) called 'the intrinsic difficulty of words' (see page 25) and the interaction between new and previously learned words. A key focus of Higa's research, however, was on the learning burden created by the interactions between words presented at the same time. Higa (1963) found that if opposites or near **synonyms** were presented together, they were more difficult to learn than unrelated words. Similarly, Thomas Tinkham (1993, 1997), Robert Waring (1997b), and Ismail Erten and Mustafa Tekin (2008) found that learning items in a **lexical set**, such as the names of fruit, colours, or articles of clothing, required more repetitions than learning unrelated words. Tinkham (1997) also found that if words were connected as though by a story (for example, 'frog', 'green', 'slimy', 'pond', 'splash', 'croak'), they were easier to learn than unrelated words. Nation (2000) looked at these studies to examine the degree of difference between learning related and unrelated words and found that relatedness (for example, near synonyms, opposites, and lexical sets) made learning 50–100% more difficult. Clearly, the kinds of words that are learned or presented together can have a strong effect on the learning burden.

The source of difficulty is likely to be in the interference between the meanings of the words. When we learn opposites at the same time, such as 'hot' and 'cold', there is the challenge of learning the individual words and also the added difficulty of not getting them mixed up with each other (which one means 'hot'?). Higa (1963) found that the greatest degree of interference was between near synonyms (for example, 'advance' and 'progress'), probably because they share the most meaning but differ in key aspects. Opposites also share meaning but represent different ends of a scale. Members of a lexical set, such as fruit, share their membership to the set but differ in many important ways. Interestingly, Tomoko Ishii (2013) found that learning the names of fruit of a similar shape ('apples' and 'oranges') was more difficult than learning the names of fruit of very different shapes ('apples' and 'bananas'). Experience shows that where there is interference between the meanings of words as well as their forms, the overall degree of interference is even greater. For example, when learning the days of the week (a lexical set), there is likely to be the strongest interference between 'Tuesday' and 'Thursday' because of their similarity in form (they both begin with *T*, and the first syllable ends with *s*).

The increase in learning burden caused by the interference between related words can be reduced by presenting items individually at different times. Initially, it may seem counter-intuitive not to teach all the days of the week at the same time; but there is no particular reason, except for learning the order of the days, why they cannot be learned one at a time as they are needed, or according to their frequency in that language. The same applies to the months of the year, numbers, colours, and various other lexical sets.

The possibilities of interference can be further reduced if the presentation of related items is not only separated in time but also done in ways which increase the distinctiveness between the items. For example, when learning numbers, the number 'four' can be learned with the collocate 'seasons', while the number 'five' can be learned with the collocate 'minutes'. In addition, items which are likely to have strong interference between them can be related to some kind of **mnemonic** which helps to keep them separate. For example, explaining the etymology of 'Thursday' (derived from the Norse god Thor) in a simple way in the L1 may make it sufficiently memorable to stop it interfering with other items.

Another way to reduce the potential for interference to occur is to learn the words in lexical sets in context. For example, it might help to differentiate between the meanings of 'fast' and 'slow' by learning these words in a sentence, such as 'Rabbits are fast and tortoises are slow.'. Receptive and productive learning of words with related meanings in contexts that reveal the differences between them is subject to less interference.

ACTIVITY 2.3   Identifying interference

Look at the following groups of words which may appear as 'sets' in various sections of a coursebook. Which sets contain items that are likely to interfere with each other? What could you do to reduce the possible interference? Compare your ideas with the notes at the end of the chapter.

1	open the door close the door open the window close the window	2	cloud office risky social lose erase	3	kitchen living room dining room bathroom bedroom
4	branches roots bark leaves trunk	5	job satisfaction challenge security social status being promoted	6	bark walk dog park big

---

Some implications of the learning burden

Dealing with the learning burden of words involves striking a balance between two types of focus. With regard to particular items, the learning burden encourages a focus on exceptions and irregularity, because these are sources of difficulty. On the other hand, with regard to knowledge of linguistic systems, the learning burden encourages a focus on regularity, because this knowledge requires familiarity with rules and patterns. Irregular features tend to be frequent but small in number; for example, past tense forms and irregular plurals. In general, rules should receive more attention than exceptions, because rules can have wide application, while exceptions tend to interfere with the application of rules. In addition, gaining control of rules leads to independence in language use. Giving deliberate attention to rules and exceptions is a part of language-focused learning. Deliberately focusing on irregularities and exceptions should only make up a small part of this strand of a vocabulary learning programme.

There are several ways in which teachers and materials writers might apply the analysis of the learning burden.

- Systems: Prioritize the development of knowledge of the systematic aspects of the language. Paying deliberate attention to pronunciation, spelling, core meanings, morphology, word choice, collocations, and vocabulary learning strategies can be of benefit in vocabulary growth. Much of this learning of language systems will come from using the language both receptively and productively in normal language use and through fluency development activities.
- Difficult words: Analysing the learning burden of particular words can help to focus the deliberate teaching of those words. Such focus, which is typically on points of difficulty, can make teaching and learning vocabulary much more efficient.
- Patterns: Analysing the learning burden highlights the value of giving deliberate mnemonic-related attention to items that are difficult. Some items are easily learned because they readily fit into known systems. Annette de Groot (2006) found that L2 words that followed L1 spelling patterns were easier to learn and, more importantly, were well retained. This seems to go against the 'levels of processing' hypothesis (Craik & Lockhart, 1972; Craik & Tulving, 1975), which can be interpreted as arguing that the greater the effort that goes into learning, the better the **retention** will be. Fitting items into familiar patterns is, in fact, a form of deep processing, because the new is made more meaningful through its **association** with the known. Where the irregularity of an item makes it difficult to learn, then using mnemonic devices like the **keyword technique**, **word part analysis**, looking for formal patterns like alliteration and rhyme, and exploring the etymological origin of words and multi-word combinations can make learning easier.
- Context: The research on interference between words with related meanings provides guidance on how teachers and materials writers might want to organize the vocabulary that is covered in lessons. In normal language use, we do not typically use vocabulary in lexical sets or bring opposites or synonyms together. Such groupings occur when teachers and course designers draw on their own mental associations to choose vocabulary to focus on. It is these mental associations that cause the problem of interference. The simplest way of reducing the learning burden caused by interference is to choose vocabulary as it occurs in normal conversation and reading texts.

(A further means of reducing the learning burden relates to the conditions of learning, which will be explored in later chapters.)

Summary

Knowing a word involves knowing the form, meaning, and use of the word. The learning burden of an L2 word is affected by similarities between the L1 and L2. Cognates generally make learning easier, and words that make use only of L1 sounds and sound combinations are easier to learn. The learning burden of a word also depends on whether its form and use fit into regular, predictable L2 patterns. Learning a word for receptive use in listening and reading is typically easier than learning a word for productive purposes (speaking and writing). The manner in which words are presented also affects their learnability. Words in lexical sets are more difficult to learn together than to learn separately, because when presented together there is the added burden of distinguishing between their similarities and the need to avoid mixing them up. This problem of interference can be reduced by increasing the distinctiveness between items and presenting them on different occasions. The problem can generally be avoided if words are learned as they occur in cohesive texts or via spoken language, where lexical sets do not typically appear together. By focusing on the systematic nature of language and giving deliberate attention to difficult words via an understanding of their learning burden, teachers can make their students' vocabulary learning more efficient.

Questions for reflection

1   Your students' first language may have many words that are similar in form and meaning to English words. Suggest two things you can do to help them notice and use the similarities to facilitate vocabulary learning.

2   You have to plan a reading course and want to give systematic attention to vocabulary during the course. How will you choose the vocabulary?

Keys to activities

ACTIVITY 2.1   Learning difficult words

Although perceptions of word difficulty will vary, Webb's research (2007b) indicated that 'abhor', 'boulder', 'crave', and 'sob' might be easier to learn than 'lick', 'mourn', 'pawn', and 'reef'. The reason for this is that the words in the first group have higher-frequency synonyms ('abhor'–'hate', 'boulder'–'rock', 'crave'–'want', 'sob'–'cry'). This makes them potentially easier to learn, as students can use a higher-frequency synonym as a model for a lower-frequency word. The words in the second group do not have higher-frequency synonyms, making them more difficult to learn.

ACTIVITY 2.2   **Analysing the learning burden of words**

The following notes about the features of these four words and phrases suggest where difficulties might arise and thus where attention could be directed during learning.

	'meet'	'yacht'	'transportation'	'run the company'
Form–meaning connection	unlikely to have a similar or borrowed form does not contain word parts a homophone of 'meat' two common meanings: 'encounter' and 'fulfil'	a loanword between some languages	contains word parts: • trans- (between) • -port- (carry) • -tion (signals the noun form)	there are other meanings of 'run' the meaning of 'run' in this combination may not be transparent phrases with similar meanings: • 'run a business' • 'run a campaign' • 'run smoothly'
Word form: sounds and spelling	regular sound–spelling relationships	irregular spelling unpredictable sound–spelling relationship easy to pronounce for most learners	regular sound–spelling relationships	knowledge of the sounds and spellings of the individual words will facilitate learning
Collocation	common collocations (encounter): • nice to ~ • pleased to ~ common collocations (fulfil): • ~ a need • ~ a requirement • ~ a standard • ~ a demand	common and predictable collocations: • sailing ~ • ~ club • ~ race • ~ marina	common collocations: • public ~ • ~ costs some less transparent collocations: • ~ system • mass ~ • regional ~	predictable collocations, e.g. 'run the company effectively'

Receptive and productive use	high-frequency; useful to learn receptively and productively	lower-frequency; more likely to be encountered than used for most learners	high-frequency; useful to learn receptively and productively	lower-frequency; more likely to be encountered than used for most learners

ACTIVITY 2.3   Identifying interference

Interference is likely to make sets 1, 3, and 4 more difficult to learn. Here are some ideas for reducing the potential for interference:

• learn the items at different times (all sets)
• use mnemonics (all sets)
• learn the words in context by making a sentence for each item; for example, in set 1:

I open the door to let my friend into my house.
I close the door and lock it when I leave.
I open the window to let some fresh air in.
I close the window to stop mosquitos coming in.

• create a visual or logical ordering; for example, in set 4 (bottom to top):

roots, trunk, bark, branches, leaves

• create a personal narrative; for example, in set 3:

I go into my house. The living room is on the left and the kitchen is on the right. Behind that is the dining room. The bathroom is upstairs opposite the bedroom.

Suggestions for further reading

Higa, M. (1965). The psycholinguistic concept of 'difficulty' and the teaching of foreign language vocabulary. *Language Learning, 15(3–4)*, 167–179.

This article presents a very interesting review of factors that make vocabulary learning difficult. Higa's doctoral research compared various meaning relationships such as near synonyms, opposites, and free associates to determine which helped and which hindered learning. This article sets this in its wider context.

Laufer, B. (1997). What's in a word that makes it hard or easy? Intralexical factors affecting the difficulty of vocabulary acquisition. In N. Schmitt & M. McCarthy (Eds.), *Vocabulary: description, acquisition and pedagogy* (pp. 140–155). Cambridge: Cambridge University Press.

Laufer's discussion of difficulty is strongly research-based and carefully weighs up the evidence for and against various factors. Later research shows that yet another factor affecting the likelihood of learning is the depth of processing involved, and this is affected by the intrinsic difficulty of a word. (The whole book by Schmitt & McCarthy (Eds.) is well worth reading.)

Nation, I. S. P. (2000). Learning vocabulary in lexical sets: dangers and guidelines. *TESOL Journal, 9(2)*, 6–10.

This review of the research on interference has the very practical aim of working out what teachers and learners should do about lexical sets. It attempts to quantify how serious the effect of learning words in lexical sets can be.

3 VOCABULARY SIZE AND GROWTH

Introduction

The way we learn words in our first language is usually different from how we learn words in another language. One of the reasons for this is that there are varying amounts of language input for learners in different contexts. For example, in the first language learning context, we typically receive both spoken and written input each day. In a second language learning context (i.e. learning the L2 in a country where it is generally used), learners have the potential to receive a large amount of L2 input, although this depends on the motivation of learners to communicate in the target language. In a foreign language learning context (i.e. learning the L2 in a country where it is not generally used), learners may receive little input, and this may rarely occur outside the classroom. These differences in the amount of input mean that teachers and learners in different contexts may need to approach vocabulary learning in different ways. In this chapter, we look at incidental vocabulary learning, which is how we typically learn words in L1. We begin by examining L1 and L2 vocabulary size and growth. We then move on to consider the fundamental distinction between incidental and deliberate learning, and examine the degree to which each contributes to vocabulary growth in the different learning contexts. We conclude the chapter by refining our understanding of incidental vocabulary learning theory, and suggest that increasing the amount of input to enhance effective incidental learning may be the key to improving L2 lexical development.

L1 vocabulary growth

In Chapter 1, we noted two different ways of counting words: using word families and lemmas. We now introduce a third: **word type**. It is worth recapping the distinction between these terms. When counting with word types, every word form is counted as a separate item, so 'accept', 'accepts', and 'accepted' would be counted as three different items. When counting with lemmas, headwords and inflections are counted as the same item, so 'accept', 'accepts', and 'accepted' would be counted together. When counting with word families, headwords, inflections, and derivations are counted together, so 'accept', 'accepts', 'accepted', 'acceptable', and 'unacceptable' would be counted as a single item.

This highlights a crucial point, which is that estimates of the vocabulary size of native speakers can vary considerably, since researchers count words in different ways. Those who use word types (the smallest unit of counting) may suggest that it is possible to learn as many as 5,000 words per year (Smith, 1941; Templin, 1957), while those who use word families (a larger unit of counting) may suggest a growth rate of around 1,000 word families per year (Biemiller & Slonim, 2001; Goulden, Nation, & Read, 1990).

So which method of counting should be used to measure vocabulary size? There is a strong argument for counting with word families, because learning a new word family indicates a clear increase in lexical knowledge. In contrast, if we use the other units of counting (word type or lemma), an increase in vocabulary size might simply represent an accumulation of knowledge of word parts, rather than a growth in the learner's knowledge of new word meanings. Indeed, the most carefully designed studies of receptive vocabulary size and growth have been conducted using word families. Researchers estimate a vocabulary growth rate of about 1,000 word families per year for young L1 learners of English (Biemiller & Slonim, 2001; Goulden, Nation, & Read, 1990). Learners may know at least 3–4,000 word families before they can read, at around five or six years of age; and by the time they reach university, they may know around 15–20,000 word families (d'Anna, Zechmeister, & Hall, 1991; Goulden, Nation, & Read, 1990).

Another way of looking at vocabulary size is to consider how many words we need to know to do different things. For example, corpus-driven research has investigated the vocabulary sizes required to understand speech and writing. This line of research is based on the premise that we tend to learn words according to their frequency in language (Schmitt, Schmitt, & Clapham, 2001); and, as we have seen in Chapter 1, we usually learn words which are higher in frequency before those which are less frequent. This is beneficial in terms of helping us to improve our comprehension of speech and writing, because the highest-frequency words are repeatedly encountered in all discourse types, while there are likely to be long intervals between our encounters with lower-frequency words. Knowing high-frequency words therefore ensures that a high proportion of the words that are encountered will be known.

Table 3.1 summarizes the evidence for how knowledge of word families by frequency enables understanding.

Word families	Discourse/text type	Evidence
the most frequent 3,000	conversation	Nation (2006), van Zeeland & Schmitt (2013)
	television	Webb & Rodgers (2009a), Rodgers & Webb (2011)
	films	Webb & Rodgers (2009b)
the most frequent 4,000	academic spoken discourse	Dang & Webb (2014)
the most frequent 8–9,000	written texts, e.g. newspapers and novels	Nation (2006)

Table 3.1 Knowledge of discourse/text type by word family frequency

These figures are relevant to both L1 and L2 vocabulary growth. In terms of L1 vocabulary growth, by the time they are ten years old, L1 learners might be able to understand a large proportion of written text. Of course, vocabulary is just one of many factors that affect comprehension, so reaching a certain vocabulary size cannot guarantee a certain level of comprehension. However, the figures do provide a useful gauge as to whether or not different types of discourse and text are likely to be understood. They also indicate the lexical challenges of learning an L2; few L2 learners are able to learn the 9,000 most frequent words (their average target is closer to 3,000).

ACTIVITY 3.1   Check your vocabulary size

Read the words in the table below in order from 1–50. Cross out any words you do not know. Add up the number of words you do know, and multiply this number by 500 to get your total vocabulary size. Then read the notes on this activity at the end of the chapter.

1	as	11	abstract	21	aviary	31	comeuppance	41	cupreous
2	dog	12	eccentric	22	chasuble	32	downer	42	cutability
3	editor	13	receptacle	23	ferrule	33	geisha	43	regurge
4	shake	14	armadillo	24	liven	34	logistics	44	lifemanship
5	pony	15	boost	25	parallelogram	35	panache	45	atropia
6	immense	16	commissary	26	punkah	36	setout	46	sporophore
7	butler	17	gentian	27	amice	37	cervicovaginal	47	hypomagnesaemia
8	mare	18	lotus	28	chiton	38	abruption	48	cowsucker
9	denounce	19	squeamish	29	roughy	39	kohl	49	oleaginous
10	borough	20	waffle	30	barf	40	acephalia	50	migrationist

Adapted from Goulden, Nation, & Read (1990)

L2 vocabulary growth

One of the key questions about lexical development is: 'How many words can L2 learners be expected to know after learning the language for different periods of time?' Surprisingly, there are relatively few studies of L2 vocabulary growth; and questions such as 'How many words should be learned per week/per year/during a course?' remain unanswered. One reason for this is that there appears to be a great deal of variation in our capacity to learn L2 vocabulary; while some people are able to make great progress, others appear to struggle. Another factor that complicates findings was discussed at the start of this chapter—that is, the variation in the unit of counting used to measure vocabulary growth, with some studies using lemmas, some using word families, and others not specifying at all. This makes it difficult to generalize across contexts.

Several studies using lemmas as the unit of counting have been conducted with L2 learners in Europe.

- James Milton (2006a) measured the vocabulary knowledge of EFL learners in Greece who received around 100 hours of English language instruction each year. He found differences of approximately 500 lemmas among students at seven different levels, with learners at the highest levels knowing about 3,500 out of the 5,000 most frequent lemmas. This suggests a lexical growth rate of around 500 lemmas per year. However, Milton reports that growth varied considerably among students; some were able to learn more than 1,000 lemmas in a year, while others never progressed beyond a vocabulary size of 400 to 500 lemmas.
- In the Hungarian EFL context, Andrea Orosz (2009) found that primary school children were able to learn around 300 to 400 lemmas per year,

with a large degree of variation in growth among those tested. Some children were able to learn as many as 1,000 lemmas in a year, and knew about 3,500 out of the 5,000 most frequent lemmas after four years of primary school study. In contrast, others had very little growth and remained at a vocabulary size of several hundred lemmas.

- In the British context, Milton (2006b) found that, on average, secondary school students learning French as a foreign language initially knew around 300 lemmas after one year of study, with growth thereafter ranging from 0–500 lemmas per year. Studies in several other EFL contexts have revealed annual growth rates from 150–200 words in Saudi Arabia to 520–600 words in Japan (Milton & Meara, 1998).

Several studies that have used word families as the unit of counting have found that EFL learners make limited progress in vocabulary learning.

- Lise Danelund (2013) found that after at least nine years of English language instruction, only 48% of Grade 13 students in Denmark could demonstrate mastery of the 2,000 highest-frequency word families on a test of vocabulary knowledge.
- George Quinn (1968) found that university students in Indonesia who had received about 600 hours of English language instruction over six years knew about half of the 2,000 most frequent word families. Ari Nurweni and John Read (1999) had rather similar findings. They showed that university students in Indonesia knew approximately 1,000 of the 2,000 most frequent word families after receiving six years of English language instruction. H. Barnard (1961) found slightly better results in India, where first year university students knew approximately 1,500 of the 2,000 most frequent word families.
- In the only **longitudinal study** that involved tracking EFL learners' vocabulary learning progress, Stuart Webb and Anna Chang (2012a) found considerable variation in yearly lexical gains among learners in Taiwan, with the amount of growth ranging from 18–430 word families. As would be expected, those who received more English language instruction tended to have greater gains. However, after nine years of instruction, only 47% of the learners had mastered the 1,000 most frequent words; and only 16% of the learners demonstrated mastery of the 2,000 most frequent words.

As mentioned earlier in this chapter, native speakers of English typically learn between 15–20,000 word families. In contrast, many EFL learners never manage to learn the 2,000 most frequent word families. In light of the studies above, it seems to be the case that vocabulary learning in many EFL contexts is neither particularly effective nor efficient. Certainly, some learners are able to make outstanding progress. However, these learners appear to be a small minority in EFL classrooms. Vocabulary growth for EFL learners is, of course, unlikely to reach the annual growth target of 1,000 word families that can reasonably be expected of most young L1 learners, but learning 500 word families per year should be an attainable target as long as they receive the monitoring and support they need in order to achieve this goal. Indeed, Webb and Chang (2012a) suggest that institutional L2 vocabulary learning programmes are necessary to ensure that L2 learners gain knowledge of the high-frequency vocabulary they will need to make progress in all aspects of the language learning process.

Deliberate and incidental learning

Although we might first think of vocabulary learning as being deliberate, researchers agree that we learn the vast majority of L1 words incidentally (Nagy, Herman, & Anderson, 1985; Nation, 2001; Schmitt, 2000). Definitions of incidental vocabulary learning vary, but perhaps the most common definition is 'learning words as a by-product of a task' (Ellis, 1999). For example, when we read or listen, our focus is on understanding the message, but we might gradually learn words that are encountered in the message by seeing and hearing them again and again in context. In these cases, our aim is to understand the input, not to deliberately learn words. Thus, vocabulary learning is seen as being incidental rather than intentional. The amount of incidental vocabulary learning is dependent on the amount of input; more input provides greater opportunity to encounter words repeatedly, and therefore a greater likelihood of words being learned (Webb & Chang, 2015a).

When we learn additional languages, there is often insufficient input for much incidental vocabulary learning to occur, and the limited amount of L2 input has led some to suggest that in the EFL learning context, deliberate learning might be responsible for most vocabulary growth (Cobb, 2007; Laufer, 2003, 2005; Webb, 2008a). We might do this on our own by focusing on a single aspect of vocabulary knowledge, such as spelling, and analysing the written form of the word so that we remember how to spell it the next time we need to use it. Similarly, we might also try to work out the meaning of the word on our own, by using a dictionary, or simply by asking someone. At other times, we might attempt to learn how the word is used with other words and pay attention to its grammatical functions and collocations, or compare it with words or word parts we already know. At school, teachers might intentionally extend our vocabulary by giving us specific tasks to complete, such as looking up words in a dictionary, cloze activities, crosswords, word search, or matching activities. In the L2 learning context, deliberate vocabulary learning activities such as learning with flashcards, word part tables, and **semantic mapping** are very common. (We will discuss deliberate learning in more detail in Chapters 4 and 5.)

In comparisons between the gains made by L2 learners in incidental and deliberate learning conditions, the deliberate learning gains are always much larger (Webb, 2002; Laufer, 2003). However, this is less clear when we consider what might be gained over the long term. Intentionally learning the form and meaning of words will certainly lead to greater knowledge of the form–meaning connection of words in the short term, but it remains to be determined whether deliberate learning accounts for greater knowledge of the form–meaning connection of words than encountering words repeatedly over a long period of time. Learning the form–meaning connection of words incidentally through reading and listening takes time and is most effectively achieved through reading and listening to large amounts of the language (Webb & Chang, 2015a). Moreover, certain aspects of vocabulary knowledge, such as grammatical functions, collocation, and association, might be better developed through repeated encounters in spoken and written input.

In comparing deliberate and incidental learning, it is perhaps most useful to consider the value that each provides. We are able to make relatively large and rapid gains in vocabulary knowledge through deliberate learning. However, we might not learn many things about the words through quick study. For example, some frequent collocates of 'lose' include: '~ weight', '~ sight (of)', '~ control', '~ interest', '~ track', '~ touch', '~ faith', '~ hope', '~ confidence', '~ ground', and '~ patience'. Most deliberate learning activities are unlikely to contribute to knowledge of more than one or two collocates. Similar arguments can be made about learning the various derivations, associations, and senses of words through deliberate instruction. On the other hand, while the amount of knowledge that might be gained through encountering words repeatedly in spoken and written input might be considerable, this is a time-consuming process and is dependent on learners receiving sufficient input. Having weighed the two methods of learning, it seems clear that both incidental and deliberate learning provide benefits and should therefore be included together in a vocabulary learning programme.

ACTIVITY 3.2   Compare your own experiences of deliberate and incidental learning

Complete the table with one or more examples of your own experiences of deliberate and incidental learning. Which type of learning do you think has contributed the most to your L1 and L2 lexical development?

	L1	L2
Deliberate		
Incidental		

Incidental Learning Hypothesis: input through reading

In a seminal series of studies on L1 lexical development, William Nagy, Patricia Herman, and Richard Anderson investigated how and to what extent incidental vocabulary learning occurs. This led them to formulate the **Incidental Learning Hypothesis**, proposing that 'incidental learning from context during free reading is the major mode of vocabulary acquisition during the school years, and the volume of experience with written language, interacting with reading comprehension ability, is the major determinant of vocabulary growth' (Nagy, Herman, & Anderson, 1985, p. 234). The key word here, it seems, is 'volume'. In their studies, Nagy, Herman, and Anderson estimated that children may read as many as one million L1 words per year. Crucially, such volume of input increases opportunities for repeated encounters with words, allowing for incidental learning to take place. While it is possible to learn a word after a single encounter, such cases are exceptions to the general rule that vocabulary knowledge is gained in small increments until eventually there is sufficient knowledge to understand and use words. Many other studies have also demonstrated that vocabulary can be learned incidentally through reading (for L1, see Jenkins, Stein, & Wysocki, 1984; for L2, see Day, Omura, & Hiramatsu, 1991).

For Nagy, Herman, and Anderson, the quantity of reading is clearly key to vocabulary growth. Another key factor is quality. Not all reading materials are equal, and it is important to consider how much of a text can actually be used to learn words, as this has been shown to affect whether or not lexical development can occur (Webb, 2008b). Some sentences will provide useful information that will facilitate learning; others may provide insufficient information, or even mislead learners about the meaning of an unfamiliar word. For example, consider the following two sentences.

1 'Every song she sang was beautiful and perfect,' Jennifer said, sincerely.
2 'Every song she sang was beautiful and perfect,' Jennifer said, mockingly.

In the first sentence, a learner may infer (correctly) that the word 'sincerely' conveys a positive meaning based on the information available. However, in the second sentence, learners may potentially make the same assumption about 'mockingly', which in fact conveys the opposite meaning.

Time is also an important factor. If words are not re-encountered for a long period of time, there is potential for knowledge to decay. Thus, knowledge does not always move forward, but probably moves back and forth along a continuum (Nation & Webb, 2011). Moreover, while Nagy, Herman, and Anderson's studies focused exclusively on the learning of form–meaning connections, more recent studies have revealed that other aspects of word knowledge, such as written form, grammatical functions, and collocations, are also gradually learned through repeated encounters in context (Pigada & Schmitt, 2006; Webb, 2007a). Together, the research in this area reveals that there is no dichotomy between knowing and not knowing a word; rather, there is a continuum along which a learner's knowledge of a word moves from the absence of knowledge, to degrees of partial knowledge, and finally to complete knowledge (Nation & Webb, 2011). In all likelihood, most words are only learned to a partial degree.

So what evidence do we have to support the argument that incidental learning through reading accounts for the vast majority of L1 vocabulary growth? Although many studies have shown that incidental vocabulary learning can occur through reading, there is little real evidence that it is responsible for the huge gains in L1 lexical growth experienced by most children. Because of the lack of empirical support for this claim, the Incidental Learning Hypothesis has also been labelled the Default Learning Hypothesis (Jenkins & Dixon, 1983; Jenkins, Stein, & Wysocki, 1984), with the argument being made that incidental learning must be the 'default' learning mode in childhood, because children do not deliberately learn thousands of words each year, not least because there is insufficient time to do so. So incidental learning through reading must account for the huge L1 vocabulary growth that occurs in childhood.

Research indicates that L2 learners are also able to learn words incidentally through repeated encounters in context (Horst, Cobb, & Meara, 1998). However, the majority of studies have shown that incidental vocabulary learning gains in L2 tend to be very small, with relatively few words being learned. This is because L2 learners, particularly in the EFL context, receive a relatively small amount of L2 input, which limits the potential for incidental vocabulary learning to occur. Although **extensive reading** programmes provide a means for them to encounter more input, L2 learners typically read about one book per week. For foreign language learners to read a million words in a year, as L1 learners may do, they would need to read approximately 166 6,000-word graded readers. Unsurprisingly, few L2 learning programmes are capable of providing the time and resources for learners to read this amount of text. This means there is a clear limitation in the extent to which incidental learning solely through reading can facilitate L2 vocabulary growth in the EFL context, though it should not be dismissed altogether, for the reasons given earlier in this chapter (see page 50).

Spoken input and incidental vocabulary learning

In the literature on incidental vocabulary learning in L1, there is little discussion of the contribution of spoken input. Although lexical growth among pre-literate children is solely achieved through receiving large amounts of spoken input, it is written input that is believed to be the source of the vast majority of later gains (Nagy & Herman, 1987). This is surprising, because there is general agreement that children learn about 25–30% of their total adult vocabulary before they can read (Biemiller & Slonim, 2001; Goulden, Nation, & Read, 1990). This would suggest that we learn very effectively through listening before we can read, and then learn very little through listening once we can read. The reason why there is relatively little focus on incidental learning through listening is that spoken input has been found to provide fewer encounters with lower-frequency words than written input (Hayes, 1988); and if speech is made up of words that tend to be known by school-age children, then it is surely unlikely to contribute to much further lexical development.

However, this argument neglects to take into account the different proportions of spoken and written discourse that are encountered by L1 learners. Consider the following points:

- Television programmes and films do include encounters with lower-frequency words. Stuart Webb and Michael Rodgers (2009b) found that 1.12% of the words in a corpus of 312 films were beyond the 10,000 word frequency level. Similarly, Rodgers and Webb (2011) found that 1.22% of the words in 288 television programmes were outside the 10,000 word frequency level; that is, in one hour of television we might hear about 6,000 words, of which 73 might be relatively low in frequency. This may seem insignificant. However, if L2 television is watched regularly, the number of unknown words that are encountered will continue to increase, and the potential for learning will rise sharply as these words are encountered again and again.
- Incidental learning from repeated encounters has been shown to occur through watching television and films. Studies examining the potential for incidental vocabulary learning through watching television and films indicate that, with sufficient input providing repeated encounters with low-frequency words (Rodgers & Webb, 2011; Webb, 2010a; Webb & Rodgers, 2009a), incidental learning is likely to occur. Moreover, research consistently demonstrates that both L1 and L2 learners can learn vocabulary incidentally through watching video (Neuman & Koskinen, 1992; Rice & Woodsmall, 1988) and that the gains may be similar in size to those made through reading (Rodgers, 2013).

- People listen to spoken input much more than they read. For example, Americans and Canadians watch television five times as much as they read (Statistics Canada, 1998; United States Bureau of Labor, 2006).

It is certainly true that the proportion of words beyond the 10,000 word frequency level in written text in the Wellington Written Corpus is higher, at 1.76% (Webb & Macalister, 2013), or just above 0.50% more than the proportion encountered in television programmes and films. However, while spoken input might not provide as high a proportion of lower-frequency words as written input, the much greater amount of time spent listening to spoken input might actually lead to a similar number of encounters with low-frequency words.

ACTIVITY 3.3   **Spoken versus written input and incidental vocabulary learning**

Think of a typical or recent class of students. Look at the chart below and tick the activities that you used with these students. Next, draw a pie chart showing the rough proportions of different types of spoken and written language input over a series of your lessons, and answer the questions below. Then read the notes at the end of the chapter.

Written input		Spoken input			
Reading		**Listening**		**Viewing**	
Short texts		Short passages		Excerpts from television programmes and films	
Graded readers		Audio versions of graded readers		Full-length television programmes and films	

1 What do you think about the balance of spoken versus written input for these students in relation to incidental vocabulary learning?

2 What could you do to increase the amount of input in the different categories?

How 'intentional' is incidental vocabulary learning?

Much of the research on the topic appears to suggest that incidental learning is unintentional. But in an interesting discussion of incidental vocabulary learning, Susan Gass (1999) proposes that incidental vocabulary learning may be more intentional than we might think.

Attention

According to incidental learning theory, we learn words by encountering them repeatedly over an extended period of time. This might seem to imply an absence of deliberate attention; however, if we consider our own vocabulary learning experiences, we find that this is rarely the case. When we see or hear a new word, we may well focus considerable attention on that word and deliberately try to learn it. Moreover, on some occasions we might immediately check the meaning of an unknown word in a dictionary, or ask someone what the word means.

Teacher explanation

In the L2 classroom, teachers often increase the potential for students to learn new words by deliberately explaining their meanings, and research clearly shows that when incidental vocabulary learning is supported in this way, it is more likely to be successful. Craig Chaudron (1982) investigated the extent to which teachers explained the meanings of words to their students in the ESL classroom. He found that teachers often deliberately explained the meanings of L2 words using L1 translations and L2 definitions, or implicitly signalled and explained word meanings using techniques such as **paraphrase**, **parallelism**, and **apposition**. John Flowerdew (1992) examined the speech of lecturers in biology and chemistry lectures given to L2 learners. He found that in just over ten hours of lectures, 315 of 329 words or concepts were defined, at a rate of about 20 definitions per lecture. Analysis of these lectures also indicated that the teachers provided explanations of word meanings using both syntactic and lexical signals.

Research has also examined the degree to which words are learned through reading and listening to passages, stories, and lectures with and without explanation of word meanings. Studies consistently show that teacher explanation of word meaning increases the extent of both L1 (Elley, 1989) and L2 (Biemiller & Boote, 2006) vocabulary learning. The way in which words are explained also affects the likelihood that they will be learned. For example, deliberate explanation of a word's meaning has been found to lead to greater vocabulary learning than implicit explanation (that is, using synonyms, paraphrases, etc.) (Vidal, 2003, 2011). It also appears to be the case that learners tend to learn more words when they are translated from the L2 into the L1 than when words are defined in the L2 (Sawada, 2009).

Dictionary use

Learners may consult dictionaries during or after reading to check words that they have encountered. Dictionaries are provided as a resource for learning in most classrooms, and students often bring their own copies with them in foreign language learning situations. Consulting a dictionary does not ensure that a word will be learned, but it usually has a positive effect on vocabulary learning (Knight, 1994). So although research on incidental vocabulary learning demonstrates that students can learn words without the use of dictionaries, their availability in most learning contexts and the positive effect they have on vocabulary learning in general suggests that they have a role to play in both L1 and L2 lexical growth through reading and listening.

Taken together, research suggests that vocabulary learning is enhanced through the support of dictionaries, teachers, parents, and peers. While the use of these resources during or after reading and listening still conforms to our definition of incidental vocabulary learning as a by-product of a task, they may help to better explain the impressive lexical growth that is believed to occur incidentally.

Expanding on incidental vocabulary learning theory

As we saw earlier in this chapter (see page 51), there is a lack of empirical evidence supporting the view encapsulated by the Incidental Learning Hypothesis that L1 (and L2) lexical growth mainly depends on incidental vocabulary learning through reading; and it has been shown that relatively small gains are made through reading individual texts. In spite of this, the Incidental Learning Hypothesis remains widely accepted, and surprisingly little theoretical development has been made in this area. However, recent studies provide information that may allow us to expand on existing theory. The following sections outline points that should be included.

An incremental process
Incidental vocabulary learning is a gradual process, and there is no dichotomy between knowing and not knowing a word. Instead, vocabulary knowledge is gained in small increments; it can increase through further encounters and decrease if a word is not encountered for a long period of time. It is also important to note that knowledge of different components

of a word, such as written form, form–meaning connection, collocation, and grammatical functions, may be gained to varying degrees through each encounter (Webb, 2007a). Moreover, gaining knowledge of one aspect does not ensure that knowledge will be gained of another.

Quantity of input

The amount of input is central to whether words can be learned incidentally or not. In the L1 environment, the abundance of input ensures that lexical growth is driven through repeated encounters with words in context. In the foreign language learning environment, a lack of input may limit learners' incidental vocabulary learning gains. The key to facilitating lexical growth for these learners may be to increase L2 input; so, for example, implementing both extensive reading and **extensive viewing** of television programmes in the curriculum may help to improve on current rates of L2 lexical growth.

Written versus spoken input

It is likely that written and spoken input both contribute considerably to L1 incidental vocabulary learning. Written input provides the greatest potential for encountering unknown words, because it contains a higher proportion of low-frequency words than spoken input. However, most people are likely to encounter more words through spoken input than written input. Spoken input may therefore provide similar or greater potential for repeated encounters with words. The degree to which each type of input contributes to incidental vocabulary learning is not clear, but research has shown that both written and spoken input contribute to incidental vocabulary learning gains and that there is greatest potential for incidental vocabulary learning to occur when the two types of input are combined (Webb & Chang, 2012b).

Varied encounters

Repeated and varied encounters with unknown words are essential for incidental vocabulary learning to occur, because the knowledge that can be gained through just a few encounters is not sufficient to fully learn a word. To demonstrate this point, let us look at four sentences that include the word 'lost':

a She <u>lost her purse</u> at the park. (= not find)
b They <u>lost the game</u> in extra time. (= not win)
c I have <u>lost touch</u> with her over the last few years. (= not keep)
d He <u>lost</u> a lot of <u>weight</u> when he was sick. (= have less)

These four sentences show variation in meaning and collocation which cannot be captured in any one sentence. Because there is much to learn about most words, it may be the case that, while repetition is extremely important, different encounters may not repeat the same information but may instead introduce new information, and knowledge might not necessarily be consolidated between encounters. For example, a first encounter with 'lost' in the collocation 'lost control' may not be reinforced by other collocates such as those mentioned on page 49. Although other aspects of knowledge, such as form–meaning connection, collocation, and written form, might be gained through these encounters, reinforcement may only occur when 'lost control' is encountered again.

A long-term process

Incidental vocabulary learning gains that are made through encountering a word several times in a single text are likely to be very small, as there is much to be learned about each word; and in most cases the amount of learning that occurs in the short term will be a fraction of what can be gained in the long term. Measuring vocabulary growth after a short period of reading or listening can show that learning has occurred, but this cannot be considered an accurate evaluation of incidental learning, because it is only measuring one moment in a very long process. Instead, we need to consider lexical development through repeated encounters over the long term: increased input is likely to lead to increased vocabulary learning, as words are encountered a greater number of times and knowledge is further strengthened (Webb & Chang, 2015a).

Incorporating deliberate learning

Research shows that incidental vocabulary learning is probably enhanced by support from deliberate learning techniques and resources that help to develop lexical knowledge, though the degree to which these techniques and resources help to consolidate knowledge gained through reading and listening is not clear. It may be more accurate to suggest that, while deliberate learning is not responsible for the huge L1 lexical growth experienced by young children, learners may deliberately learn the words that they first encounter during reading and listening to enhance learning to a certain degree.

Language learning experience

Incidental vocabulary learning may become easier with increased vocabulary size, and this could in turn speed up the rate of learning (Webb, 2007b). As people become more proficient in a language, and as their vocabulary size increases, they may be able to focus more attention on any unknown words they encounter. Moreover, the accumulation of lexical knowledge may reduce the learning burden of unknown words. Having a larger vocabulary size means there is greater potential for learners to understand the language that is encountered (Webb & Paribakht, 2015); and knowing more words may also enhance their ability to learn any unknown words they encounter (Liu & Nation, 1985). In fact, one study found that a difference in vocabulary size of about 500 words made a significant difference in the proportion of words that were learned in an extensive reading programme (Webb & Chang, 2015b). Although the students were in the same school year and had a similar English language learning profile, those who knew more words learned around 50% of the unknown words they encountered during reading, while those who knew fewer words learned around 20% of the words. This is an example of what is known as the **Matthew effect** (Merton, 1968), which explains why advanced learners may be more successful at vocabulary learning than beginners. It also helps to better explain the massive L1 lexical growth that occurs between the ages of 6–18.

Summary

There is a significant difference between the number of word families that native speakers may learn and the number that many EFL learners manage to learn. Context is a key factor. In the process of learning our first language, we learn many words through repeated encounters during reading and listening. Although we might initially gain just a small fraction of knowledge about a new word, encountering the same word again and again over time will lead to greater and deeper knowledge of that word. When we receive large amounts of input, incidental vocabulary learning may be the most effective means of facilitating lexical growth. Foreign language learners, however, may not receive sufficient input to learn many words through reading and listening. Consequently, deliberate learning may play a larger role in L2 lexical development. Because learning vocabulary incidentally in our first language is so effective, perhaps the key to improving L2 lexical development is to find ways of vastly increasing the amount of L2 input.

Questions for reflection

1 How often do you encounter unknown L2 words in speech or in writing? Do you think you tend to learn more words incidentally through one than the other?

2 Incidental vocabulary learning is typically a slow process where we gain knowledge in small increments. We may learn more about words in some situations than in others. What do you think affects the degree to which you gain lexical knowledge when you encounter unknown L2 words?

3 Consider an unknown L2 word that you recently encountered. What did you learn about it? Think about the context in which you encountered it, the form of the word, how it related to other words, and how it was used.

Keys to activities

ACTIVITY 3.1 **Check your vocabulary size**

Compare your vocabulary size to that of native speakers of English at different stages of learning:

Pre-literate children: 3–4,000 word families

Ten-year-olds: around 8–9,000 word families

Educated adults: 15–20,000 word families

ACTIVITY 3.3 **Spoken versus written input and incidental vocabulary learning**

Language learning materials tend to include shorter texts and listening passages that serve to teach different aspects of language, and there are often a greater proportion of written texts than spoken texts. Perhaps your responses reflect this. However, it is useful to also consider the value of including more input to fuel vocabulary learning, because incidental learning is dependent on the amount of input that learners receive. It is also useful to think about the extent to which we have learned words through listening and the importance that spoken input may have in the learning process.

Suggestions for further reading

Nagy, W. E., **Herman, P. A.**, & **Anderson, R. C.** (1985). Learning words from context. *Reading Research Quarterly*, *20(2)*, 233–253.

This seminal study on incidental vocabulary learning describes the key issues that are involved in researching this area. Nagy, Herman, and Anderson also theorize about the extent to which incidental vocabulary learning is responsible for L1 vocabulary growth.

Nation, I. S. P. (2006). How large a vocabulary is needed for reading and listening? *Canadian Modern Language Review*, *63(1)*, 59–82.

This article examines the number of words that are required to understand different types of discourse. The research highlights the importance of knowing the most frequent words and the lexical challenges that L2 learners face when trying to understand English.

Webb, S. A., & **Chang, A. C.-S.** (2012a). Second language vocabulary growth. *RELC Journal, 43(1)*, 113–126.

This study looks at the extent of L2 vocabulary growth, as well as the proportion of words that EFL students learn at different word frequency levels. Webb and Chang outline principles to consider when setting up an effective vocabulary learning programme.

4 CONDITIONS CONTRIBUTING TO VOCABULARY LEARNING

Introduction

What has to happen for vocabulary learning to occur? Activities may be used to facilitate vocabulary learning, but more specifically it is the learning conditions that these activities set up which result in the learning itself. A major goal of this book is to show how a range of very useful activities make use of learning conditions, and how these activities can be used and adapted to maximize the occurrence of such conditions. This chapter looks at how learning conditions occur in activities. Awareness of the conditions that contribute to vocabulary learning should help teachers and learners to see how effective (or ineffective) an activity may be, as well as to find ways to modify exercises to make them more likely to facilitate learning.

Framework of vocabulary learning conditions

Vocabulary learning occurs because certain conditions are established which facilitate learning. These are repetition, **noticing**, **retrieval**, **varied encounters** and **varied use**, and **elaboration**. These learning conditions are themselves underpinned by two key factors:

1 repetition, i.e. the number of encounters with each word
2 the quality of attention at each encounter.

The greater the number of encounters, the more likely learning is to occur; and the deeper the quality of the encounters, the more likely learning is to occur. The few experiments comparing the effects of the number of encounters (repetitions) with the quality of the encounters suggest that, of the two factors, quality has the stronger effect (Laufer & Rozovski-Roitblat, 2015; Webb, 2008a). See Table 4.1 for a framework of how these factors break down into the various vocabulary learning conditions.

Repetition	= number of encounters (first encounter + repetition)	
Quality of attention	Incidental	Deliberate
Noticing		
Retrieval (receptive or productive)		
Varied encounters (receptive) or varied use (productive)		
Elaboration (receptive or productive)		

Table 4.1 Framework of vocabulary learning conditions

Quality of attention depends primarily on whether the learner gives incidental attention or deliberate attention to a word they encounter. There are a few situations where it is not easy to distinguish between the two; but, as seen in Chapter 3, incidental attention generally applies when the learner's focus is on some other aspect of communication besides individual words and phrases, while deliberate attention applies when the learner consciously focuses on particular aspects of a word or phrase. In general, deliberate attention in an activity is more likely to result in learning than incidental attention. However, in a well-balanced vocabulary learning programme, the opportunities for learning from incidental attention should be much greater than those for learning from deliberate attention.

It is also worth noting that the four learning conditions relating to quality of attention—noticing, retrieval, varied encounters and varied use, and elaboration—are largely cumulative. For example, retrieval also involves noticing, and varied use involves retrieval and noticing; elaboration certainly involves noticing and may involve retrieval if the elaborated words have been met before; and deliberate elaboration can also involve varied use. However, because elaboration can occur when the word is **decontextualized**, deliberate elaboration does not necessarily involve varied use.

There are other important conditions which contribute to learning, such as the similarity of L1 and L2 concepts, the existence of cognates and **loanwords**, patterning within L2 words, and interference between related words, but these largely affect the learning burden of a word (see Chapter 2). The lighter the learning burden of a word, the less repetition and attention will be required to learn it.

ACTIVITY 4.1   **Analysing quality of attention**

Which of the following situations involve incidental attention and which involve deliberate attention? Justify your classifications. Then check your answers at the end of the chapter.

1 learning a word using a flashcard app

2 looking up a word in a dictionary while reading

3 hearing a word during a lecture

4 asking someone the meaning of a word they have just used in a conversation

5 breaking down a word into word parts

6 hearing a word used in a discussion

7 subconsciously guessing a word from context

8 using a word without being sure of its meaning

Table 4.2 gives examples of activities which make use of the learning conditions aligned to quality of attention. (For a more detailed explanation of some of the activities, see Chapter 5.)

Repetition	= *number of encounters (first encounter + repetition)*	
Quality of attention	Incidental	Deliberate
Noticing	Guessing from context	Highlighting words in a text
	Noticing a gap when speaking or writing	Focusing on the form or meaning of a word on a flashcard
		Using a dictionary or glossary
		Being taught words
Retrieval	Seeing a previously encountered word while listening or reading, and recalling its meaning	Remembering words on flashcards
		Doing cloze exercises after reading a text
	Recalling and using a recently encountered word as part of conversation or writing	Playing games that involve remembering the names of objects (e.g. Kim's Game)
		Recalling a list of words

Varied encounters	Seeing a previously encountered word in a new form or context while listening or reading, and recalling its meaning (e.g. linked skills) Extensive reading	Looking at different examples of the word used in context Doing an exercise consisting of true/false sentences
Varied use	Recalling and using a recently encountered word in a new way in conversation or writing (e.g. linked skills)	Doing cloze exercises Doing topic-based continuous writing Giving a presentation
Elaboration	Encountering and using a word to communicate Describing pictures Reading interactively (reading and discussing in a group)	Using memory techniques to link L1 and L2 words (the keyword technique) Creating a chart or map of related words (semantic mapping) Analysing word parts Looking at the different senses of a word to determine its core meaning

Table 4.2 Vocabulary learning conditions with example activities

These learning conditions provide a very useful framework for evaluating a range of activities, and in the remainder of this chapter we will look closely at each of the conditions, following the order shown in Table 4.1.

Repetition

There is plenty of L1 and L2 research showing the importance of repetition (Brown, Waring & Donkaewbua, 2008; Kweon & Kim, 2008; Laufer & Rozovski-Roitblat, 2011; Pellicer-Sánchez & Schmitt, 2010; Pigada & Schmitt, 2006; Rott, 1999; Waring & Takaki, 2003; Webb, 2007a). Common sense also suggests that the more often you encounter or use a word, the stronger your knowledge of it will be.

ACTIVITY 4.2   **Using repetition**

Think of a class you teach, or a group of learners that you know. Suggest three activities you could use to make sure that the words the learners encountered during their reading session have a chance of being used or encountered again later on. Then read on and check your ideas.

It is useful to distinguish repetition in incidental learning from repetition in deliberate learning. In principle, fewer repetitions are needed in deliberate learning than in incidental learning.

Repetition and incidental learning

A major feature of incidental vocabulary learning is that learning the meaning of a word typically requires the learner to infer the meaning from **contextual clues**. A commonly asked question is: 'How many repetitions are necessary for learning to occur?' Research does not provide a clear and obvious answer to this question, largely because the salience of the word, the availability of information about it, the quality of the encounters with it, and the learning burden of the word itself are also very important factors affecting learning, and it is not easy to separate their effects from that of repetition. However, besides the general consensus that the greater the number of repetitions, the more likely learning is to occur, research does suggest the following:

- Learning is supported if, in the initial encounter(s) with a word, information is readily available about the word, such as its form and meaning. This information provides basic knowledge which can then be strengthened, added to, and retrieved in later encounters (Royer, 1973).
- In general, the value of repetition is limited by the law of diminishing returns. That is, the first few encounters with a word are likely to add significantly to lexical knowledge, with each subsequent repetition making a smaller contribution. Karina Vidal (2011) found that the greatest increase in vocabulary learning from reading occurred at around two or three repetitions, and from listening at around five to six repetitions. Another very innovative study takes us a step closer to what actually happens when learners encounter new vocabulary in texts. Ana Pellicer-Sánchez (2016) used eye tracking technology to reveal how long learners focused on new words. She found that at around the third to the fifth repetition, there was a significant increase in the speed of retrieval. After eight encounters with the word in the text, the retrieval time started to approach that of known words. In her study, Pellicer-Sánchez found that eight repetitions (all target words in the study were repeated eight times) resulted in high scores on form and meaning recognition tests and moderate scores on meaning recall tests.
- Studies have shown that there is probably a useful intermediate repetition goal for incidental learning of around 12 or more repetitions. Marlise Horst, Tom Cobb, and Paul Meara (1998) found that words repeated eight

times or more showed the greatest gains. Thomas Saragi, Paul Nation, and Gerold Meister's data (1978) and Stuart Webb's data (2007a) suggested at least ten repetitions. Pellicer-Sánchez and Schmitt (2010) found that words occurring more than ten times showed the greatest gains.

- It has also been shown that repetition similarly affects the incidental learning of multi-word combinations (Durrant & Schmitt, 2010; Sonbul & Schmitt, 2013; Webb, Newton, & Chang, 2013).

What is common in all of these studies is the recognition that, although repetition is clearly an important factor affecting vocabulary learning, there are plenty of words that are readily learned with a very small number of repetitions and some words that are not learned, even after many repetitions. Ronan Brown, Rob Waring, and Sangrawee Donkaewbua (2008) found that well over 20 repetitions may be needed for some words, especially in listening. Any proposed number of repetitions will be more than enough for some words and not enough for others, although it may serve as a reasonable estimate for most words. In general, there seem to be medium-strength correlations between repetition and learning (Saragi, Nation, & Meister, 1978; Webb, 2007a).

Repetition and deliberate learning

In deliberate learning, a smaller number of repetitions—around seven—appears to be required to learn most words (Crothers & Suppes, 1967; Lado, Baldwin, & Lobo, 1967; Tinkham, 1993, 1997; Waring, 1997a), although learners differ greatly in their aptitude for deliberate vocabulary learning (Thorndike, 1908; Tinkham, 1989; Webb, 1962). Even the first pass through a list of word pairs can result in substantial learning, especially if the language being learned is related to the learner's L1, as is the case with English, German (Thorndike, 1908), and Spanish (Crothers & Suppes, 1967). Warwick Elley (1989) found that two deliberate encounters had a notable effect on learning when a teacher quickly explained a word encountered in a listening text. Note, however, that most of the studies concerned focused on measuring knowledge of the written form and meaning of words, and largely involved choosing the correct meaning in a multiple-choice test or providing a meaning in a recall test. While recognizing the form of a word and recalling its meaning are central to reading, there are many other aspects of vocabulary knowledge to be gained.

Spacing of repetitions

Within a deliberate learning session, retention is better if the repetitions of a word are not all massed together but spaced. In other words, if several words are being learned at the same time, it is better to give attention to each of the words and then come back to the first one again so that there is an interval between each encounter with a particular word. This is better than concentrating on one word at a time, repeating it over and over. It used to be thought that the spacing of words within a learning session needed to be gradually increased, but more recent research has shown that evenly spread spacing is sufficient (Nakata, 2015).

Increasing repetition

Repetition is important in learning, and the more repetitions there are, the more likely learning is to occur. We will now look at a few ways of increasing repetition. (See Chapter 5 for an in-depth overview of activities and how learning conditions contribute to their effectiveness.)

Using graded readers

In incidental learning, we now know that repetition is primarily related to quantity of input; that is, the more learners listen and read, the more often words will be repeated. Unfortunately, as we know from Zipf's law, at least half of the different words in any text are likely to only occur once. This means that a very large proportion of the new words encountered in a text are not likely to be repeated in that text, or even in texts which follow. A key solution to this problem is to read texts that are specially prepared for language learners, namely graded readers. Although Zipf's law still applies to graded readers, every word in a graded reader is likely to be useful to the learner and worth learning. Graded readers are now available up to the 8,000 word frequency level, beyond which learners should move on to reading unsimplified texts.

Repeated reading

Re-reading the same text effectively doubles the repetitions of words. Reading similar texts (that is, on the same topic) will reduce the number of different words in the text by at least 50% (Sutarsyah, Nation, & Kennedy, 1994). While this only has a minor effect on repetitions, it does avoid a lot of the distraction that can come from having to deal with large numbers of unknown words. The focus here is on verbatim repetition (repeatedly encountering the word in exactly the same context) to strengthen learning. Repeated viewing of the same film or television programme achieves the same result.

Linked skills

Activities such as the **linked skills** activity (see Chapter 5), where learners deal with the same content across different language skills, build in repetition by focusing on the same topic several times during the activity. This is varied (rather than verbatim) repetition, i.e. encountering the word in various unfamiliar contexts, which enriches learning. Combining incidental learning and deliberate learning can ensure that words which do not get enough repetitions in incidental learning can be strengthened through deliberate learning.

Deliberate learning

Repetition is much more easily controlled in deliberate learning. In deliberate strategies, such as learning words with flashcards, repetition is a key element.

Quality of attention

Repetition needs to be supported by high-quality encounters with the words. As we saw in Table 4.1, four learning conditions contribute to the quality of attention involved in vocabulary learning: noticing, retrieval, varied encounters and varied use, and elaboration. We will now look at each of these in turn and give a few examples of activities to illustrate.

Noticing

Noticing involves paying attention to a word. As a key component of vocabulary learning, it has been the focus of considerable speculation and research in applied linguistics (Ellis, 1991; McLaughlin, 1990; Schmidt, 1990). In incidental learning, noticing occurs when guessing from context and when retrieving the meaning of a familiar or partially familiar word. Looking up a word in a dictionary or glossary makes noticing more deliberate, as does encountering words which have been highlighted in the text, for example in bold, italics, or colour. Although noticing by itself is not one of the deeper levels of quality of attention, it is still very important, because where we give our attention largely determines what will be learned (Barcroft, 2009). If we focus on the form of a word, then we are more likely to learn that than its meaning. If we focus on the meaning of the word, then this necessarily takes our attention away from its form. We will now look at the various ways in which noticing can occur.

Decontextualization

The more deliberate acts of noticing involve some kind of decontextualization. This means looking at a word in isolation, rather than as part of the context in which it appears. For example, when we look up a word in a dictionary, or have it explained to us, we view that word as a specific language item, rather than as a component of the surrounding text.

Word consciousness

Noticing is encouraged by **word consciousness** (Scott & Nagy, 2004; Graves, 2006). This refers to a general meta-linguistic awareness of words and various aspects of what it means to know a word. For example:

• an awareness of the value of dictionaries and of the usefulness of looking up words

- an awareness that many words can be broken down into parts and that the meanings of these parts relate to the meaning of the whole word
- a recognition that words have many senses, but that these senses share a common core meaning
- an awareness that there are many aspects of word knowledge
- the realization that some words are formal and others informal, and that the choice of words strongly affects a message.

Word consciousness is developed by doing activities with a deliberate focus on these kinds of knowledge. Strategy training also raises word consciousness. The goal of word consciousness training is to make learners excited about encountering and learning new words, to make them aware of how to go about learning words, and to get them interested in exploring the many aspects of the words that they already know.

Negotiation

Group work activities also provide the opportunity for noticing to occur, particularly when learners negotiate the meanings of words that are unfamiliar to them. **Negotiation** of vocabulary involves what some call 'language-related episodes'. These occur when, in the context of a communication task, learners clarify and explain language features to each other, such as what a word means or how to spell it. Importantly, learners do not have to actively engage in negotiation in order to gain the benefits; observing others negotiating seems to be as effective as actively taking part (Ellis & Heimbach, 1997; Newton, 2013; Stahl & Clark, 1987). Vocabulary which is negotiated is more likely to be learned than vocabulary which is simply encountered in context (Newton, 2013). However, negotiation takes time (Ellis, Tanaka, & Yamazaki, 1994) and therefore cannot account for as much learning as simply guessing from context.

Many activities that are used to facilitate vocabulary learning do not go much beyond the level of noticing. For example, learning words in bilingual lists, where L2 words and their L1 translations can be seen at the same time, only requires a quality of attention at the level of noticing. Similarly, repeating words over and over to oneself does not go beyond the level of noticing. As we shall see in the sections that follow, it is not difficult to increase the quality of noticing.

Retrieval

The second learning condition contributing to quality of attention is retrieval (see Table 4.1). Retrieval can only occur on the second or subsequent encounters with a word, because it involves recalling what was encountered before. This reliance on the recollection of previous learning explains why retrieval is sometimes called the **testing effect** in the field of psychology. There are two types of retrieval: receptive retrieval involves seeing or hearing a word form and having to retrieve its meaning, as when reading or listening; productive retrieval involves needing to express a meaning and having to retrieve the appropriate word form, as in speaking or writing.

Reading and listening activities in general set up ideal conditions for retrieval. When reading, for example, the meaning of an unfamiliar word may be guessed from context, or looked up in a dictionary. The next encounter with that word in the text provides an opportunity for retrieval to occur, and subsequent encounters provide further opportunities. Research by Joe Barcroft (2007) has shown that making such retrievals is more effective for learning than being provided with the meaning of the word each time it is encountered. Retrieval is a powerful learning condition, which becomes even more powerful when the retrievals are spaced in time. Retrieval can also be enhanced if learners are aware of cognate or loanword relationships between L2 and L1 words. Many of these are so obvious that the connection does not need to be pointed out (for example, 'table' in English and French), but some are not so obvious (for example, English 'coast' and French 'côte').

One of the skills that a teacher needs to develop is knowing how to provide learners with opportunities to make retrievals. At the most basic level, this may simply involve pausing before completing a sentence, in order to give learners enough time to make the retrieval. It also involves making it possible for repetition to occur so that these repetitions become opportunities for retrieval. Let us consider a few ways of creating such opportunities.

Re-telling

Re-telling activities provide opportunities for retrieval, and teachers can usefully spend a reasonable amount of time on getting learners to re-tell and reflect on previous work. During re-telling, the 'pause–prompt–praise' procedure is an important tool for both the teacher and the learners. This procedure involves pausing in order to give the learner a chance to retrieve, providing a prompt or clue to help if the retrieval seems unlikely to occur, and finally, giving praise for a successful retrieval.

An effective way to encourage re-telling if the learners are working from a text is to get them to put the text away and then recall what they have been working on. If the teacher handles this skilfully, this can be used as an opportunity to go beyond retrieval to enrich and elaborate on the previous learning. In any lesson, the old material is much more important than the new material, because the old material is further along the path to being learned, so the attention given to it is more likely to result in well-established learning. The new material is just beginning this journey.

Digital glossaries

Digital reading texts provide excellent opportunities for retrieval. When **glossing** words in hard-copy texts, the glosses are likely to appear in the margin next to the line where the glossed word occurs, or in a box next to a reading text. Such glosses eliminate the need for retrieval. Hyperlinks to glosses in e-readers such as Kindle and Kobo, however, allow users to retrieve the meaning of a word before tapping on the word to bring up the gloss. This retrieval with feedback when needed is likely to be more effective than retrieval by itself.

Flashcards

The use of flashcards to deliberately learn vocabulary makes strong use of the condition of retrieval. Receptive retrieval occurs when looking at the L2 word and trying to retrieve its meaning. This is easier than productive retrieval, which involves looking at the L1 meaning (the translation) and trying to retrieve the L2 word form. Research comparing receptive retrieval and productive retrieval with flashcards has shown that if only one kind of retrieval is to be used, then it should be productive retrieval (Griffin & Harley, 1996). This is because, even though productive retrieval is more difficult, it includes the knowledge that is needed for both productive and receptive retrieval. Doing well on receptive retrieval, on the other hand, does not ensure successful productive retrieval.

Varied encounters and varied use

As we saw in Table 4.1, the third learning condition is divided into varied (receptive) encounters and varied (productive) use. Both involve retrieval but differ from it in the important sense that they also involve encountering or using a word in different forms or contexts. The degree of difference between current and prior encounters or use will affect how much is learned about the word (Hall, 1991; Joe, 1998); the greater the difference, the stronger the learning. The strength of learning is probably accounted for by the strengthening effect of retrieval plus the enriched information about the word provided by the variation in encounter or use. As noted earlier, verbatim retrieval provides the strengthening effect of retrieval, but not the enrichment.

As Angela Joe (1998) found, there are many degrees of variation which affect our knowledge of a word. Words can vary in their form, meaning, and use. Forms can vary in their spoken form, written form, and word parts. Meanings can differ according to the various senses of a word. Word use can vary according to variations in grammatical context and collocation. Several of these aspects are interdependent. For example, a different grammatical context may require the use of a different form of the word as well as different collocations and perhaps a different sense.

Informal **concordance** studies of the occurrence of words in graded readers and novels show that the vast majority of encounters with content words within a text are varied. This is why extensive reading is a good way of expanding receptive vocabulary knowledge. The opportunities for varied encounters with words in reading could be increased by reading different texts on the same topic, such as topical articles from different online newspapers and magazines. For listening and speaking, group work activities which encourage negotiation provide opportunities for varied encounters and varied use. When learners negotiate the meaning of a word, they move from a topic-focused discussion to a language-focused discussion. This requires them to consider the word in two different ways.

Differences between the L1 and L2 are likely to contribute positively to the opportunities for varied encounters. What seems to be the same concept in two different languages is highly likely to differ in the range of referents from one language to the other. For example, 'branch' in English ('tree branch', 'branch of a company', 'branch of a bank', etc.) is represented by several words in Indonesian. These differences can seem very striking to a language learner; and besides being part of the fun and educational value of learning another language, they can also serve to enrich vocabulary knowledge.

In essence, opportunities for varied encounters and varied use are created by any activity which involves revisiting the same topic or material in a way which ensures that vocabulary is recycled and, crucially, that differences are introduced in the process. A linked skills activity, for example, involves dealing with the same material across a range of different language skills. The changes at each step need to be sufficient to allow for varied encounters with recurring words and to encourage varied use of them.

An activity like re-telling will result in varied use if certain features of the activity are adapted. One feature examined by Joe (1998) was the presence of written material for the activity. One group had a handout in front of them while they did the re-telling, while another had to put it away and work from memory. The group with the handout in front of them used more of the target words but used them in the same way as they appeared in the handout. The group without the handout used fewer target words but with variation. This clearly shows that having to rely on recall can present opportunities for varied use. Another way of encouraging varied use involves re-telling from a different perspective or presenting the material in a different way. So if the original material is a description of an incident, the re-telling could involve giving an account of it in the first person rather than in the third person, presenting it as a formal report, or acting it out as a dialogue in pairs or groups (for example, as two people who were involved in an incident, or between a reporter and a witness). The value of these changes would be measured by the resulting amount of varied use.

Elaboration

The final learning condition concerns the enrichment of knowledge of a word by encountering more aspects of its form, meaning, and use. Just as varied encounters and use are, cumulatively, forms of retrieval, elaboration is a form of varied encounters and use. Similarly, just as there are degrees of varied encounters and use, there are degrees of elaboration. It is also worth noting that the difference in effectiveness between elaboration and retrieval in a hierarchy of quality of processing may not be very large. In their study of memory in relation to learning content (not vocabulary specifically), Jeffrey Karpicke and Janell Blunt (2011) found that retrieval actually produced better results than the elaborative technique of linking words with related meanings in the semantic mapping activity (see Chapter 5). Let us consider a few ways in which elaboration can be stimulated in vocabulary learning.

Pictures
Pictures can help to reinforce and elaborate on the use of a word in a text. In some circumstances, pictures have a negative effect on learning, in that they divert attention from what needs to be learned. But in the most useful circumstances, a picture can provide a memorable image of the meaning and context of the word.

Keyword technique
One of the most striking ways of stimulating elaboration is the keyword technique (Pressley, 1977) (see Chapter 5). This is a memory technique that involves choosing an L1 'keyword' that sounds like the beginning of the L2 word you want to learn, then linking the keyword to the meaning of the L2 word by means of a visual image incorporating both. For example, a Japanese learner wanting to learn the English verb 'cite' (= to quote) might choose the keyword 'Saito' (a Japanese surname) and then visualize 'Mr Saito' with quotation marks around him (i.e. being cited).

Word parts
Elaboration can also occur when looking at the origins (or etymologies) of words and their relationships with other words which share the same word part (Wei & Nation, 2013).

Core meanings
Similarly, elaboration can occur when looking at the various senses of a word listed in a dictionary in order to identify the common core meaning that runs through all of the senses.

Deliberate or incidental elaboration?
All of the activities for generating elaboration described above involve looking analytically at a word form or meaning and relating it to other forms

of knowledge. So what about incidental elaboration? One form of incidental elaboration involves using words in authentic, memorable language, such as **instantiation** (Anderson, Stevens, Shifrin, & Osborn, 1978). Instantiation occurs when, in directing our attention towards a particular use of a word, we think of a specific instance of its use—that is, a specific referent. For example, the word 'rollercoaster' may be instantiated if learned through riding a rollercoaster at an amusement park. Thus, the memory associated with the word contributes to it being learned. It seems to be the case that instantiation is more likely to occur in the 'here and now' use of spoken language; encountering words in reading, particularly in reading fiction, is unlikely to result in instantiation because the learning experience is less likely to be memorable. **Content-based language teaching** (CBLT) and **content and language integrated learning** (CLIL) can both provide excellent opportunities for vocabulary learning, particularly where the instruction involves doing and applying. This is because genuine, objective-focused language use provides learners with the opportunity to instantiate and thus develop a rich range of associations with a particular concept.

ACTIVITY 4.3   Identifying conditions of learning

Quickly review Table 4.2, then think of three different vocabulary learning activities that you have done with a class. For each activity, decide which conditions of learning were involved.

Effects of errors and wrong examples

It is important to be aware that the learning conditions of noticing, retrieval, and varied use are likely to work with errors and wrong examples in the same ways as with correct forms. This means that activities which involve choosing between two or more items, where the false choice is lexically or grammatically incorrect, can cause learners to learn incorrect forms. Where choices share lexical or formal similarities, there is also the risk of interference between correct and incorrect forms and meanings: the more similar the choices, the greater the likelihood of interference. There is some evidence for the effect of interference from research on collocations. At the very least, it seems advisable not to create or use activities that include incorrect forms. Activities involving incidental learning from input are likely to largely involve correct forms.

Implications for learning collocations

Frank Boers, Murielle Demechleer, Averil Coxhead, and Stuart Webb (2014) argue that deliberate attention should be given to collocations because they are difficult to learn incidentally. The reasons for this are as follows:

1 We have seen that most collocations are low in frequency compared to the frequency of the individual words that make them up. Very large amounts of input would be required to get a reasonable number of repetitions of the same collocation, and the lengthy intervals between the repetitions would weaken the effect of repetition.
2 When the collocation is composed of known parts, the importance of each part is not high, particularly if it has a rather vague meaning, as with the verbs in verb–noun collocations such as 'make a mistake', 'take your time', and 'have a rest'.
3 The vagueness of the meaning of a high-frequency member of a collocation may make it difficult to keep it distinct from semantically related high-frequency members of other collocations, thus encouraging interference (for example, 'take a break', 'have a rest').

On the positive side, some of the formal features of multi-word combinations that make them memorable, such as alliteration, have a positive effect on incidental learning as well as deliberate learning (Boers, Lindstromberg, & Webb, 2014). Noticing these formal features is a form of elaboration, in that it enriches knowledge of the multi-word combination.

Summary

Vocabulary learning depends on the occurrence of a range of learning conditions relating to the two key factors of repetition and quality of attention, and on whether the repetition or attention is incidental or deliberate. The quality of encounters with words can be shallow where the word is simply noticed, and deeper where aspects of knowledge retained from previous encounters are retrieved. Retrieval is more effective if it involves encountering words in new contexts or using them in different ways. Deliberate learning in particular is more effective if the learner actively processes the word, for example by breaking it down into its constituent parts, using mnemonic devices such as the keyword technique, or by identifying its core meaning. Part of good vocabulary pedagogy involves making sure that activities include plenty of repetitions of the target vocabulary, and that these repetitions involve high-quality encounters with the words. In the following chapter, we will examine a range of common language learning activities that set up optimal vocabulary learning conditions.

Questions for reflection

1 How important is interaction among learners in setting up good conditions for vocabulary learning?

2 How should a children's story book be designed to support vocabulary learning? Suggest four major design features.

3 How can a teacher incorporate aspects of repetition and quality of attention (noticing, retrieval, varied encounters/use, elaboration) into a reading aloud activity so as to maximize the opportunities for vocabulary learning? Consider strategies involving both deliberate and incidental attention.

Keys to activities

ACTIVITY 4.1   Analysing quality of attention

The answers depend on the degree of conscious attention paid to the word and its meaning.

1 deliberate	4 deliberate	7 incidental
2 deliberate	5 deliberate	8 possibly incidental
3 incidental	6 incidental	

Suggestions for further reading

Barcroft, J. (2007). Effects of opportunities for word retrieval during second language vocabulary learning. *Language Learning, 57(1),* 35–56.

Barcroft's research looks at whether it is good to have a gloss with a word each time it occurs, or whether it is better for learners to have to make retrievals. His research has very practical implications for the way in which glossing is used in texts.

Pressley, M. (1977). Children's use of the keyword method to learn simple Spanish vocabulary words. *Journal of Educational Psychology, 69(5),* 465–472.

This is one of a number of early pieces of research examining the keyword technique. Michael Pressley continued researching this technique, making it the most researched vocabulary learning activity. In this carefully designed study, he separates the parts of the technique to see which part has the greatest effect.

5 ANALYSING VOCABULARY LEARNING ACTIVITIES

Introduction

As we saw in Chapter 4, certain learning conditions must be established for vocabulary learning to take place. These conditions involve repetition and significant encounters with words. These general conditions are put into practice in particular vocabulary learning activities, and the ways in which these activities are done can affect the amount and quality of learning that occurs from them. In this chapter, we look at a range of the most common vocabulary learning activities and analyse them to see what learning conditions they give rise to. We consider in particular how the activities can be used and adapted to provide the best opportunities for vocabulary learning.

Principles for the selection of activities

The activities included in this chapter were selected on the basis of their ability to promote both incidental and deliberate vocabulary learning. Many of the activities centre around the use of strategies and techniques which are discussed elsewhere in the book, such as dictionary use, the keyword technique, and flashcards. A further important point to note is that the activities are not mutually exclusive; many activities are enhanced by the use of additional strategies and techniques which are the focus of other activities.

The analysis of each activity follows the same format. First, a quick-reference chart provides the following information.

- **Programme strand:** Identifies how the activity fits within a balanced vocabulary learning programme and what skill is primarily involved, where relevant. The choice of activities in this chapter is guided by the principle of the four strands (Nation, 2007), which is discussed in more detail in Chapter 8. According to this principle, a well-balanced programme should provide equal opportunities for both incidental and deliberate learning through 1) **meaning-focused input**, 2) **meaning-focused output**, 3) **language-focused learning**, and 4) **fluency development**. Incidental learning occurs through meaning-focused input, meaning-focused output, and fluency development. Deliberate learning occurs in the language-focused learning strand.

- **Learning goal:** Specifies the purpose of the activity; for example, learning new words, developing knowledge of the spoken and written forms of words, and strengthening knowledge of partially known words.
- **Learning conditions:** Lists the most salient learning conditions set up by each activity. A key aim here is to clarify how vocabulary is learned, in order to develop a greater awareness of what makes the activity work so that it can be evaluated and used in ways which maximize its effects.
- **Research evidence:** Provides information, where relevant, on research that justifies the inclusion of the activity in this chapter.
- **Further reading:** Gives some suggestions for those interested in learning more about each activity.

This chart is followed by a description of the activity, some comments on the lexical dimension, further details about the learning conditions that occur in the activity, and, most importantly, suggestions for how the activity might be used to optimize vocabulary learning.

Note on skill focus

Many of the activities in this chapter can be adapted for use across a range of skills and strands of a vocabulary learning programme. It is worth making some general points, however.

- Listening activities tend to fit into the meaning-focused input strand of a course, where learners incidentally acquire vocabulary by encountering it in context. Meaning-focused input requires a low density of unknown words (2% or less) so that learners can focus on comprehension.
- Speaking activities tend to fit into the meaning-focused output strand of a course, where learners further develop vocabulary knowledge by producing words in context. Learning through meaning-focused output is more difficult than learning through meaning-focused input, because it requires extensive knowledge of the words and the words they can be used with.
- Reading activities can fit into multiple strands; the conditions present within the activity will indicate which strand it belongs in. For example, in reading activities where all of the words are known and there is a focus on increasing speed, the appropriate strand would be fluency development. As with listening, reading activities are classified as meaning-focused input when there is a focus on comprehension and a low density

of unknown words (2% or less). Reading activities can also fit into the language-focused learning strand when the aim is to deliberately learn vocabulary through reading.

* Writing activities tend to fit into the meaning-focused output strand of a course. The vocabulary component of these activities requires a depth of knowledge of words that is often beyond what has already been gained, making the activities particularly challenging. Moreover, because greater accuracy is usually expected in writing than in speech, writing activities are typically used after learning has occurred through listening, reading, and speaking.

ACTIVITY 5.1   **Analysing vocabulary activities in a coursebook (1)**

Look at an English language coursebook that is used in your context. Make a list of the different activities that are used for vocabulary learning. Then answer the questions. Compare your answers with the notes at the end of the chapter.

1 To what extent are activities in each of the four skills of listening, speaking, reading, and writing used for learning vocabulary?

2 To what extent is vocabulary likely to be learned incidentally and deliberately within the coursebook?

Vocabulary learning activities

1 Extensive listening

Programme strand	Meaning-focused input from listening
Learning goal	Learn new words, strengthen knowledge of partially known words, develop knowledge of form, meaning, and use
Learning conditions	Repetition, varied encounters
Research evidence	The little research available suggests that L2 learners do learn words incidentally through listening (van Zeeland & Schmitt, 2013). Research on the scope and range of vocabulary in films and television programmes (Webb & Rodgers, 2009a, 2009b) indicates that such input is a good potential source of learning.
Further reading	Elley (1989), van Zeeland & Schmitt (2013)

Description

Extensive listening involves learners receiving large quantities of comprehensible spoken input that consist of at least 95% of known words (see also *7 Extensive reading*). Extensive listening can come from a wide variety of sources, such as listening while reading, watching films or television, listening to recorded novels, listening to stories read aloud by the teacher, participating in conversations, activities focusing on spoken interaction (see *4 Task-focused spoken interaction*), and listening to recorded talks and dialogues. Such listening should focus on what is being said and is best not accompanied by language-focused activities which take time away from the listening. Extensive listening can involve comprehension checks, such as questions about the content or information transfer activities (see *3 Information transfer*), but the main focus should be on understanding large quantities of spoken input.

Lexical information

Because dictionary look-up is not really possible during listening activities, the main source of information about words will be gained through guessing from context. If listening is accompanied by reading, as when watching a film with captions, or reading a book while listening to an audio version, then knowledge of the written form of the words can support learning of the spoken form.

Learning conditions

Vocabulary learning is supported by repetition (Brown, Waring, & Donkaewbua, 2008) and by varied encounters with words. Both unscripted and informal spoken language tend to use a more limited range of vocabulary than written language (Nation, 2006), and also make greater use of high-frequency words and phrases (Shin & Nation, 2008). This means that informal spoken input is likely to provide more favourable conditions than more formal scripted input for vocabulary learning through listening.

Improving vocabulary learning

1 Quantity of comprehensible input is a major factor in learning vocabulary through listening; using longer texts provides more opportunities for repeated retrieval of topic-related words and more varied encounters.
2 If listening is accompanied by the written form of the text, then vocabulary learning will be much greater (Brown, Waring, & Donkaewbua, 2008). Webb and Chang (2012b) found that repeated reading while listening resulted in more vocabulary learning than repeated reading without listening.
3 Where listening is not a well-developed skill, repeated listening is likely to result in better vocabulary learning. Elley (1989) had learners listen to

a story three times, in order to make sure that some degree of vocabulary learning would occur.

4 Adding an element of deliberate language-focused attention is usually effective as a way of enhancing learning. Elley (1989) also found that vocabulary learning increased significantly if the teacher briefly explained the meaning of unfamiliar words that learners encountered as they were listening to a story.

5 Preparation for listening can result in more vocabulary learning, especially if the preparation is vocabulary-focused (Chang, 2007).

2 *Classification*

Programme strand	A mixture of strands and skills
Learning goal	Learn the form and meaning of new words, strengthen knowledge of partially known words, learn associations between words
Learning conditions	Noticing, receptive retrieval, elaboration
Research evidence	Interaction can contribute to vocabulary learning through negotiation of form and meaning (Newton, 2013). The best opportunities for vocabulary learning through interaction occur in small group work (Dobao, 2014a).
Further reading	Nation & Hamilton-Jenkins (2000), Sokmen (1992)

Description

In a classification activity, learners work in small groups to organize words in some clearly determined way under headings or in categories. This is one of the most efficient ways of getting learners to focus on thematically related vocabulary (around 30 or 40 words is appropriate). The words should be gathered from a coherent text, the topic of which will naturally determine the scope and focus of the activity. Learning words by theme should also help to avoid interference, as there will be greater semantic differentiation between the words. (See Chapter 2 for more on interference.)

Lexical information

During the activity, learners typically discuss the meanings of words, explaining them to each other when necessary, and consider how they relate to each other. The learners focus on words that cause problems for them and skip over those which are already familiar; this is much more efficient than the teacher trying to go through a large list systematically, giving equal time to each word.

Learning conditions

For words that are already at least partially known, there is the opportunity for receptive retrieval, with some elaboration occurring as a result of doing the classification activity. For words that are unfamiliar, there is the opportunity for noticing (of the form and hopefully the meaning), with the help of others in the group, or a dictionary.

Improving vocabulary learning

Having a dictionary available can be useful for words which are unfamiliar to the learners. It is also useful to know four or five adaptable ways of getting learners to deal with a large group of words in a structured manner. Here are some examples:

1 Learners organize words from a coherent text type; for example, they could organize words from a problem–solution text according to 1) background to the problem, 2) the problem itself, 3) possible solutions to the problem.
2 Learners arrange words on a scale based on the degree to which they are related to the topic of the text or some other criterion.
3 Learners map out the vocabulary in a **graphic organizer** based on the source text.
4 Learners focus on form during the activity, classifying words according to whether they contain specified word parts.

Classification activities may also be used to further develop knowledge of the meanings of partially known words. Specifically, this occurs through noticing the semantic associations that each word has.

3 Information transfer

Programme strand	A mixture of strands and skills
Learning goal	Strengthen knowledge of partially known words
Learning conditions	Elaboration
Research evidence	Not researched. However, Stahl and Vancil (1986) found that the discussion stimulated between learners in similar activities had great potential to contribute to learning.
Further reading	Palmer (1982)

Description

Information transfer activities can be receptive or productive. Receptive information transfer activities involve transferring information gained from listening or reading to a different format. In a receptive information transfer activity based on listening input, learners could listen to a monologue or a dialogue and use the information gained to fill in a table or form; for example, they might listen to someone talking about the subjects they study at school and fill in a school timetable, or listen to someone being interviewed and fill in a passport application form for that person. Productive information transfer activities involve transferring information gained from, say, a form or a table to spoken or written output. Information transfer activities are very effective for all skills. The most useful are those that relate to the lives and needs of the learners, not only because they will focus attention on directly meaningful language but also because they are likely to be more motivating.

Lexical information

During a receptive information transfer activity, information about the target words will come largely from the input, through guessing from context. The format of the input (for example, a table or diagram) will also provide contextual information to support learners' comprehension, again through guessing from context, drawing strongly on knowledge of the wider world.

Learning conditions

The major justification for using information transfer activities to facilitate vocabulary learning is that the process of transferring information from a linguistic form to a non-linguistic form involves a kind of elaboration that results in **dual coding** (d'Agostino, O'Neill, & Paivio, 1977; Nation, 1988). The quality of the verbal and non-verbal information about particular words will depend on how they are encoded (for example, in a visual or diagrammatic format), and whether their linguistic form is retained or altered. Encoding in visual or diagrammatic form would allow for deeper elaboration. The weakness of many information transfer activities is that they simply involve transferring information from one linguistic context to another without the target words themselves being changed, thus precluding any need for elaboration. However, the change in context from linguistic to diagrammatic may be enough to make a word more memorable, as a striking example of a varied encounter.

Improving vocabulary learning

1 Information transfer activities can be used to further develop knowledge of words which have already been encountered. Knowledge of the spoken and written forms of the words is likely to be improved through hearing the words and writing them down; and the form–meaning connection is also likely to be strengthened by determining the vocabulary that is necessary to complete the activity.

2 Including some delay between listening to or reading the input and encoding it in a different format allows for retrieval to occur. This can be a three-step process: 1) learners listen to or read the input; 2) they talk

about it in small groups to clarify it; 3) they transfer the information into a different format. (This is comparable to the process in *5 Linked skills*.) The process also increases repetition and provides opportunities for the negotiation of any problematic vocabulary.

3 Filling in an information transfer diagram as a pair or small group activity is likely to involve repetition and increase accuracy through negotiation.

4 By extending the information transfer activity to make it a three-step procedure, the opportunities for vocabulary learning can be increased. For example: 1) learners listen to or read the input; 2) they transfer the information to a non-linguistic format; 3) they use the non-linguistic output to produce a piece of writing or speaking. Having a delay (perhaps a day or two) between Steps 2 and 3 will increase the opportunities for spaced retrieval and varied use.

4 Task-focused spoken interaction

Programme strand	Meaning-focused input from listening, meaning-focused output through speaking
Learning goal	Learn the forms and meanings of new words, strengthen knowledge of partially known words, learn to use words in speech
Learning conditions	Repetition, noticing, receptive and productive retrieval, varied encounters and use
Research evidence	There is evidence of vocabulary learning being facilitated by this activity type from studies of negotiation (Newton, 2013; Ellis & He, 1999; Ellis & Heimbach, 1997; Ellis, Tanaka, & Yamazaki, 1994) and from studies involving **pre-tests** and **post-tests** (de la Fuente, 2002; Kim, 2008a; Newton, 2013).
Further reading	Nation (1991a), Newton (2013)

Description
Task-focused spoken interaction activities usually involve learners working in pairs or small groups to solve a problem presented to them. The outcome of the activity may be a list of suggestions, a choice between options, a ranked list, or a yes/no decision. Such activities are easy to design, and they provide excellent opportunities for the incidental learning of vocabulary.

Lexical information
The handout for the activity and the learners' discussions can be useful sources of information about words, with guessing from context being a key strategy. During the activity, there is the opportunity for negotiation, as learners explain words to each other as a standard part of solving the task. In

general, most, though certainly not all, of the negotiation will be successful, providing useful information about the negotiated words (Newton, 2013; Kim, 2008b).

Learning conditions

Task-focused spoken interaction activities are characterized by language-related episodes where noticing can occur, particularly through negotiation, which sets up excellent conditions for language learning. Most negotiation involves receptive and productive varied use. When negotiating the meaning of a word, for example, the word becomes the focus of deliberate attention: the word form occurs in a kind of **metalanguage** ('What does "shed" mean?'), and it is often repeated, perhaps with a morphological inflection ('Sheds are…'). Repetition within an episode provides opportunities for retrieval, albeit without much time between retrievals. Importantly, as was mentioned in Chapter 4, the results of studies focusing on negotiation have shown that the observers learn just as well as the active negotiators (Ellis & Heimbach, 1997; Newton, 2013). However, it is worth noting with regard to Newton's findings that the majority of vocabulary learning in his communicative tasks occurred without overt language-related episodes. Most vocabulary learning occurred from learners quietly guessing from context, or perhaps in having previous knowledge stimulated through their encounters with the words in use.

Improving vocabulary learning

The design of spoken tasks can have a striking effect on vocabulary learning.

1 Having a written worksheet for the task provides the opportunity for teachers to include vocabulary for learners to focus on; this vocabulary is much more likely to be negotiated than vocabulary that the learners happen to use which is not in the worksheet (Newton, 2013). Consider the following guidelines for designing a task-focused spoken interaction activity with a worksheet (adapted from Nation, 2013a):

   • have a worksheet with around 12 target words on it
   • use tasks that draw heavily on the written input
   • have small groups of students of a similar proficiency
   • include outcomes that require the written input to be changed so that there is opportunity for varied use
   • divide the task into steps so that there is opportunity for repetition and retrieval at each step.

2 The information distribution in a task influences what is negotiated. Newton (2103) found that split information tasks, where each person in a group has different information, were more likely to result in a focus on word form, while shared information tasks, where each member of a group has the same information, provided more opportunities to focus on word meaning.

3 It is possible to design interactive tasks that focus on one particular word; for example, consider the following task focusing on the word 'qualification' (from Nation & Hamilton-Jenkins, 2000):

> Work together to group these jobs into those that you think require a formal qualification (such as nursing) and those that do not.
>
> teacher   doctor   shop assistant   salesperson   plumber
> bus driver   cleaner   engineer   computer programmer

5 Linked skills

Programme strand	A mixture of strands and skills
Learning goal	Learn the forms and meanings of new words (in particular, topic-related vocabulary), learn to use new words in speech and/or writing, develop understanding of known but rarely used words
Learning conditions	Repetition, retrieval, varied encounters and use
Research evidence	The **narrow reading** involved in this activity type (Hwang & Nation, 1989; Schmitt & Carter, 2000) provides a small increase in repetitions without increasing the number of different words (Sutarsyah, Nation, & Kennedy, 1994), thus reducing the **vocabulary load** of the activity.
Further reading	Nation (2013, Chapter 15)

Description

Linked skills activities involve working on the same material using several different language skills. Issue logs are a particular kind of linked skills activity that continues over an extended period of time. Both are ideally suited to use in content-based language teaching (CBLT) and content and language integrated learning (CLIL) contexts, and provide excellent conditions for incidental vocabulary learning.

In a linked skills activity, learners work on the same piece of material using a range of different language skills. For example, they might talk about what they know of a particular topic, such as the Amazon Jungle, then read about the same topic, and finally use the information to write about it.

In an issue log activity, each learner chooses a topic of interest to them. Over the next few weeks, they research this topic, report on it to their classmates, and eventually present a written assignment on the topic. This is typically done as independent study in pre-university language courses, but it can also be done in secondary schools where the students have access to computers and library resources. The activity is called an issue log because the learners choose an issue that is relevant and interesting to them and keep a 'log', or running record, of information that they have gathered on the topic. It can be considered a form of linked skills activity because the learners read, listen, speak, and write during the different stages.

Lexical information

In linked skills activities, information about the words can come from a variety of sources. Teachers may pre-teach topic-related vocabulary, students might negotiate the forms and meanings of words during discussion, or refer to a dictionary, and knowledge is likely to be gained and strengthened through varied encounters and uses.

Because issue log activities are typically done independently, dictionaries and guessing from context tend to be the main sources of information about words.

Learning conditions

Linked skills activities encourage repetition. Because the same material is focused on in each step of the activity, the same vocabulary is likely to occur again and again. In fact, if the same vocabulary does not recur, then this is an indication that the activity needs to be redesigned. When the same vocabulary does recur, there will be opportunities for retrieval; and since linked skills activities include both receptive and productive steps, this retrieval can be both receptive and productive. A well-designed linked skills activity should also provide varied encounters and opportunities for varied use, because although the same material is focused on in each step, what the learners do with the material will vary. The inclusion of productive steps (speaking or writing) in a linked skills activity encourages the learners to read and listen purposefully, with the awareness that they will have to talk or write about the material later on at the forefront of their minds. This means they are more likely to pay attention to the form of the language used when listening and reading as well as the meaning.

Improving vocabulary learning

1 For a linked skills activity, it is best to use a reading text as a starting point and keep closely to the same topic in each step.
2 If the final step in the linked skills activity involves productive use of the language (speaking or writing), then Step 1 or 2 of the activity should also involve productive use of the language. For example, if Step 3 of the activity is to be a piece of writing, then having Step 2 as a speaking activity will make the transition to writing much easier.

6 4/3/2

Programme strand	Fluency development from speaking
Learning goal	Learn to use words in speech in a more fluent manner
Learning conditions	Repetition, productive retrieval, varied use
Research evidence	Research shows that the 4/3/2 activity increases the speed of speaking (Arevart & Nation, 1991; Boers, 2014; Nation, 1989). Boers compared 4/3/2 with 3/3/3 in order to separate the effects of repetition and time pressure in this activity type. He found that decreasing the time between each step of the activity was the main contributor to fluency development, not repetition.
Further reading	Boers, F. (2014)

Description

In the 4/3/2 activity (Maurice, 1983), learners work in pairs, with a speaker and a listener in each pair. An easy topic is chosen for the activity so that the learners will have no difficulty in finding something to talk about and in identifying the language they need. When the teacher says 'go', the speaker in each pair talks to their partner about the topic. The listeners do not interrupt or ask questions but listen attentively. At the end of four minutes, the teacher says 'stop'. The speakers swap seats so that they have a new partner. The teacher says 'go', and the speakers now give exactly the same talk but in only three minutes. At the end of the three minutes, the speakers move once more to join a new partner, and they now have two minutes to give the same talk. So, during the activity, each speaker talks three times to three different partners for a total of nine minutes. Each listener hears three different talks from three different people. The next time the activity is done, the speakers and listeners should swap roles, with the listeners becoming speakers and vice versa.

This activity has the typical fluency development criteria of 1) working with known language items, 2) involving some pressure to speed up, 3) being message-focused, and 4) involving a large amount of practice time. (See *1 Extensive listening*, *7 Extensive reading*, and *16 Ten-minute writing* for fluency development activities involving the use of other language skills.)

Lexical information

For speakers, improvements in vocabulary knowledge are likely to come solely from opportunities for the retrieval of words under time pressure. For listeners, vocabulary knowledge is likely to be strengthened through varied encounters with words used in the spoken input.

Learning conditions

The 4/3/2 activity involves the productive retrieval of words and phrases that should be reasonably familiar to learners. The retrieval is done under time pressure, which increases fluency of access to the words used. Repetition, particularly repetition over the three steps of the task, is also a factor strengthening knowledge of the words. The first (four-minute) step provides an opportunity for varied encounters and use, but the subsequent three-minute and two-minute steps will most likely involve verbatim repetition.

Improving vocabulary learning

1 Having each speaker give three talks in a row, rather than alternating with the listener, allows for more repetition.
2 To further enhance fluency development, invite speakers to give another two-minute delivery of the talk in the following 4/3/2 session, just before the listeners from the previous session take over as speakers and give the three deliveries of their talk.
3 Allowing some preparation time for the first delivery of the talk will help to reduce error. This can involve writing out the talk or making notes including useful words and phrases, incorporating it into a linked skills activity focusing on the same topic (as a final step), or practising the talk with feedback from a partner before the 4/3/2 activity begins with a new partner.
4 Adjust the time allowed to accommodate the proficiency level of the learners. In its original form (Maurice, 1983), the 4/3/2 activity was actually the 5/4/3 activity, but because of the lower proficiency level of the learners that Supot Arevart and Paul Nation focused on in their research, the time was reduced to make it more manageable. So, for more advanced learners, longer times could be given, and for less proficient learners, shorter times such as 3/2/1.5 could be used.

ACTIVITY 5.2 **Analysing a speaking activity**

Based on the information in the chapter so far, analyse the learning conditions set up by the following activity. Think about a) repetition (number of encounters), and b) quality of attention. Then read the notes on this activity at the end of this chapter.

Preparing a talk

In this activity, learners gather information to prepare for a talk. They then practise the talk with another member of the class as their audience, who gives them feedback. When they are happy with what they have prepared, they present the talk to the class and answer questions.

---

7 *Extensive reading*

Programme strand	Meaning-focused input from reading, fluency development from reading
Learning goal	Learn the forms and meanings of new words, strengthen knowledge of partially known words
Learning conditions	Repetition, deliberate noticing, varied encounters
Research evidence	Research has shown that L2 words can be learned incidentally through reading a single text (Brown, Waring, & Donkaewbua, 2008; Waring & Takaki, 2003) and that the amount of learning is likely to increase through reading a greater number of texts (Webb & Chang, 2015a).
Further reading	Day & Bamford (2002), Nation & Waring (2013), Waring (2000), the Extensive Reading Foundation website (see Website references)

Description

Extensive reading involves learners reading books which are at the appropriate level for them. Ideally, each learner reads a different book of their own choice which they find interesting and enjoyable to read. Each learner keeps a record of the books they have read and their evaluation of each book. Learners should be introduced to extensive reading during class time; once the teacher is satisfied that the learners understand what extensive reading involves and see the value in doing it, some or all of it can be done as homework. In a well-designed extensive reading programme, around two-thirds of the time should be spent on reading material which contains a small proportion of unknown words (around 2% of the **running words**), and around one third should be spent reading very easy material containing few or no unknown words, with a focus on fluency development.

It is essential for low- and intermediate-level learners to use books written within carefully controlled vocabulary levels (graded readers), which exclude words that are well beyond the learners' current level. In general, lower-level graded readers cover the 3,000 most frequent words, and mid-level readers focus on words in the 4–8,000 word frequency levels. Specially prepared graded readers are much more accessible for foreign language learners than books written for young native speakers (Webb & Macalister, 2013). As we have seen in Chapter 3, books written for young native speakers of English typically use a range of vocabulary which is much larger than the vocabulary size of foreign language learners.

Lexical information

During extensive reading, vocabulary gains are made through guessing from context and through dictionary use. Guessing from context can develop knowledge of unfamiliar family members of previously known words. As Pigada and Schmitt (2006) have shown, guessing from context can also strengthen and enrich knowledge of partially known words; it involves drawing on a wide variety of clues including information from both the immediate and wider linguistic contexts, knowledge gained from earlier parts of the text, knowledge of the wider world and particular subject areas, common sense, and morphological clues.

Learning conditions

Vocabulary learning from extensive reading is primarily enabled by repetition and varied encounters (see also *8 Guessing from context*). In terms of repetition, reasonably large quantities of input are needed to encounter most of the words at a particular 1,000 word frequency level, and to encounter them enough times for learning to have a chance to occur (Nation, 2014). Table 5.1 shows the time requirements for learning the 9,000 most frequent word families. For example, to learn the second 1,000 most frequent words in a year, learners would need to read 200,000 words per year, at a rate of 33 minutes per week over 40 weeks. This assumes a relatively slow reading speed of 150 words per minute, and that learners would encounter each word around 12 times.

Frequency level	Reading goal	Reading time per week over 40 weeks (150 words per minute)
2nd 1,000	200,000 words	33 minutes
3rd 1,000	300,000 words	50 minutes
4th 1,000	500,000 words	1 hour 23 minutes
5th 1,000	1,000,000 words	2 hours 47 minutes
6th 1,000	1,500,000 words	4 hours 10 minutes
7th 1,000	2,000,000 words	5 hours 33 minutes
8th 1,000	2,500,000 words	6 hours 57 minutes
9th 1,000	3,000,000 words	8 hours 20 minutes

Table 5.1 Amount of reading input and time needed to learn the 9,000 most frequent word families (adapted from Nation, 2014)

Table 5.1 shows that from the fourth 1,000 word frequency level onwards, the amount of reading would need to increase by 500,000 words per year; and from the seventh 1,000 word frequency level onwards, over an hour a day, five days a week, 40 weeks of the year would need to be devoted to reading, assuming that this quantity of input comes only through reading. This is substantial, but possible nonetheless. Of course, spoken sources are available, but these provide less intensive input; it takes around two hours to watch a film featuring around 10,000 running words (a rate of around 83 words per minute, or just over half the reading rate of 150 words per minute).

Besides repetition, extensive reading usefully sets up the condition of varied encounters. When a word occurs again in an extensive reading text such as a graded reader, it typically appears in a context which is different from the previous context(s) in which it occurred. This finding can be easily confirmed by doing a concordance search on a graded reader for words which are likely to be new at the level of that reader. Thus, each new encounter with a word during extensive reading is highly likely to enrich knowledge of that word through the variation in context, as well as strengthen knowledge through repetition.

Extensive reading also provides opportunities for deliberate noticing through the use of dictionaries to look up the meanings of words. In the case of e-books, the ease of instant touch access to the dictionaries built into e-readers and tablets makes it much more likely that learners will look up words and thus add a deliberate element to vocabulary learning during extensive reading. Dictionary use greatly increases the chances of learning (Hulstijn, Hollander, & Greidanus, 1996; Knight, 1994; Laufer & Hill, 2000; Peters, 2007). Some advocates of extensive reading actively advise against dictionary use on the grounds that it takes time away from reading and discourages guessing from context (Luppescu & Day, 1993). But the benefits to vocabulary learning of dictionary use outweigh this concern, particularly if learners are given training and encouragement to guess from context and thus see the dictionary as a way of confirming a guess rather than substituting for it. Besides, looking up words in a digital dictionary is now so quick that it takes very little time away from reading.

Improving vocabulary learning

1 The most important way of increasing vocabulary learning from extensive reading is to simply do more of it. The minimum target should be around one graded reader every two weeks. This is irrespective of the proficiency level of the learners, because as the level of graded readers increases, so too does their length: graded readers written for beginners feature no more than a few hundred words, while graded readers for intermediate learners are several thousand words long. (See also *9 Speed-reading*.)

2 Deliberate learning elements are worth incorporating into an extensive reading programme. For example, unknown words encountered during extensive reading could be put on flashcards with their translation on the other side so that they can become the focus of deliberate study later on. If the learners are reading graded readers, then almost every word they read

will be useful and worth learning. Dictionary use will help in the making of flashcards and in remembering the words through focused noticing.

3 If the learners are reading unsimplified texts, there is value in doing narrow reading; that is, reading within a very limited topic area. This will dramatically reduce the number of different words that the learners encounter—generally by around 50% of the number they would encounter if they were reading the same amount on a wide variety of topics (Sutarsyah, Nation, & Kennedy, 1994).

4 Rereading books is a good way of improving reading fluency. It also has the positive effect of increasing repetition and allowing for the receptive retrieval of previously encountered words. The rereading should probably be done within a few weeks of the first reading for receptive retrieval to be successful.

8 *Guessing from context*

Programme strand	Meaning-focused input from listening and reading
Learning goal	Link the forms of unknown words to their meanings, develop knowledge of new words
Learning conditions	Repetition, noticing, retrieval, varied encounters
Research evidence	Research has shown that the meaning of L2 words can be inferred through reading (Waring & Takaki, 2003), listening (van Zeeland & Schmitt, 2013), and viewing (Rodgers, 2013), and that different aspects of vocabulary knowledge (form, meaning, and use) are gained in the process (Webb, 2007a).
Further reading	Nation (2013a, Chapter 8)

Description

Guessing from context occurs while listening and reading, when learners use clues from the linguistic context, background knowledge of the topic, or their own common sense, to infer the meaning of unknown or partially known words or multi-word combinations that they encounter in meaning-focused input. Such guessing can occur consciously or subconsciously. During the process, learners may link the forms of unknown words to their meanings, as well as notice and remember different forms of a word (its inflections and derivations), its grammatical function, and its collocations. Guessing from context accounts for the majority of L1 vocabulary learning.

Lexical information

Guessing typically involves using contextual clues. These are usually located in the immediate context of the word, within the same clause. However, the wider context beyond the clause also provides important contextual information. This kind of guessing draws largely on linguistic clues and is sometimes described as a bottom-up approach to guessing. Guessing can also draw on background knowledge if the learner's existing schema of the topic makes such guessing possible (a top-down approach). Haastrup (1989) argued that guessing from background knowledge of the topic is less likely to result in retention of the word form and its meaning, because the learner's attention is focused on top-down contextual knowledge rather than on the word form itself and on memorable linguistic clues. Subsequent research, however, has not provided support for this argument (Pulido, 2003, 2007). Drawing on knowledge of the wider world which is not necessarily closely related to the topic can result in partially correct guesses, such as 'this has something to do with people', or 'this is a good rather than a bad thing'. Such small increases in knowledge are an important part of learning through the guessing from context strategy.

Learning conditions

Noticing is the key factor affecting learning through guessing from context, as words that are consciously guessed are more likely to be retained. Repetition is, unsurprisingly, another major condition affecting guessing from context (Waring & Takaki, 2003). The most reliable finding is that the more repetitions there are, the more likely learning is to occur through guessing from context. However, there is evidence that some learning can occur through just one encounter. Zipf's law works against the guessing from context strategy, in that many of the unknown words are not likely to be repeated within the same text. So a critical factor in learning through guessing from context is ensuring that the quantity of input is aligned to the proficiency level of the learner, because increasingly large amounts of input will be needed to get enough repetitions of the next most useful words to learn.

Each occurence of a word after the first encounter provides an opportunity for a combination of guessing from context and the retrieval of information about words gained from previous encounters. Success is dependent on the ability of the learner to see the connection between the present and previous contexts, and there is some evidence to suggest that learners differ in their ability to do this (van Daalen-Kapteijns & Elshout-Mohr, 1981). Research on glossing has shown the importance of retrieval (Barcroft, 2007): better retention was found for words that were glossed on the first encounter only, as this allowed retrieval to occur at subsequent encounters. (Glossing removes the need for retrieval to occur because the meaning is provided.) Where a word occurs several times within the same text, or even across different texts, in the vast majority of cases the linguistic contexts will not be the same. Such variation in context is likely to be the strongest factor affecting the quality of vocabulary learning through guessing from context; and this underlines the importance of quantity of input in learning through guessing from context, because the larger the amount of input, the greater the number of opportunities will be for repetition and encountering the word in varied contexts. This range of varied contexts will make guessing from context a richer means of learning than, say, using flashcards, where each word is either decontextualized or presented in a single context.

Improving vocabulary learning

The likelihood of learning and retaining information about a word from encountering it once in context is thought to be rather low—somewhere between 10–20% (Nagy, Herman, & Anderson, 1985; Swanborn & de Glopper, 1999). Most contexts, however, do tell you something about a word. To gain the greatest benefit from learning through guessing from context, learners need to develop their guessing skills. Nation (2013a) describes four important approaches through which a teacher can help their students improve: 1) the ease approach, 2) the practice approach, 3) the skill approach, and 4) the deliberate training approach.

1 Guiding learners in choosing material at the appropriate level of difficulty could be considered an example of the ease approach. If a text contains too many unknown words, then it is likely to be difficult for learners to comprehend and they will thus have difficulty in guessing the unfamiliar words that they encounter in the text. As we have seen in Chapter 1, research suggests that learners need to know around 98% of the running words in a text for the vocabulary not to be a major issue in comprehension (Hu & Nation, 2000; Schmitt, Jiang, & Grabe, 2011). There is growing debate over whether lexical coverage is a sensitive enough factor for determining the difficulty of texts. The development of mid-frequency reading texts is an attempt to provide material at the right level of difficulty even for learners of high proficiency (Nation & Anthony, 2013), though Jez Uden, Diane Schmitt, and Norbert Schmitt (2014) suggest that these may not be necessary. Nonetheless, successful guessing does require contexts that do not contain a high density of unknown words.

2 Encouraging learners to read and listen to large amounts of input could be considered an example of the practice approach. Quantity of input is key to providing repeated opportunities to practise the strategy of guessing from context, and thus, through incidental learning, to become better at guessing and reading more generally.

3 Working with learners to improve their reading and listening skills is an example of the skill-based approach. This approach sees guessing from context as an integral part of comprehension. It is indeed possible to argue that guessing from context is indistinguishable from reading comprehension, because most guesses from context depend on successful

comprehension of the context; and once this is achieved, most of the available clues to the meaning of the unknown word will have been revealed. In any case, training in guessing from context will not compensate for poor comprehension skills.

4 Training learners in using the guessing from context strategy follows the deliberate training approach. L1 research (van Daalen-Kapteijns, Elshout-Mohr, & de Glopper, 2001) suggests that while all L1 readers have the skill of guessing from context, some are more proficient in using it than others. It has also been argued that the size of a learner's working memory plays a role in determining the amount of vocabulary learning achieved through guessing from context (Daneman & Green, 1986; Gathercole & Baddeley, 1989; Service, 1992). The most common strategic error that learners make when guessing from context is to allow the form of the word rather than the context to determine their guess (Laufer & Sim, 1985). Research shows that training in guessing from context results in better guessing (Fukkink & de Glopper, 1998; Kuhn & Stahl, 1998). However, no one system of training has been shown to be better than another (Walters, 2006).

Some additional notes on enhancing guessing from context:

• If learners confirm the meaning of a word—for example, by looking it up in a dictionary after they have guessed its meaning from contextual clues—this will greatly increase the effectiveness of the guessing from context strategy (Fraser, 1999; Mondria, 2003).

• The success of learning vocabulary in listening texts through guessing from context can be improved if learners are able to see a written version of the text at the same time. Brown, Waring, and Donkaewbua (2008) found much less vocabulary learning on immediate post-tests from listening only (multiple-choice: 8.2 out of 28; translation: 0.56) than from reading only (12.54; 4.10) and reading while listening (13.31; 4.10).

• Guessing from context is likely to improve as learners' vocabulary sizes increase (Webb & Chang, 2015b). There are several related reasons for this. First, the density of unknown words in each context will be smaller. Second, learners will have a deeper understanding of the words that they already know, making it easier to interpret each new context. Third, learners' skill in guessing from context is likely to improve as their vocabulary size increases. Fourth, learners' understanding of the systems underlying spelling, morphology, and word meaning will be better established, thus reducing the learning burden of new words.

9 *Speed-reading*

Programme strand	Fluency development from reading
Learning goal	Learn to process words in a more fluent manner (by increasing reading speed)
Learning conditions	Repetition, varied encounters
Research evidence	Speed-reading can contribute to vocabulary learning by speeding up access to known words, particularly high-frequency words, and by pushing learners to process language in meaningful chunks rather than word by word (Chung & Nation, 2006; Tran, 2012).
Further reading	Tran (2012)

Description

A speed-reading activity typically involves learners reading short texts about 500 words long under timed conditions. In a typical session, each learner chooses a passage that they have not read before. They wait until the teacher says 'go', and then start reading. When they have finished reading, they write down the time taken to read the passage. They then turn the passage over and answer the ten multiple-choice questions on the back to check their comprehension. They get the answer sheets and mark their answers themselves. The learners' goal is for their comprehension to be around seven or eight out of ten; a higher score means that they are reading too slowly, and a lower score means they are not comprehending well enough. They then enter their comprehension score on a comprehension graph, convert their reading time into words per minute using a conversion chart, and enter their reading speed on their reading speed graph. At regular intervals, the teacher should look at the learners' graphs and give them feedback and encouragement on their reading progress.

Speed-reading is a fluency development activity (see also *6 4/3/2*), so the materials used should be well within the learners' vocabulary knowledge. Most learners of EFL read at speeds of less than 100 words per minute, while the upper limit of normal reading for native speakers is around 300 words per minute (Nation, 2005). Speed-reading trains learners to increase their reading speed to at least 200 words per minute. Free speed-reading courses at various word frequency levels, plus the Academic Word List, are available from Paul Nation and Sonia Millett's websites (see Website references).

Lexical information

Knowledge about the words comes from retrieval with a small amount of guessing from context. The focus on reading at a faster rate can contribute to an increased speed of retrieval, which should be considered an important gain in a learner's lexical development.

There is a largely unproven argument that fluency development activities are one of the major ways of developing knowledge of multi-word combinations. This argument is based on McLaughlin's idea of restructuring (1990), which proposes that if we want to improve our fluency in a language, we will at some point need to restructure the language units we are working with in order to be able to deal with them more fluently. That is, if we read on a word-by-word basis, we will be able to reach a certain speed through practice; to go beyond that, we will need to move from word-by-word processing to processing phrasal chunks. Even though fluent readers physically focus on almost every word in a text, they process language at the phrase and clause level. Fluency development activities can thus achieve more than simply increase the speed of language processing. They can also provide a subconscious motivation to make fundamental changes to the nature of language processing. We need to be cautious in accepting this argument, however, because there is still very little evidence to support it.

Learning conditions

The major learning condition set up by a speed-reading activity is varied encounters, because the known words will appear in new contexts. The other learning condition involved is repetition, both within the text and in the accompanying comprehension questions, which are likely to provide repetition of some of the topic-related vocabulary. However, it is important to reiterate the point made earlier in the book (see Chapter 1) that repetition is affected by Zipf's law, as it is in all meaning-focused activities, with over half of the different words appearing only once or twice, even over multiple series of speed-reading activities. The use of material written using a controlled vocabulary does little to change this spread of repetitions, but controlling vocabulary should at least ensure that most of the words will be familiar.

Improving vocabulary learning

1 The major way of maximizing the effects of speed-reading is to simply do more of it. Research by Chung and Nation (2006) and Tran (2012) found that, over the course of around 20 speed-reading sessions, there was a noticeable improvement in reading speed across the full range of sessions. In general, most of the increase occurred in the first ten sessions, but there was still improvement in the later sessions.

2 The series *Reading for speed and fluency* (Nation & Malarcher, 2007) provides sets of five passages on the same topic for learners to use to increase

their reading speed and fluency. Covering the same topic five times is an attempt to maximize the effect of the background knowledge learners bring to each text, and to allow for repetition and varied encounters, although this effect is likely to be small and largely focused on topic-related vocabulary.

3 Speed-reading needs to be seen as a tool with a wider purpose, which is to initiate and support a long-term process that extends beyond the vocabulary learning programme, with fluency development occurring through everyday reading. This process is likely to be optimized if speed-reading activities are accompanied by substantial amounts of extensive reading. This should include easy extensive reading where the learners read texts which are well within their vocabulary level, and extensive reading where a small proportion of the running words (2% or less) are beyond their current vocabulary knowledge.

10 *Vocabulary-focused comprehension questions*

Programme strand	Meaning-focused input from reading and listening
Learning goal	Learn the forms and meanings of new words, strengthen knowledge of partially known words
Learning conditions	Repetition, varied encounters and use
Research evidence	Not researched
Further reading	Kraus-Srebrič, Brakus, & Kentrič (1981)

Description

Comprehension questions can take many forms, including pronominal questions (*wh*-questions), true/false questions, yes/no questions, and multiple-choice questions. Comprehension questions also vary in terms of focus: they may focus on details within the text, on the general ideas and gist of the text, on the application of ideas in the text, or on critiquing the text. The most straightforward way of using comprehension questions is for the learners to read the text and then answer the questions. This is likely to be followed up by the teacher marking the questions or getting the learners to mark them themselves using an answer sheet or based on feedback. In some cases, learners may be encouraged to look at the questions and think of possible answers before they read the text.

Vocabulary-focused comprehension questions are designed so that the target vocabulary in the text occurs in the questions and/or in the answers to them. The questions can still have the range of forms and levels of focus described above, but particular thought is given to vocabulary learning when formulating the questions. Because vocabulary learning is the central goal, there is value in the teacher discussing the answers with the learners after they have answered the questions. This increases the potential for target words to be repeated and used in different ways, thus increasing the likelihood that they will be learned.

Lexical information

This activity can focus on partially known words or unfamiliar words. Information about the words can come from the use of the words in the text, in the questions and answers, and in any follow-up discussion of the answers. The teacher can make a special point of focusing on the target words in the discussion. The information gained, largely through guessing from context, might be about the meaning of the words, or about how the words are used.

Learning conditions

The occurrence of the target words in the text, the questions, the answers, and the discussion should amount to plenty of repetitions of the words. Vocabulary-focused comprehension questions provide ideal conditions for varied encounters. Ideally, the contexts in which a target word occurs in the text, in the questions, and in the answers would differ enough to provide varied encounters of a deeper quality with the word. The discussion could also provide opportunities for varied productive use.

Improving vocabulary learning

1 Using *wh*-questions provides opportunities for productive retrieval and productive varied use. Whereas multiple-choice questions, yes/no questions, and true/false questions all contain the answers within the questions, *wh*-questions require learners to formulate their own answers, thus allowing for productive retrieval to occur; and if the answers cannot be copied verbatim from the text, then there is also the opportunity for productive varied use.

2 If reading texts are turned over during the discussion part of the activity, the potential for productive retrieval will be much greater. This means that when discussing the answers, the learners should not be able to look back at the text, or even at the questions and answers.

3 Using the pyramid procedure (Jordan, 1990) creates greater opportunities for repetition. This procedure involves learners checking their answers with their partner, then with another pair, and finally in a whole class discussion.

The teacher's skill in formulating the vocabulary-focused comprehension questions will be a key factor in determining the amount of repetition and the quality of the processing that occurs during the activity. The following checklist can be useful as a rough guide to making good-quality questions.

- Are *wh*-questions used rather than yes/no, true/false, or multiple-choice questions?
- Do the target words occur in the questions and/or answers?
- Are the target words used in the questions or answers in different ways from how they are used in the text (for example, in a slightly different form, with different collocates, in a different grammatical pattern, or with a slightly different sense)?
- Has the discussion of the answers been arranged so that there will be plenty of opportunities for the target words to be used, including productive use?

11 Interactive reading

Programme strand	Meaning-focused input from reading and listening, meaning-focused output through speaking
Learning goal	Learn the forms and meanings of new words
Learning conditions	Repetition, noticing, retrieval, varied encounters and use
Research evidence	Research by Elley (1989) with young native speakers of English showed that vocabulary learning occurred through listening to stories, even without teacher explanation of the vocabulary, but that the inclusion of teacher explanation resulted in much larger gains.
Further reading	Mol, Bus, & de Jong (2009), Samuels (1970)

Description

Interactive reading involves learners actively engaging with a story as it is read to them by the teacher; for example, clarifying the language and ideas involved, talking about the pictures in the book, predicting what will happen in the story, reading aloud, and discussing what has happened. The activity mirrors what occurs when a parent reads a book with their child; by making reading a group activity, learners are encouraged to learn from each other and reflect on the text. The interactive characteristics distinguish this activity from those which simply involve listening or reading while listening to a story. The activity is widely used by teachers of young L1 learners and goes by several names, including shared reading, shared-book reading, interactive reading, and 'blown-up books' (because of the large-format books sometimes used in the activity). As there are so many variants, it is worth defining the key characteristics:

1 The teacher reads the story aloud to the learners.
2 The learners can at least see the pictures in the book and if possible the text.
3 The teacher interacts with the learners about the content of the story.

4 The teacher interacts with the learners about the language in the story.
5 The same book is usually read again on several occasions using the same interactive technique.

The person often credited with developing the activity is Don Holdaway (1979). It is not difficult to adapt for use with older learners, the main adaptation being the choice of the reading text (Smith & Elley, 1997).

Lexical information

In interactive reading, information about words can come from the story itself, from the teacher's explanations, and from one or more of the learners listening to the story. Elley (1989) found that words which were illustrated in the pictures accompanying the story had a greater chance of being learned, though it should be noted that pictures accompanying a written text do not always have positive effects on comprehension and learning. This is because we largely learn what we focus on (Barcroft, 2006), and pictures can distract from the text (Samuels, 1970). It is also useful to consider the evidence that learners learn vocabulary from each other in speaking activities (Newton, 2013). This has been shown to occur even for learners who are not actively participating in the interaction but who are simply listening. The information provided by learners needs to be accurate, though not necessarily complete. As vocabulary learning is very much a cumulative process, even small amounts of relevant information can usefully contribute to learning.

Learning conditions

There are two kinds of repetition that can occur during interactive reading: 1) repetition within the story and its presentation, and 2) repetition from re-telling the story. Repetitions within the story and its presentation are likely to provide varied encounters with the words, whereas repetitions from re-telling the story are more likely to be verbatim repetitions of the first presentation of the story. While verbatim repetitions can lead to the successful retrieval of word meanings, varied encounters are likely to have a stronger effect on learning.

The interaction between the teacher and the learners during the reading provides opportunities for noticing via the negotiation of the meanings of words, which may include writing words on the board to clarify both spoken and written forms.

Improving vocabulary learning

1 To increase repetition when doing interactive reading, each sentence in the book could be said at least twice if this can be done while still keeping the listeners' interest.
2 If the interactive reading of a story continues over several days, the teacher can begin each session with a summary of what has happened so far in the story. When making the summary, the teacher should encourage the

learners to help by asking what happened next. This provides opportunities for retrieval to occur and increases the repetition of target vocabulary. Each suggestion that the learners make should be repeated by the teacher to ensure that it is heard by all members of the class, with everyone benefiting from the repetition.

3 The same book could be used for interactive reading two or three times, with a gap of a week or two between each reading. This will increase both the quantity and quality of retrievals and repetition.

4 When the learners have heard the story a few times, they can try re-telling the story as a class activity. The pictures in the book can be used to support the productive retrieval of words.

12 *Reading with text highlighting*

Programme strand	Meaning-focused input from reading
Learning goal	Learn the forms and meanings of new words
Learning conditions	Deliberate noticing
Research evidence	Research on highlighting has shown that it seems to have little effect on vocabulary learning or comprehension (Rott, 2007; de Ridder, 2002). However, highlighting multi-word combinations does increase the likelihood that they will be noticed and looked up in the dictionary (Bishop, 2004).
Further reading	Peters (2012)

Description
Highlighting is a form of **textual enhancement** which increases the chances that unknown words will be noticed and learned. Words can be highlighted in a text through the use of colour, bold, italics, capital letters, or underlining. As the learner reads, their attention is drawn to the highlighted words or phrases, and this does two things: first, it signals that the highlighted word or phrase has some extra information attached to it, such as an accompanying gloss; second, it gives prominence to the form of the word.

Lexical information
As noted above, highlighting encourages a focus on word form. The greatest source of learning is likely to be the written form of the word, as that is where attention is directed; and the chances of learning the meaning of the word rests on the readers' ability to infer it from the context.

Learning conditions
Because what we learn is what we focus on (Webb & Boers, 2013), highlighting a word is likely to result in some gain in knowledge of the form of

the word through deliberate noticing. Where highlighting signals a gloss, it increases the likelihood of the gloss being looked at and learners noticing the meaning of the word. However, this noticing is likely to have only small effects on learning (see *13 Glossing*); and if there is a large number of highlighted words with glosses, competition or interference between the glosses may limit their effectiveness.

Improving vocabulary learning

1 Highlighting is worth doing as a way of drawing attention to target words, or to signal glosses within the text. However, it is important to avoid having an excessive number of highlighted words in a text.

2 There appears to be little inherent difference between the various forms of highlighting in terms of their effectiveness in improving vocabulary learning. Any difference that occurs may be the result of learners' interpretation of the meaning or significance of highlighting, or because the form of highlighting used is inappropriate on an individual level. For example, using italics and underlining may be inappropriate for learners with dyslexia; and a significant proportion of males are colour-blind, so the use of colour for highlighting is probably not a good idea.

3 Because highlighting (particularly with italics or capital letters) slightly changes the form of the word, it may create the condition of varied use if the word has already been encountered in a non-highlighted form.

4 Frequency-based text analysis using lexical profilers such as *AntWordProfiler* (see Website references) can be used to highlight words of a particular frequency level; in this way, the learner's attention would be directed towards words in the profiled text which are at the frequency level that is most appropriate for their current vocabulary size.

13 *Glossing*

Programme strand	Meaning-focused input from reading
Learning goal	Learn the forms and meanings of new words
Learning conditions	Noticing, receptive retrieval, varied encounters
Research evidence	The evidence is generally in favour of glossing contributing to vocabulary learning (Bowles, 2004; Hulstijn, Hollander, & Greidanus, 1996; Jacobs, Dufon, & Hong, 1994; Ko, 2005; Watanabe, 1997). Glossing is a kind of incidental learning, because learners are likely to see a gloss not as a means of learning a word, but as an aid to comprehension of the text (Bowles, 2004).
Further reading	Hulstijn, Hollander, & Greidanus (1996)

Description

A gloss consists of a brief explanation of a word or phrase in a text. The gloss may be given in the learners' L1 or in the language of the text. A gloss may also be a picture, or be accompanied by a picture. The glossed word is typically highlighted (see *12 Reading with text highlighting*), but not all occurrences of the target words are necessarily glossed. Glosses are used in hard-copy and digital texts in a variety of ways. The favoured position for a gloss in a hard-copy text is in the margin next to the line containing the glossed word, largely because it is less disruptive to reading compared with having to go to a glossary at the end of the text. In a digital text, the gloss is accessed by touching or clicking on the glossed word. As the learners read, they can access the glosses to support their comprehension. Glossing has many attractions as a technique for allowing learners to deal with texts which would otherwise be too difficult for them. It is a quick way of clarifying the meaning of a word which might not be easy to guess correctly from context, with minimal interruption to the reading process. It thus supports reading comprehension and may have the additional benefit of encouraging vocabulary learning by increasing the chances that unknown words are noticed, and helping readers to link form to meaning.

Lexical information

A gloss provides information about the word—essentially its meaning, though additional information may also be provided. Research by Marjolijn Verspoor and Wander Lowie (2003) supports the view that the core meaning rather than the contextual meaning of the word should be provided. This would then require the reader to adapt the meaning to the context, thus deepening the mental processing involved.

Glossing provides a greater chance that readers will be able to link the form of a word to the meaning than textual enhancement, because in the former case, both are provided, while in the latter, readers still need to work out the meaning.

Learning conditions

Noticing occurs when glossed words are highlighted, because highlighting increases the possibility that the gloss will be looked at (de Ridder, 2002). Because glosses are easier to access than dictionary entries, they are much more likely to be used (Hulstijn, Hollander, & Greidanus, 1996).

Particularly in the case of hyperlinked glosses in digital texts, there is the potential for retrieval and varied encounters to occur when glossed words are repeated. The very process of dealing with a gloss ensures that the word is attended to at least twice (look at the word, look at the gloss, then come back to the word again), and that attention is given to the decontextualized meaning and then its contextualization (look at the gloss, then consider its application to the context). Research by Barcroft (2007, 2015) shows that it is preferable to gloss the first occurrence of a word and perhaps the second, with subsequent occurrences left unglossed, to encourage retrieval and strengthen learning.

Improving vocabulary learning

The following is an adaptation of Nation's guidelines for using glosses (Nation, 2013a):

1 Use glosses, highlighting them if the goal is vocabulary learning.
2 Use marginal glosses for hard-copy material and hyperlink glosses for digital material.
3 Use L1 glosses for learners with vocabulary sizes of less than 2,000 words, and either L1 or L2 glosses for more proficient learners. Keep the glosses simple and clear.
4 Avoid using multiple-choice glosses.
5 Provide the core meaning of the word in the gloss.
6 Where possible, gloss words which are likely to be repeated in the text, but do not gloss every occurrence.
7 Where possible, use a combination of glossing and text simplification, with the simplification replacing low-frequency words (beyond the ninth 1,000) that are not repeated and glossing being used for high-frequency and mid-frequency words (Nation & Anthony, 2013).

Adapted from Cambridge Applied Linguistics: Learning Vocabulary in Another Language by I. S. P. Nation, © Cambridge University Press 2001.

There is a downside to glossing, which is that it may get in the way of comprehension (Taylor, 2010)—particularly if too many words are glossed and highlighted and if the glosses are too elaborate. A study by Frank Boers, Anna Siyanova-Chanturia, and Paul Warren (2013) using eye tracking technology found that pictures in glosses resulted in poorer learning of word forms. It is therefore essential that glossing is used in a principled manner, following the guidelines provided above.

ACTIVITY 5.3   Analysing vocabulary activities in a coursebook (2)

Look again at the vocabulary learning activities in the coursebook that you examined for Activity 5.1 and answer the questions. Then compare your answers with the notes at the end of the chapter.

1 Can you determine any principles behind the selection and sequencing of these activities?

2 Are you satisfied that the words which are focused on within the book are likely to be learned by your students? Why (not)?

---

14 *Writing with feedback*

Programme strand	Meaning-focused output through writing
Learning goal	Improve the accuracy and sophistication of words in writing
Learning conditions	Noticing, repetition
Research evidence	Not researched
Further reading	Zhou (2009)

Description

It is not easy to convert receptive knowledge of vocabulary to productive knowledge, largely because learners are often unwilling to take risks with vocabulary that they do not know well (Coxhead, 2007; Horst & Collins, 2006; Rott, Williams, & Cameron, 2002). However, because writing allows time for reflection and opportunities for the teacher to provide encouraging feedback, there is a great deal of benefit to be gained from developing productive vocabulary knowledge through writing. So there is value in providing productive vocabulary learning goals within the goals that are set for learning from writing.

Feedback on writing covers the correction of vocabulary-based errors and the choice of vocabulary items; it can be used to reveal how knowledge of form, meaning, and use might be lacking for any misused words. Vocabulary-based errors include misspellings, the use of **synforms**, unusual collocations, failure to make countable/uncountable distinctions, and morphological errors. The teacher can directly correct such errors on the piece of writing, or use some kind of marking system that indicates where the error is and what kind of error it is but leaves it to the learner to make the correction. Common errors can also be dealt with through direct teaching in class. Feedback on the choice of vocabulary items can include praise on the use of a particularly apt word or phrase, and suggestions for replacing less effective words with words more suited to the topic and discourse type of the text. The feedback technique known as 'reformulation' (Cohen, 1989) involves the teacher rephrasing parts of the text. Although this is very labour-intensive and time-consuming for teachers, it can provide useful models for learners. Besides, the quality of vocabulary use in writing plays a significant role in the assessment of writing (Astika, 1993; Engber, 1995), so it is worth taking the time to provide encouraging and constructive feedback.

Lexical information

Information about vocabulary used in writing typically comes from the teacher, although peer feedback is another potential source. Learners' dictionaries may also be a source of information, particularly example sentences.

Learning conditions

Learning from feedback on writing is a form of deliberate learning which largely occurs at the level of noticing. Suggestions concerning vocabulary choice are not really examples of varied use, because they suggest a change in vocabulary, rather than variation in the use of the same word. If the suggestions on vocabulary choice and corrections of vocabulary errors are used in the production of a final draft, then repetition can play a useful role in learning.

Improving vocabulary learning

1 Lee (2003) and Lee and Muncie (2006) found that doing lots of preliminary activities, such as watching a film, doing a cloze activity, reading a closely related text, doing a comprehension activity, writing the first draft, discussing vocabulary based on a writing frame, writing the second draft, and then getting feedback and correction, resulted in a large number of the target words being used in the final piece of writing. This suggests that activities such as the linked skills activity, where writing can be done as the third step in the series, can help learners transfer receptive vocabulary knowledge into written productive use.

2 Word consciousness activities could play a useful role in getting learners to increase the sophistication of the vocabulary they use in their writing. One such activity, 'Reading like a writer', involves reading a text somewhat similar to the one that needs to be written and noting useful features and vocabulary that could be used.

15 Computer-mediated written interaction

Programme strand	Meaning-focused input from reading, meaning-focused output through writing
Learning goal	Learn the forms and meanings of new words when relevant to comprehending input or to engage in written interaction; learn to use words in writing
Learning conditions	Noticing, receptive and productive retrieval, varied encounters and use
Research evidence	Learners tend to see computer-mediated written interaction as being akin to spoken interaction (Kötter, 2003). McDonough and Sunitham (2009) found close to 50% retention of the words involved in successful language-related episodes. Smith (2005) also found evidence of vocabulary learning through computer-mediated written interaction. De la Fuente (2003) found that negotiation is much more likely to be abandoned in written interaction than in spoken interaction, although the success rate of negotiation is generally high, as it is in spoken interaction (McDonough & Sunitham, 2009; Newton, 2013).
Further reading	de la Fuente (2003), McDonough & Sunitham (2009)

Description

In computer-mediated written interaction, learners are given a task to complete by communicating with each other using computers or mobile devices rather than speaking. They may also have a worksheet which guides and supports their interaction (see *4 Task-focused spoken interaction*). Research suggests that this kind of spontaneous written communication shares several features with spoken communication: it is unrehearsed and informal, is often synchronous, and allows language-related episodes to occur where words are negotiated and explained.

Lexical information

As with spoken interaction, information about words can come from the negotiation between those involved in written interaction, through guessing from context, and from any written information given on an accompanying worksheet. The information provided through written negotiation seems to be largely accurate and thus contributes to vocabulary learning.

Learning conditions

We might expect computer-mediated written interaction to result in more learning, because of the more permanent nature of reading and writing compared to listening and speaking. In fact, the small amount of research comparing spoken and written interaction (de la Fuente, 2003) did not find any significant difference, although those in the spoken interaction group tended to learn somewhat more. This is probably because written interaction takes longer and results in less language use.

Computer-mediated written interaction provides opportunities for retrieval, varied encounters, and varied use. During a language-related episode, vocabulary can be the focus of deliberate noticing, and the questioning and explanation of a word sets it in a variety of contexts, even if these are meta-linguistic contexts (where language is used to talk about language).

Improving vocabulary learning

1 Because quantity of language input and output is such an important variable affecting repetition and opportunities for learning in general, it is worth training learners to touch-type so that they can speed up their written communication. This will help to increase the overall quantity of language input and output, thereby enhancing vocabulary learning through computer-mediated written interaction.

2 Getting learners to work in groups of three or four can increase the amount of interaction that occurs, and also the opportunities for successful nego-tiation, because there are likely to be more people with knowledge of the negotiated words.

3 Having a pair of learners on each computer can have positive effects on learning. One learner can do the typing (preferably the faster typist), and they can orally discuss the written messages they receive from another pair and agree on what they are going to send in reply. This mixture of spoken and written interaction is likely to increase the quantity of language input and output, as well as increase the number of repetitions of the target words. Working in pairs may also enhance learning, particularly for the learner who is not typing, because the cognitive load of the activity is reduced for each learner, allowing them to give more time and attention to language use. Being too deeply absorbed in a task can take attention away from what really needs to be learned, or the incidental learning goal. Indeed, Jonathan deHaan, W. Michael Reed, and Katsuko Kuwada (2010) found in a non-interactive activity that the learner observing their partner playing a music video game recalled three times more of the song lyrics encountered than the learner actually playing the game.

4 It is also worth teaching the language of negotiation so that learners are able to negotiate in the L2. Teachers may also want to talk to learners about the value of using the L2 whenever possible during the task.

5 Learning is likely to be enhanced if there is some follow-up reflection for reporting on what happened during the activity and the outcome, as this will provide opportunities for repetition and varied use.

16 Ten-minute writing

Programme strand	Meaning-focused output, fluency development through writing
Learning goal	Learn to use words in writing in a more fluent manner
Learning conditions	Repetition, productive retrieval, varied use
Research evidence	Not researched
Further reading	Nguyen (2015)

Description
This fluency development activity involves learners writing continuously for ten minutes, two or three times a week for several weeks, and tracking their progress on a graph. The topics chosen should be ones which allow the learners to bring existing background knowledge to the writing, as well as the vocabulary they need to deal with the topic. A list of easy topics (see Nation, 2013a) could be put up on the classroom wall for learners to choose from if they are wondering what to write about. Each learner can write on a different topic.

The writing is done under carefully timed conditions. When the learners are ready to begin writing, the teacher says 'go' and makes a note of the time. When exactly ten minutes are up, the teacher says 'stop' and the learners quickly finish the sentence they are writing. Each learner then counts the number of words in their piece of writing and adds the total to a graph, with the date of the piece of writing and its topic along the horizontal axis and the number of words along the vertical axis. The goal is to try to increase the amount of writing done in each session. The pieces of writing should not be corrected for errors, because focusing on correctness is likely to slow down the speed of written production. Instead, the teacher can give positive feedback on the content of the writing, encouraging the learner to write more.

Lexical information
Dictionary use should not be encouraged during ten-minute writing, as this would clearly slow down fluency of output. This means improvements in vocabulary knowledge are likely to come solely from the opportunities for the retrieval of words under time pressure.

Learning conditions

Ideally, fluency development activities make use of known vocabulary, with the goal being to make this vocabulary more fluently accessible and to encourage learners to work with larger phrasal units rather than single words. As the topic vocabulary in a written text is likely to be repeated, repetition can contribute to the speed of access to vocabulary.

As they write, the learners have to retrieve the words they need to use, and this productive retrieval can strengthen word knowledge. There are also likely to be opportunities for varied use, as learners use familiar words to express new ideas.

Improving vocabulary learning

1 The type of repetition used in the 4/3/2 activity (see *6 4/3/2*) can be used, modified to allow more time for writing—for example, to 10/9/8 or 7/6/5. The three pieces of writing need not be done in the same session, and the learner could be allowed to quickly read the piece of writing from the previous session before rewriting it within the shortened timeframe. The teacher could also ask learners to make some corrections before rewriting so that errors are not repeated.
2 The quality of the writing is likely to be improved if the learners talk about their topic with a partner for a few minutes beforehand. The discussion can focus on both form and content.
3 Ten-minute writing can be based on work recently done in class so that there is more opportunity for repetition and retrieval to occur.

17 Flashcards

Programme strand	Language-focused learning from reading
Learning goal	Link the forms of L2 words to their meaning, learn written forms of words (for beginners)
Learning conditions	Spaced repetition, receptive and productive retrieval, deliberate noticing
Research evidence	The flashcard activity is a rote-learning procedure, and there is over 100 years of research showing its efficiency and effectiveness (Nation, 2013a, Chapter 11).
Further reading	Nakata (2011)

Description

The flashcard activity typically involves writing an L2 word on one side of a small card and its L1 translation on the other. A set of these cards is then used to go through each L2 word and try to recall its L1 translation. Once a learner can do this with a high degree of success, the cards are turned over, and the learner looks at the L1 translation and tries to recall the L2 word form. Learners need some training to use flashcards well, and this should focus on the principles of 1) spacing the learning, 2) using retrieval, 3) varying the order of the words in the pack, 4) using elaboration techniques where necessary, 5) avoiding interference, and 6) saying the words aloud.

There is plenty of flashcard software that can be used. Not all apply good principles of learning; Tatsuya Nakata (2011) outlines a valuable set of criteria for evaluating such software and also applies these criteria to a wide range of existing software. Digital flashcards are likely to be at least as effective as the paper versions, and they may even be better if used properly, because they often include adaptive recycling features and motivational record-keeping functionality that enables learners to track their progress.

Lexical information
The focus of the flashcard activity is to strengthen learners' knowledge of the form–meaning connections of words. This is achieved through repeated retrieval. Other aspects of vocabulary knowledge such as collocation and association may also be gained when there is overlap between the L1 and L2 words (Webb, 2007b).

Learning conditions
Research overwhelmingly supports the practice of spacing repetitions rather than grouping or massing them together to be learned in one session. This means that the best procedure to follow when using flashcards is to spend a few minutes working through them, put them away for a few hours, then work through them again, rather than spending an extended period of time going through the cards over and over again. There are two kinds of spacing to consider: the spacing between items within a learning session, and the spacing between learning sessions. It was previously thought that, for both of these kinds of spacing, the spacing should be increased incrementally with each repetition. However, recent research (Nakata, 2015) has shown that the amount of spacing is in fact more important than gradually increasing the spacing. Moreover, Ulf Schuetze (2015) has shown that when learning sessions are spread over the course of a few days, equal spacing is better for long-term retention. Nevertheless, there is still value in increasing the spacing between each consecutive learning session, particularly between later learning sessions.

Retrieval can occur through recall. Successful receptive retrieval occurs when a learner sees an L2 word form and is able to recall its L1 translation. Productive retrieval occurs when a learner thinks of, or sees, the L1 meaning and is able to recall the L2 word form. It has been argued (Baddeley, 1990) that each successful retrieval strengthens the connection between the form of a word and its meaning. This is one reason why flashcards are superior to word lists or vocabulary notebooks. Flashcards encourage retrieval, because the word form is on one side of the card and the meaning is on the other; and seeing one prompts the learner to retrieve the other. With word lists and vocabulary notebooks, both the form and the meaning are seen together, so there is no such opportunity for retrieval. Research has shown that receptive retrieval and productive retrieval have different effects, so there will be value in incorporating both when using flashcards, to ensure that learners make progress in using vocabulary for both receptive and productive purposes. But if only one type of retrieval is used, then productive retrieval may provide the greatest benefit to learners (Webb, 2009a, 2009b).

Deliberate noticing works best when attention is focused directly on what needs to be learned—in this case, form–meaning connection. For a simple learning task, a deliberate focus is considerably more effective than incidental learning. However, it is important to remember that incidental learning is required for skill improvement, content learning, and to develop familiarity with a range of aspects of word knowledge.

Improving vocabulary learning

1 As noted above, learners need to be trained in using flashcards effectively (Nation, 2008). They should understand the reason for using flashcards to encourage retrieval and recognize the importance of spaced retrieval. They should practise using flashcards, allowing time for retrieval before turning the card over, changing the order of the cards in the set as they recall words, saying the word quietly to themselves, and making use of other techniques (see *18 Keyword technique, 19 Word parts*) when an item proves difficult to remember. They should also be aware of interference and understand that closely related items such as near synonyms, opposites, and members of a lexical set should not be included in the same set of cards (Nation, 2000).

2 Flashcards are most effective when learners themselves can choose the words on the flashcards, when the words chosen are at the right level for the learners so that they get the best return for their efforts, and when they are supported by learning from meaning-focused input, meaning-focused output, and fluency development. If learners make their own flashcards, some learning may occur during the process of making them. However, it may be more efficient to choose from a set of ready-made cards, or to use flashcard software, because more learning is likely to occur when using the cards than when making them.

3 Teachers should monitor learners' use of flashcards, for example by asking them to bring their cards to class and checking how many cards they have made and what words they have put on the cards. Learners should also be given the opportunity to discuss how they feel about using flashcards and the degree of success that they have experienced in using them.

4 Learners can test each other on their cards.

5 It is essential that learning with flashcards is well integrated into a vocabulary learning programme. Deliberate learning using flashcards needs to support and enrich incidental learning through both input and output. This can be done in several ways: by choosing words for deliberate study from reading and listening input, by using deliberate vocabulary learning as preparation for extensive reading and listening, and by ensuring that the choice of words to learn is strongly guided by frequency lists and **needs analysis**.

18 *Keyword technique*

Programme strand	Language-focused learning from reading
Learning goal	Learn the forms and meanings of new words
Learning conditions	Deliberate elaboration
Research evidence	The keyword technique is the most thoroughly researched vocabulary learning activity, with the vast majority of experiments indicating that it outperforms any default deliberate learning activity by around 20%.
Further reading	Pressley (1977)

Description

We briefly described the keyword technique in Chapter 4. This deliberate learning technique is a mnemonic device for relating the form of a word to its meaning in a memorable way. It draws on four components:

1 the form of the L2 word to be learned
2 a keyword that the learner chooses from their L1 (or is provided for them) which resembles all or the beginning of the L2 word form
3 a visual image that links the meaning of the keyword with the meaning of the L2 word
4 the meaning of the L2 word.

For example, in order to learn the L2 word 'funds' (= money), a Thai learner might choose the Thai keyword 'fun', which means 'teeth'. The next step is to visualize an image combining the Thai keyword with the meaning of 'funds', for example someone sinking their teeth into a pile of banknotes. The effect of this is that whenever the learner encounters the word 'funds', the form of the word will remind them of the keyword, and this will prompt them to visualize the associated image, which conveys the meaning of the L2 word. While this may seem a rather clumsy and elaborate process for memorizing a word and its meaning, it has proved to be very effective. It need not be used to learn every word—only for those that do not stick readily in memory. (The keyword technique can be used very effectively in conjunction with *17 Flashcards*, though it is not limited to being used in this way.)

Lexical information

In order to use the keyword technique, the learner needs to have both the form and meaning of an L2 word available for processing. This means the keyword technique does not provide new information about the word; it simply provides a memorable way of linking the form and meaning of words.

Learning conditions

The major learning condition underpinning the keyword technique is deliberate elaboration. Pressley's research (1977) looked at the various components of the keyword technique to see what made it work, and he concluded that the image combining the meaning of the L1 keyword and that of the L2 word was central to the effectiveness of the technique. Simply providing an image of the meaning of the L2 word was not nearly as effective as the linking image created using the keyword technique.

Repetition is not an integral part of the technique, although once the keyword technique has been applied to a word, coming back to the word again and again using flashcards is an effective way of ensuring that the word is learned. However, supporters of the keyword technique might argue that if the linking image is truly memorable, then repetition would be rendered unnecessary.

Improving vocabulary learning

1 The effectiveness of the keyword technique initially depends on the choice of keyword and then on the memorability of the linking image. In most studies of the keyword technique, the keyword is an L1 word. Some languages, like Mandarin, which are largely monosyllabic and have a very limited range of syllable structures, may not provide a rich source of keywords to match to L2 words. In these cases, learners can be encouraged to choose keywords from other languages they know, or from the words they already know in the L2.

2 Learners need a reasonable amount of guided practice with the keyword technique before they become comfortable using it. The goal of the practice should be to make it so easy for them to use the technique that they use it whenever they have the opportunity to do so. Teachers can model choosing keywords, interacting with the class, and eventually get learners to work in groups and choose keywords themselves. Similar practice can be done in creating linking images.

3 An important part of the keyword technique is visualizing the linking image rather than just describing it. Learners should therefore be encouraged to close their eyes and visualize the linking image as a way of making sure that it will truly work. This visualization is thought to result in dual coding (Paivio & Desrochers, 1981), whereby information about the word is stored both linguistically and visually.

19 *Word parts*

Programme strand	Language-focused learning through reading
Learning goal	Learn the forms and meanings of words; develop knowledge of word form
Learning conditions	Deliberate noticing, deliberate elaboration
Research evidence	Wei (2015) found that using the word part technique was as effective as the keyword technique and deliberate rote-learning.
Further reading	Wei & Nation (2013)

Description

The word part technique is not a way of working out the meaning of the word; rather, it is a technique for making new words (especially complex words) easier to retain in memory (Wei, 2015). It involves breaking down a complex word into its constituent parts and then deliberately connecting the meaning of each part to the meaning of the whole word. For example, 'autograph' can be broken down into the parts *auto-* and *-graph*. Awareness of the meanings of these parts (*auto-* = 'self', *-graph* = 'write') allows learners to better recognize and remember the meaning of the word as a whole. The technique is based on the fact that around 60% of English vocabulary comes from French, Latin, or Greek, so being familiar with the common prefixes, suffixes, and word stems of English can make vocabulary learning more effective. Research by Wei (Wei & Nation, 2013) found that around 2,000 of the third 1,000 to the tenth 1,000 most frequent word families in English are related to the 2,000 most frequent word families, through having shared word stems. In addition, a small number of common prefixes (for example, *non-*, *un-*) and suffixes (for example, *-able*, *-less*) have been found to account for a very large proportion of affix use in English (Bauer & Nation, 1993; Stauffer, 1942). This means a relatively small amount of word parts knowledge has the potential to make a very useful contribution to vocabulary learning.

In order to make the connection between the meanings of the parts and the whole, the meaning of the whole word needs to be looked up in a dictionary or guessed from context, and the learner needs to memorize the most useful word parts and their meanings. That said, knowing the most useful, regular, and productive prefixes and suffixes can make it possible for a learner to deal with low-frequency members of a word family if they already know one or two members of the family. If an unfamiliar family member is encountered in context, then the combination of the contextual clues and a familiarity with word building affixes can make it possible for a learner to do what Anglin (1993) calls 'morphological problem-solving'.

The first step in learning to use the word part technique is to deliberately learn the most frequent prefixes, suffixes, and stems (for lists of the most frequent prefixes and suffixes, see Bauer & Nation, 1993; Nation, 2013a; Sasao & Webb, 2017). A list of useful word stems is provided in Appendix 3 (taken from Wei & Nation, 2013). Affixes and stems can be learned using flashcards (see *17 Flashcards*).

Lexical information

Information about the word comes from the meaning of the parts and also from looking up the word in a dictionary or using some other deliberate method of identifying the meaning of the word. In many ways, the word part technique is a decontextualized method of memorizing the meanings of words.

Learning conditions

Word part analysis is a form of deliberate elaboration, involving deep processing of the form of a word and its meaning. The elaboration occurs through identifying known parts of the word which also occur in other known words and relating the meanings of these parts to the meaning of the whole word. This effectively entails connecting new knowledge to old knowledge, with the former represented by the unfamiliar word and the latter by the known parts. The word part technique has many similarities with the keyword technique (Wei, 2015). For example, the word parts are form-based, at least to some degree, and the interactive linking involves the combination of the meaning of the parts and that of the whole word.

The use of prefixes and suffixes to deal with members of the same word family could eventually become a method of incidental learning, once enough practice makes the information readily available to the learner. However, the use of stems, particularly bound stems such as *-cess-* ('go') and *-dict-* ('say') where the forms and meanings are less transparent, is likely to always be a deliberate learning activity.

Improving vocabulary learning

1   The successful application of any technique will come from having plenty of opportunity to understand and practise it. It is thus essential that learners get plenty of training in using the word part technique over many weeks, preferably longer.
2   The successful application of the technique will also depend on the selection of word parts to be studied and memorized, and on the quality of the deliberate learning of these parts. If the word parts occur in many words, then the benefits will far outweigh the cost of learning. If these word parts are thoroughly learned, practised, and tested, then this knowledge will be readily available whenever the word part technique needs to be applied.

3 The study of word stems is a significant step towards understanding the etymology of words and making use of this etymology to help make learning memorable. Research on multi-word combinations (Boers, Eyckmans, & Stengers, 2007) has shown that understanding their origin (for example, knowing that 'left high and dry' comes from sailing) helps with their retention. There is every reason to expect that a similar approach will work for single words, especially complex words.

20 *Dictionary use*

Programme strand	Language-focused learning from reading
Learning goal	Learn the forms and meanings of new words
Learning conditions	Deliberate noticing, repetition, varied use, deliberate elaboration
Research evidence	Dictionary use results in vocabulary learning (Bruton, 2007; Hulstijn, Hollander, & Greidanus, 1996; Knight, 1994; Laufer & Hill, 2000; Peters, 2007). Studies show that learners do not use dictionaries well and that the amount and quality of dictionary look-up depends on the salience of words in the text and learners' view of the goal and importance of the reading task (Peters, 2007).
Further reading	Laufer & Hill (2000)

Description

There are two major kinds of receptive dictionary use. The more common of these involves simply gaining quick access to the meaning of a word, or some other information about it. The other is focused on learning and can be considered a vocabulary learning strategy. It involves using a dictionary to help remember a word, and it is probably best used with words that are already partially known. Lower-level learners should use a **bilingual dictionary**, because in order to understand the definitions in a **monolingual dictionary**, a learner needs to have a vocabulary size of around 2–3,000 words. A good dictionary allows the learner to look through the various senses of the word in order to discern the core meaning—that is, the meaning that runs through all of the senses. The learner can also look at the form of the word and at nearby entries to find words which share the same word stem. If the dictionary contains easily accessible and comprehensible etymological information, then the learner can look at this to enrich their knowledge of the word. Most learner dictionaries contain plenty of examples, and looking at these should give some idea of the use of the word and its collocations. Dictionary use is a deliberate learning strategy and learners need training to use it well.

Lexical information

When a dictionary is used while reading, both the reading text and the dictionary are sources of information about the word. The reading text provides contextual information which would ideally prompt learners to guess the meaning of a word, before confirming or enriching their guess by referring to a dictionary.

Learning conditions

Dictionary use applies the condition of deliberate noticing, particularly when it occurs with the first encounter of a word. It has been noted that the use of glosses (and presumably dictionary use) involves looking at an unknown word in a text, looking at its entry in a glossary or dictionary, and then looking back at the text again (Watanabe, 1997), which results in a small amount of massed repetition. It is also possible to argue that there is a small degree of elaboration or varied use involved in dictionary use. This is because the meaning given for a word in the dictionary might not closely match its use in the text, which means the learner has to make a contextual adjustment in order to use the dictionary meaning. Dictionaries usually cover several senses, so the adjustment between the sense given in the dictionary and the sense of the word in context need only be small. It could be argued that providing fewer senses in the dictionary and always giving the core meaning would place more pressure on the dictionary user to make the contextual adjustment and therefore result in more thoughtful processing and better retention of the meaning of a word—Verspoor and Lowie (2003) and Serafima Gettys, Lorens Imhof, and Joseph Kautz (2001) provide some evidence to support this. Dictionary use also applies the deep condition of deliberate elaboration through various analytical procedures which enrich knowledge of a word.

Improving vocabulary learning

1 The most important way of improving vocabulary learning through dictionary use is to train and encourage learners to use dictionaries effectively. Part of this encouragement could involve getting learners to do more of their reading on e-readers, which provide instant touch access to the definition of words in the text, making dictionary look-up easier and less time-consuming. Some e-readers, notably those from Kindle and Kobo, allow abbreviated and expanded dictionary look-up while reading, which is useful in terms of minimizing the disruptive effect of dictionary use on the reading process while allowing readers to access more detailed information about a word if necessary.

2 Teachers should also measure learners' vocabulary size to assess whether they know enough words to be able to use a monolingual dictionary. As long as the bilingual dictionary is of a reasonable quality, learners should not be struggling with a monolingual dictionary if they do not have a large enough vocabulary size to be able to use it comfortably. In relation to the previous point, reading software for L2 learners would ideally offer a choice of dictionary, to allow readers to look up words in the L1 if desired.

3 Strategies for dictionary use need to be well informed and well practised. The various strategies need to be practised separately, so finding the core meaning, identifying related words, understanding etymologies, using word parts, and analysing the use of words should each be covered separately across several practice sessions.

21 Dictation

Programme strand	Language-focused learning from listening and writing
Learning goal	Learn the connection between the spoken and written forms of words
Learning conditions	Repetition, deliberate noticing, varied encounters
Research evidence	Not researched
Further reading	Nation & Newton (2008, Chapter 4)

Description

In this activity, learners listen to a text around 150 words long which is read to them three times. First, it is read through in its entirety so learners can get some idea of what it is about. Then it is read through in chunks, each chunk being roughly seven or eight words long, and learners write what they hear. The scope of each chunk should be determined by the grammar and content of the sentences. In the third reading, the text is again read as a whole and learners make additions, corrections, or changes to what they wrote during the second reading. The text is then marked; this can be done in many ways, but if dictation is a commonly used activity, then on most occasions learners should be able to mark the texts themselves so that the teacher is not over-burdened with a heavy marking load. This typically involves learners exchanging scripts (the theory being that it is easier to see someone else's mistakes than your own). Marking can be done by handing around a copy of the text, by projecting the text on the board, or by getting one student to write the text on the board as the rest of the class checks their scripts.

The focus of dictation is on deliberate learning, particularly on the connection between spoken and written language. Although learners listen and write, dictation is more a test of language proficiency than a test of listening. Oller and Streiff (1975) describe dictation as a test of 'grammar-based expectancies', underlining the idea that if dictation is delivered properly, the learners need to be processing language at the phrase or clause level in order to cope with the chunks of language they hear. From a vocabulary perspective, dictation focuses on the accurate reception of spoken words and phrases which are already largely familiar to the learners. Proof of recognition comes from having to write these words and phrases, and there has been some debate about the importance of correct spelling when marking a dictation, with the suggestion being made that small spelling errors are acceptable.

Lexical information
Information about the words in a dictation comes from the dictation text itself and from the marking feedback. Sawyer and Silver (1961) suggest that the same dictation needs to be done at least twice a few days apart in order to benefit from the feedback on the first administration of the dictation.

Learning conditions
The main learning from dictation comes from deliberate noticing. It could also be argued that dictation provides the opportunity for varied encounters, because the familiar words in the dictation text are likely to occur in contexts which are different from those in which they have been encountered before. Because each dictation session typically involves the text being delivered three times, there is also the opportunity to learn from verbatim repetition.

Improving vocabulary learning
1 For dictation to be successful, the words in the dictation should be at least partially familiar to the learners from previous encounters. It is therefore useful to choose dictation texts which are from material that the learners have already worked on, or closely related material.
2 Nation (1991b) argues that dictation and several other related activities (for example, **dictogloss**) all rely on learners getting practice in holding phrases and clauses in memory before reproducing them in a different medium. This encourages learners to become familiar with such chunks, and thus be more likely to work at phrase or clause level rather than at individual word level in their language use. So it is important to make sure that the dictation is delivered in meaningful chunks which are long enough to require the learners to repeat them in their minds before writing them down.

22 Semantic mapping

Programme strand	Language-focused learning from all four skills
Learning goal	Learn the associations among words, learn the forms and meanings of new words
Learning conditions	Repetition, deliberate noticing, elaboration
Research evidence	Stahl and Vancil (1986) found that the discussion component of the activity contributed more to learning than the semantic map itself.
Further reading	Stahl & Vancil (1986)

Description

Semantic mapping involves the teacher and learners working together to build up a map of words and phrases associated with a particular topic. A word or phrase describing the topic is placed in the centre of the map, then aspects of the topic are organized and expanded on through discussion and added to the semantic map. Particular attention is given to explaining and linking the various aspects of the topic and clarifying the vocabulary related to those aspects. The activity has two goals: content learning, including the stimulation of background knowledge, and vocabulary expansion. Stahl and Vancil's description of semantic mapping (1986) involves the teacher initially listing vocabulary related to the topic and then, through discussion, organizing the vocabulary as a semantic map. Semantic mapping activities can start from recalling a topic that the learners have recently studied or know a lot about. They can be based on a recent event or on shared cultural knowledge. In many ways, semantic mapping is the formalization of the collective knowledge produced and shared through teacher–learner and learner–learner interaction.

Lexical information

Information about each word comes from the discussion between the teacher and learners. Because semantic mapping is typically led by the teacher, they are able to check on and add to the information provided by the learners about the words. The process of arranging the words into a semantic map can also be a source of reflective lexical insights.

Learning conditions

Learning from semantic mapping is heavily dependent on the skill with which the teacher manages the activity. In terms of vocabulary learning, deliberate noticing should occur as the teacher provides and elicits explanations of the vocabulary. Semantic mapping differs from other spoken interaction activities, in that noticing is directed towards both the form of the words and phrases and their meaning. Noticing of form is supported by using both spoken forms of the words (in discussion) and the written forms (in the semantic map). Noticing of meaning derives from the explanation of the core meaning of the words and how they relate to the topic.

Another learning condition involved in semantic mapping is repetition. The teacher should aim to repeat the target vocabulary in the activity. This can be verbatim repetition from going through the map several times at various stages of its development, and repetition through varied use in discussions of the map. Looking at the different relationships between related words can also be considered a form of elaboration.

Improving vocabulary learning

1 Semantic mapping will be most effective if:

- learners are encouraged to make productive use of the target vocabulary, through having to retrieve it rather than it being supplied by the teacher
- there is plenty of repetition through having to justify and explain the connections made in the semantic map
- the map is reconstructed a few days later to allow for repetition and spaced retrieval
- the map leads on to a task that makes productive use of it, such as a piece of writing or a problem-solving discussion.

2 There is value in teachers providing much of the vocabulary for semantic mapping, because this allows learners to focus on making sure that useful words and phrases, which may already have been encountered, are included. Learners can suggest additional words and phrases, and the teacher can decide what to do with these suggestions.

3 Semantic mapping involves highlighting semantically meaningful relationships between target words, and the teacher needs to make sure that these relationships are largely ones that will have positive effects on learning (Tinkham, 1997) rather than having the negative effect of increasing interference between the target words. The teacher should not focus on near synonyms or opposites unless a member of the pair is already well known. Similarly, listing members of a lexical set should be avoided. Rather, there should be a focus on relating items in a story or on the basis of some kind of logical or sequential relationship, such as a list of instructions or a process for doing something.

23 *Intensive reading*

Programme strand	Language-focused learning from reading
Learning goal	Learn the forms and meanings of new words; learn topic-related words encountered in texts
Learning conditions	Deliberate noticing, retrieval, deliberate elaboration
Research evidence	Because **intensive reading** is primarily a language-focused activity involving deliberate learning, vocabulary taught during this activity has a reasonable chance of being remembered. Research indicates that reading accompanied by deliberate learning activities results in better learning than simply reading (Min, 2008; Paribakht & Wesche, 1996; Sonbul & Schmitt, 2010), or reading with dictionary use (Laufer & Rozovski-Roitblat, 2011).
Further reading	Nation (2004b)

Description

Intensive reading is primarily a language-focused learning activity (in contrast, see *7 Extensive reading*) in which learners read texts with the help of a teacher, other learners, a dictionary, and other forms of support. Without these, they would not be able to read the text with adequate comprehension.

When used as a teacher-led classroom activity, intensive reading usually involves short texts of a few hundred words. The teacher helps the learners understand the text by explaining the difficult words, clarifying points of grammar, explaining any figurative expressions or idioms, and explaining the ideas presented in the text. This amounts to **rich instruction**—that is, spending a considerable amount of time on developing a holistic understanding of a word by drawing attention to its form, meaning, and use.

Intensive reading can provide the basis for the deliberate teaching of language items only marginally related to the reading text and also for the development of language learning strategies; for example, the strategies described in *8 Guessing from context*, *19 Word parts*, and *20 Dictionary use* can be practised during intensive reading.

Intensive reading can also be an individual activity where the learner works through a difficult text such as a novel or an academic text with the help of a dictionary. From a vocabulary perspective, such reading can involve a lot of effort for little gain, because at least half of the unknown words that the learner encounters in the text will occur only once, and many of them may be so far outside the learner's current knowledge that they will not be encountered again for a very long time. In a typical novel of around 100,000 words, there are likely to be at least 1,000 words of no great value to the learner.

Lexical information

The main source of vocabulary knowledge in intensive reading comes from the teacher or from the dictionary, depending on whether the intensive reading is done as a classroom activity or individually.

Learning conditions

The major learning condition during intensive reading is deliberate noticing. Skilful teachers can use intensive reading as an opportunity for retrieval, by relating the new knowledge to previous knowledge, and deliberate elaboration, by devoting time to the rich instruction of particularly important words.

Improving vocabulary learning

1 Carefully choosing which words to focus on is an important way of increasing the value of vocabulary learning through intensive reading. The selection should involve consideration of the general frequency of the words in the language (high-frequency words clearly deserve attention) and the relevance of the words for the learners' future use of the language (technical words).

2 Repetition of the words during an intensive reading session will support learning, but it is even more important to come back to the words a few days later, then again a few weeks later, to provide opportunities for repetition, retrieval, and elaboration. Such revision activities can include recalling the words that were previously focused on, breaking down the words into word parts, looking at spelling patterns and irregularities in the form of the words, practising saying the words to improve pronunciation, suggesting collocates of the words, and extending their meanings.

3 Words encountered during intensive reading should go onto flashcards for individualized deliberate learning (see *17 Flashcards*).

ACTIVITY 5.4   Analysing your favourite learning activities

Based on what you have read in this chapter, see if you can successfully apply the principles discussed to your own teaching experience. Choose three of your most successful classroom activities in which vocabulary learning occurs—ones that you are familiar with or use frequently. Then answer the questions below for each activity.

1 How does the activity fit within a balanced language course in terms of incidental learning (meaning-focused input, meaning-focused output, fluency development) or deliberate learning (language focused-learning)?

2 What lexical information is generated during the activity?

3 What learning conditions occur during the activity?

Summary

This chapter has analysed activities across the four skills of listening, speaking, reading, and writing that can give rise to vocabulary learning. The way in which an activity is used can have a major effect on this learning. Activities can be used in ways which maximize vocabulary learning from the activity, or in ways which make vocabulary learning difficult or unlikely to occur. This means that teachers and learners need to understand the conditions that facilitate learning and be aware of how activities can be modified to optimize these conditions.

Questions for reflection

1 The analysis of activities in this chapter has referred to the quality of attention created by the activities in terms of noticing, retrieval, varied encounters and use, and elaboration. Are there any other criteria that you feel are important in the analysis of vocabulary learning activities?

2 What vocabulary learning activities have not been analysed in this chapter?

3 The central premise of Chapters 4 and 5 is that teachers (and perhaps learners) need to be analytical about the activities they use and how they use them, because vocabulary learning depends on the learning conditions that the activities set up. Do you agree? Or do you think that vocabulary learning simply occurs as a result of encountering and using the language? Give reasons for your answer.

Keys to activities

ACTIVITY 5.1   **Analysing vocabulary activities in a coursebook (1)**

1 Ideally, the activities in the coursebook will balance all four skills equally. Reading and listening activities should help to develop receptive vocabulary knowledge that should enable learners to recognize and understand words they encounter. Speaking and writing activities should help to develop productive vocabulary knowledge that will enable learners to use words more effectively. Moreover, reading and writing activities should contribute to learning the written forms of words, while speaking and listening activities should contribute to learning the spoken forms of words.

2 It is not always easy to distinguish between incidental and deliberate learning. For some activities, such as those utilizing flashcards, the distinction may seem very clear; however, it could be argued that incidental learning occurs even with flashcards, in that typical spelling patterns will be picked up incidentally in the process of going through a large number of words. Nevertheless, it is a useful distinction for EFL teachers to make, even in a rather rough way, because they tend to spend too much time on deliberate activities and not nearly enough on those that result in incidental learning.

ACTIVITY 5.2   **Analysing a speaking activity**

Repetition is probably the strongest factor in this activity. The preparatory stages provide opportunities for repetition. Questions asked after the talk may also provide repetition. The words will be used productively; and if the talk is given without notes, productive retrieval can occur. Answering questions can result in productive varied use.

ACTIVITY 5.3   Analysing vocabulary activities in a coursebook (2)

1 Possible selection and sequencing principles include: easy to difficult, receptive to productive, or working systematically through the four skills of listening, speaking, reading, and writing. Another possible sequence is to move from deliberate to incidental learning.

2 In most activities, the focus of attention and the learning conditions that are involved in the activity will be very important in determining what will actually be learned. It is useful to consider the degree to which the target vocabulary is focused on and the extent to which the different activities promote repetition, noticing, retrieval, varied encounters and use, and elaboration.

Suggestions for further reading

Each activity in this chapter includes brief suggestions for further reading. The following references look more generally at analysing vocabulary learning activities.

Laufer, B., & **Hulstijn, J.** (2001). Incidental vocabulary acquisition in a second language: the construct of task-induced involvement. *Applied Linguistics, 22(1)*, 1–26.

Laufer and Hulstijn describe three criteria for evaluating vocabulary learning activities: need, search, and evaluation. They propose that by looking at how well each criterion applies to a particular activity, it is possible to predict the likely effectiveness of the activity for vocabulary learning.

Hulstijn, J. H., & **Laufer, B.** (2001). Some empirical evidence for the involvement load hypothesis in vocabulary acquisition. *Language Learning, 51(3)*, 539–558.

Laufer and Hulstijn put their theory to the test in this article. The **Involvement Load Hypothesis** stimulated several published experiments as well as numerous theses testing the hypothesis, and critiquing Hulstijn and Laufer's research, particularly with regard to time-on-task. Generally, activities with a greater involvement load take longer to complete than activities with a smaller involvement load, so time-on-task needs to be controlled for when experimentally evaluating an activity.

Nation, I. S. P., & **Webb, S.** (2011). *Researching and analysing vocabulary.* Boston: Heinle Cengage Learning.

Nation and Webb sought to build on the Involvement Load Hypothesis by including other factors that were known to encourage vocabulary learning. Laufer and Hulstijn's scale involved three criteria, with each having a value of 0, 1, or 2. Nation and Webb's **Technique Feature Analysis** involves looking at an activity against 18 criteria, each being present (1 point) or absent (0). Research indicates that Technique Feature Analysis is more effective in evaluating the effectiveness of activities than the Involvement Load Hypothesis (Hu & Nassaji, 2016).

6 LEARNING VOCABULARY IN DIFFERENT CONTEXTS

Introduction

How vocabulary is learned varies between different contexts. Beginner, intermediate, and advanced students should all focus on learning different sets of words. ESL and EFL learners will learn in slightly different ways. Moreover, the way we teach words is affected by the age of the learner. Very young children tend to learn initially through listening, while older children, adolescents, and adults learn through both reading and listening. In this chapter, we will consider the different contexts in which vocabulary is learned and discuss the various approaches that teachers might use to teach words in each context.

Learning vocabulary in the EFL context

The term 'English as a Foreign Language' (EFL) applies to learners who are living in a country where English is not the first or significant language; examples include Japan, Brazil, and France. Learning vocabulary in the EFL context can be quite challenging, primarily because learners may not have much exposure to English outside the classroom. This means that teachers are likely to have a significant impact on the lexical development of their students, so having a principled plan for vocabulary learning is essential.

ACTIVITY 6.1 **Language development in the EFL classroom**

Based on what you have read so far about how vocabulary is learned, and on any classroom experience you have, what features of the EFL classroom situation in particular do you think are challenging in terms of vocabulary acquisition? Read on to check your ideas.

There are several features that make learning in the EFL context unique. Being aware of these can help teachers positively influence how their students approach vocabulary learning.

Contact with English

First, the EFL context is characterized by a relative lack of opportunities for students to learn with meaning-focused input and meaning-focused output outside the classroom. A lack of contact with English in this context means teachers must ensure that there is plenty of input inside the classroom, as well as frequent opportunities for students to use their developing knowledge of vocabulary. Familiarizing students with different resources they can use outside the classroom to learn and practise using vocabulary is also very useful, as doing so can reveal the ways in which they can autonomously develop their L2 vocabulary knowledge. Extensive learning programmes, where students read as much as possible and watch L2 television and online videos regularly, are very important in the EFL context. Through encountering large amounts of L2 input in these programmes, students' knowledge of taught words is likely to expand, as these words are encountered again and again. New words and collocations may also be learned incidentally (Webb, Newton, & Chang, 2013). More challenging, perhaps, is the need to provide plenty of opportunities for students to use target words in speech and writing. Speaking and writing activities take up precious classroom time, so it is important to ensure that activities are structured in ways which maximize the use of taught words. Including target words in the instructions is one method of ensuring that these words receive attention (Nation, 2008).

Needs

Second, EFL students may not have any clear and immediate need to learn the target language. Some language learning materials may focus on common situations, such as introductions, asking for directions, and shopping. However, students may not come across these situations unless they travel abroad. Other learning materials may concentrate on thematic topics, such as the environment, technology, or personality types. These again may not relate to any clearly defined need for the students. So although prescribed course content may require them to learn words included in commonly used learning materials, the value of these words may not be clearly apparent. Selecting materials that more effectively cater to students' needs will provide a better chance that the vocabulary encountered in the materials will be learned. If it is not possible to select alternative materials, then having students focus on learning the highest-frequency words that are unknown to them would provide the greatest value. Lower-frequency, topic-related words could simply be glossed to eliminate the need for students to spend much time on them, since these words are unlikely to be encountered, needed, and remembered once a unit of learning has been completed.

Motivation

A third feature of learning vocabulary in the EFL context is that students' motivation for learning may vary to a considerable degree. Some learners may be highly motivated and working towards living or studying in an English-speaking context in future. Some learners may be studying because they hope to communicate effectively when they are travelling for work or leisure, while others may simply be learning English because it is a required component of the curriculum. Because there is often no immediate benefit to learning English in the EFL context, it is useful for teachers to highlight the value of vocabulary learning to students. Raising awareness of how reaching certain vocabulary knowledge targets can help students to comprehend English may encourage further learning. For example, if students know that the 800 lemmas in the Essential Word List (Dang & Webb, 2016b) represent 75% of English, or that the 3,000 most frequent word families cover 95% of the words used in most types of spoken discourse, then they might feel motivated to work towards achieving a specific vocabulary learning goal.

It may also be useful to raise awareness of why selected materials and activities are used. If students understand the value in what they are doing to learn vocabulary, then they are likely to be more engaged.

Balance

Fourth, the balance between deliberate learning and other types of learning in the EFL classroom is often not optimal; deliberate learning typically accounts for a greater percentage of classroom time than it ideally should. While deliberate learning can lead to fast and efficient gains in vocabulary knowledge, these gains on their own are unlikely to be sufficient to enable students to process and use words effectively. To develop a rich knowledge of words, learning needs to occur in a variety of ways. As we shall see in Chapter 8, deliberate learning should only account for about a quarter of the time spent learning words in a well-balanced vocabulary learning programme, as it needs to be supplemented with learning through meaning-focused input (revealing to students how words are used), meaning-focused output (using words for communication), and fluency development (processing words at a faster rate). This will help to develop the productive vocabulary knowledge that is necessary for students to be able to use words effectively and fluently.

Learning vocabulary in the ESL context

The term 'English as a Second Language' (ESL) applies to learners in countries where English is the most commonly used language, such as the

United States, Canada, the United Kingdom, Australia, and New Zealand. In the ESL context, there are frequent opportunities to encounter and use English outside the classroom. The teacher's impact on vocabulary learning is therefore likely to be smaller than in the EFL context. This does not mean that teachers do not contribute to vocabulary learning in the ESL context; they simply play a slightly different role. Let us consider some key features of learning ESL that distinguish it from the EFL context (Nation, 2013b).

Contact with English

First, there may be greater scope for vocabulary learning outside the classroom than within the classroom. Students can develop vocabulary knowledge through encounters with words in meaning-focused input and by using partially known words outside the classroom. It is important for students to take advantage of the many opportunities to learn through meaning-focused input and meaning-focused output. For young learners, this may be very easy, as they are often placed in classrooms where their only option is to communicate in English, so their motivation to learn and use English is likely to be very high. This should extend beyond the classroom, because they will continue to have a great deal of contact with English and feel the need to further improve their English to fit in better at school. For adult learners, however, there may be differences in the degree to which opportunities to encounter and use English are sought out beyond the classroom. This is because adult learners may also have the opportunity to communicate in their L1 with other L2 learners in their community. The challenge for teachers, then, is to find ways for adult learners to move beyond learning the vocabulary that serves their basic needs (shopping, getting around, taking care of financial and governmental issues, etc.) to encountering and using English for convenience and pleasure.

Needs

Second, ESL students often have specific and immediate needs that require them to learn situation-specific vocabulary. They need to be able to understand and use words in different situations to cope with the basic challenges of daily life. These challenges are largely unique to the ESL context and include communicating effectively when food shopping, finding jobs, enrolling children in schools, finding places to live, making friends, and setting up and paying for utilities. ESL coursebooks often have syllabuses that involve learning the vocabulary and language that is relevant to many of these different situations. Teachers should work out which situations need to be addressed to best support their students' needs.

Motivation

Third, motivation tends to be high. Because students have to cope with many issues in English on a daily basis, there is typically an immediate need to improve their English language skills. And because vocabulary is often the key factor determining whether language can be understood (Laufer & Sim, 1985), students may be keen to learn the words that are essential for surviving in a foreign country. Although motivation will vary on the individual level, it is likely to be higher for the majority of ESL students than their EFL counterparts, particularly in the initial stages of learning.

Cultural integration

A fourth feature is the need for students to receive support in understanding the cultural and integrational aspects of ESL. Although students will have different reasons for learning ESL, one key component involves learning to function effectively in a new country. This involves understanding and adapting to the way in which native speakers of the language typically interact. It should also include understanding local customs. Although it is not necessary for students to always follow what may be very different customs from those they are familiar with, there is value in understanding them. Lexical development in the ESL context may in fact reflect the extent to which students are involving themselves in the different opportunities to integrate into the new culture. Many students will immerse themselves in the new culture and use English at every given opportunity to consolidate and expand their vocabulary knowledge. However, there will also be some students who fail to make any progress in their lexical development, despite having lived in the ESL context for many years. One reason why some students do not make much progress is that beginners may lack the confidence that would allow them to take part in opportunities to use English. Another reason is that some learners may have the support that allows them to live in an ESL context without needing to communicate regularly in English. A third reason is that some may not feel they have opportunities to interact in English regularly. An important part of teaching ESL therefore involves raising awareness of the vocabulary and language that will enable learners to live fully in the new culture.

Priorities for teaching

The many opportunities to encounter and use words outside the classroom in the ESL context should influence how vocabulary is taught in two ways: teaching vocabulary learning strategies and deliberately focusing on gaps in knowledge.

Teaching vocabulary learning strategies

Although there is greater potential for learning through meaning-focused input and meaning-focused output outside the classroom in the ESL context, this does not ensure that all students will know how to take advantage of these opportunities. Teaching vocabulary learning strategies can make students more aware of the different opportunities, have the confidence to learn and use English in these situations, and increase their potential to learn unknown and partially known words (see Chapter 7). There are three reasons why it is worth spending considerable time in the classroom to promote **autonomous learning**:

1 Although many students may have the motivation to further develop their language skills outside the classroom, some may be able to get by without encountering and using English and therefore require active encouragement to do so.

2 The greatest potential for learning in the ESL context lies outside the classroom. Students' engagement with English ought to be much higher outside the classroom, because this is where the greatest gains in lexical and language development are likely to occur.

3 Students are likely to use a variety of different strategies for vocabulary learning (Schmitt, 1997), and training them in the use of the most valuable strategies may enhance their ability to learn words. Taking the time to support autonomous learning therefore has great value.

Deliberately focusing on gaps in knowledge

Because there is more potential in the ESL context for meaning-focused input, meaning-focused output, and fluency development to occur outside the classroom, deliberate learning inside the classroom has greater value; the context allows teachers to spend more time on explicitly teaching the aspects of vocabulary knowledge that they feel their students are lacking. Let us look at some examples of deliberate focus:

• If teachers feel their students have difficulty correctly pronouncing words, they may use exercises designed to improve knowledge of spoken forms.

• If students have trouble understanding or using complex words, then teachers may spend more time on explicitly developing knowledge of word parts.

• A common need for students is to further develop fluency in what they have already learned. Those who have only recently moved to an ESL context may have learned many words but have difficulty in processing them quickly, resulting in a slower rate of speaking than might be considered normal. Teachers might therefore wish to spend more time on fluency development within the classroom.

• The demands of work or academic study in the ESL context may require students to improve their accuracy in the use of language to a greater extent than might be considered necessary in the EFL context, so another common focus for deliberate teaching in the ESL classroom is to improve the use of formulaic language (sequences of words that are frequently used together). Unusual word combinations often distinguish even very advanced L2 learners from native speakers. These are often the result of differences between L1 and L2 phraseology (Nesselhauf, 2003). For example, Japanese learners might say 'take lunch' rather than 'have lunch' or 'eat lunch', because the Japanese equivalent of 'take lunch' is a frequently occurring L1 word combination. Similarly, Chinese learners may say 'open and close the light' rather than 'turn on and turn off the light', because the former is closer to the Chinese equivalent.

ACTIVITY 6.2   Evaluating topics in EFL and ESL contexts

Consider the following topics. In your opinion, are they more useful for learning vocabulary in the EFL or ESL contexts, or both? Compare your answers with the notes at the end of the chapter.

Topic	EFL	ESL
Introductions		
Giving directions		
Getting your car repaired		
Following classroom directions		
Paying an electricity bill		
Describing everyday routines		
Ordering food at restaurants		
Describing weekend plans		
Fashion		
Asking for help when shopping		
Applying for jobs		

Teaching vocabulary to children

There is a great deal of research indicating that children are very effective vocabulary learners. As we have seen in Chapter 3, research suggests that children incidentally learn thousands of L1 words before they can read (Biemiller & Slonim, 2001; Goulden, Nation, & Read, 1990). Young learners can also make great progress in their L2 lexical development through incidental and deliberate learning approaches.

ACTIVITY 6.3   **Which activities work best with children?**

1 Make a list of five to ten vocabulary learning activities that you think are commonly used with younger children. Then check your ideas at the end of the chapter.

2 Now think about which activities on your list are likely to be the most successful. Read on to check your ideas.

There are several important differences between teaching L2 vocabulary to children and adults. These relate to children's learning needs, the role of listening, the issue of measuring vocabulary knowledge, and limitations around word knowledge and metalanguage.

Needs

First, the most useful words for adults are not necessarily the most useful words for children. Lists of the most important words for learners, such as the General Service List (West, 1953), the New-GSL (Brezina & Gablasova, 2015), and the Essential Word List (Dang & Webb, 2016b) are based on texts written for older learners. This means that the words in these lists are the high-frequency vocabulary of adults rather than children. Although there may be a reasonable amount of overlap in the words that are important for adults and children, there are also likely to be a number of differences. For example, 'monster', 'dragon', 'pirate', and 'fairy' were found to be much more frequent in children's stories than in texts written for older readers (Webb & Macalister, 2013). Similarly, words related to wildlife (for example, 'ant', 'elephant', 'monkey', 'shark') and the environment (for example, 'vine', 'twig', 'nest', 'reef') are also much more common in language directed towards children. The differences between the vocabularies of adults and children mean that teachers should be selective when choosing target vocabulary from formal word lists with children, and words that do not appear in such lists should not necessarily be excluded from teaching. For example, vocabulary that is central to children's stories deserves to be taught, because these items are likely to be encountered again and again across different stories.

Learning through listening

The vocabulary growth of children is initially stimulated through listening and direct teaching rather than reading. Several researchers (Krashen, 1989) have suggested that adults learn a large proportion of vocabulary incidentally through reading. However, children may have little or no knowledge of the written forms of L2 words. It would therefore be unreasonable to expect large gains to be made through reading in the early stages of a child's lexical development. Learning the written forms of words takes time; and, at least initially, words are likely to be learned primarily through listening.

The number of words that children learn through listening can be enhanced through the teacher's explanation of word meanings, and also through the use of pictures (Elley, 1989).

Measuring vocabulary

Following on from the previous point, it is also important to note that some things which can be done very effectively with adults, such as measuring vocabulary knowledge, are much more difficult with children who have yet to develop strong reading skills. For example, tests of vocabulary knowledge often rely on the test taker reading the written forms of target words and linking them with their meanings. For children, this can be quite challenging, because the words and the definitions may be difficult to understand. Tests that provide spoken (rather than written) L2 words together with pictures to convey meanings are likely to provide much more accurate measures of children's vocabulary knowledge than tests which have been created for more advanced learners, such as the Vocabulary Size Test (Nation & Beglar, 2007) and the Vocabulary Levels Test (Nation, 1983; Schmitt, Schmitt, & Clapham, 2001; Webb, Sasao, & Ballance, 2017). (Chapter 9 includes information on a useful test designed to measure the vocabulary knowledge of children.)

Word knowledge

Children may have much to learn about some L2 words, because they are likely to know less about most L1 words than adults. As discussed in Chapter 2, the amount of knowledge that we have about a word in L1 is likely to affect how easy it is to learn that word in the L2. Adults typically learn words that they already know well in their L1. This means that if there is overlap between the L1 and L2 meanings, their knowledge of the meaning of this word should be quite clear. In contrast, children know far fewer L1 words, so some words that they encounter in the L2 might represent new concepts for them. As such, teachers need to spend more time helping children to understand the meanings of new L2 words than they would with adults.

Abstract language and metalanguage

Another difference between teaching vocabulary to children and adults is that younger learners may have difficulty understanding the more abstract and figurative language (for example, 'a few', 'run a bath', 'of course') and metalanguage ('noun', 'verb', 'adjective', 'preposition') that is used in some texts and activities. At first, this might seem a large stumbling block to using certain texts and activities with children. However, unlike many adults, children generally do not expect to fully understand every word or sequence of words they encounter. When children learn their L1, they are usually happy to listen to stories that include a very large proportion of unknown words if the topic is of interest to them. If comprehension of a word is essential to completing an activity, then modification can provide a suitable solution. For example, explanation and gesture can be used quite easily to convey the meanings of the different parts of speech.

There are several advantages of teaching vocabulary to children. First, children tend to be highly motivated to learn through reading and listening, particularly through activities that are fun or involve some degree of competition, such as games and songs. Games that involve learning L1 concepts that they are interested in and are well known in the L1 are particularly common for teaching words to children. Concrete nouns that relate to the primary classroom in some way, such as colours, shapes, animals, numbers, and letters, as well as verbs that can be conveyed easily through simple actions, may be easily learned through games. Second, children are not usually discouraged from learning through reading, listening, and watching television when their comprehension is not perfect. This is perhaps because, in the early stages of first language learning, children may not always know all of the words that they encounter. Instead, they may be satisfied if their comprehension is sufficient to understand or enjoy the language input. The fact that children can be engaged with input that is not clearly understood may allow them to encounter relatively large amounts of input. This is quite different from some older L2 learners who have difficulty moving forward if their comprehension is not precise. A third advantage of teaching vocabulary to children is that the frequency of L2 input can be greatly enhanced through repeated reading, listening, and viewing. This may be due to their initial lack of precise comprehension when they first listen to a story, or watch a television programme. However, through repeated reading, listening, and viewing, their comprehension of the story should gradually increase, as should their understanding of the words in the story (Webb & Chang, 2012b).

ACTIVITY 6.4   Planning for small and large classes

Think of a student profile (age, context, motivation for learning, etc.) and plan a short series of vocabulary learning activities for a) a small group, b) a large class. Then read on and check your ideas.

Learning vocabulary in small classes

Ideally, language learning classrooms would all have a small number of students to allow for more teacher–student interaction and time to monitor and provide feedback to individual students. Working with small groups of students also allows teachers to tailor vocabulary learning programmes to the needs of individuals. However, there are still several challenges to teaching vocabulary in small classes:

1 Because there is less diversity within the class, it can sometimes be difficult to get students to engage with their peers. Instead, they may expect learning to occur solely through interaction with the teacher.
2 Students may tune out when topics are oriented towards others' needs.
3 Students may not see the value in learning through meaning-focused input and instead rely on deliberate learning and learning through meaning-focused output.

The greatest advantage of learning vocabulary in small classes is that there are many opportunities for students to receive feedback. Raising awareness of the different ways in which vocabulary is learned is perhaps the best way to deal with the challenges listed above. It can be useful to introduce the concept of how vocabulary is learned through meaning-focused input, meaning-focused output, language-focused learning, and fluency development activities (Nation, 2007), and also to explain that research clearly shows that students learn words through interaction with one another (Newton, 2013), as well as with the teacher (Ellis & He, 1999). This should help students to see the value in what they are asked to do in class.

Learning vocabulary in large classes

Small classes may be the ideal, but teachers often need to cope with class sizes that initially seem unmanageable. Teaching large classes can be challenging for a number of reasons. Ability levels (and levels of vocabulary knowledge) are likely to vary, making certain exercises appear less meaningful to some members of the class. Reduced teacher–student interaction makes it more difficult to monitor comprehension, monitor and evaluate the use of words, and provide individualized feedback. Moreover, because teachers have fewer opportunities to work with individual students, it can be difficult to support comprehension. There can also be challenges in using some exercises (for example, presentations) or forms of assessment (for example, face-to-face interviews) which require larger amounts of time spent working with individual students. Furthermore, students may be reluctant to speak out and use the words they are learning in front of many others that they do not know well. There are several ways in which teachers can help to improve the potential for effective and efficient vocabulary learning in large classes.

Level testing
Evaluating vocabulary knowledge using tests such as the Vocabulary Levels Test (Nation, 1983; Schmitt, Schmitt, & Clapham, 2001; Webb, Sasao, & Ballance, 2017) is particularly useful with large classes. Determining the appropriate frequency level from which to choose words for students to learn increases the chances that target vocabulary will be useful to them.

Moreover, it will also identify the students whose lexical knowledge is behind that of their peers. This information can alert teachers to the students who may struggle with certain activities and exercises due to a lack of comprehension or confidence in using words (Webb & Chang, 2015b).

Pair and group work

Providing plenty of opportunities for pair work and group activities that increase the potential for students to develop their productive knowledge of words through meaning-focused output has great value. When students work with others, their combined knowledge can scaffold learning, leading to greater performance than might be achieved by working on their own (Swain & Lapkin, 1998). Research shows that students are able to learn words by negotiating their forms and meanings in spoken interaction (Newton, 1995, 2013) and when working together to complete writing tasks (Dobao, 2014a, 2014b). Moreover, Dobao (2014b) found that when the size of groups increases from two to four students, there may be more occurrences of words being learned.

Meaning-focused input

Activities that involve learning with meaning-focused input can be used very effectively in large classes. For example, extensive reading, listening, and viewing can be done individually, with students selecting the materials that they are interested in. In such situations, it is important to guide students in selecting the most suitable materials, not those that are beyond their level. Extensive learning should be done with materials that are easy to understand so that students encounter large amounts of comprehensible language. The biggest challenge for teachers when students are learning through meaning-focused input is supporting comprehension, because if students cannot understand the input, then they may feel discouraged from continuing to learn in this way. During extensive learning periods in the classroom, teachers should move around and provide support for any students who are having difficulty understanding the input. Support might initially be best provided using class materials, where everyone learns from the same spoken or written text or television programme. Unknown vocabulary can be pre-taught, and glossaries can be provided. Breaks can also be used to check students' understanding. During extensive reading, it is best to provide audio support if possible so that students can read along as they listen to the story. There are three advantages to using audio support: it ensures that students maintain the same reading rate, helps students to process the text in chunks rather than word by word, and increases the amount of vocabulary learning (Webb & Chang, 2012b).

Explaining value

In large classes, it is vital that students understand why they are learning specific words, as well as how they are learning them. When there are more students to deal with, it is difficult to give each student individual attention and feedback. Students may not see value in the activities and exercises that they are doing and their motivation might decrease. Explaining the plan for vocabulary learning, how knowledge of words will be strengthened, and what needs to be done to promote learning, may help students to be more engaged with the process of learning words.

Engaging students in the learning process

Finally, teachers can survey students about their vocabulary learning to give them a stronger voice in a large class. Here are some useful questions to ask students about their vocabulary learning:

- Do you have any questions about the words that we are learning?
- Do you have any questions about the ways in which we are learning words?
- Did you study the words we learned this week outside class?
- Where do you encounter English outside the classroom?
- Where do you use English outside the classroom?
- Are you having any problems learning the words that we are focusing on in this class? If so, why do you think that is?

This can be done in pen-and-paper format, or using online polling software such as Poll Everywhere if the resources are available (see Website references). Online surveys allow students to answer questions and give feedback anonymously in real time via smartphones, computers, and tablets. Responses can be seen live by everyone in the class. Multiple-choice and open-ended questions can be used, with the answers displayed as percentages for multiple-choice questions and lists of responses for open-ended questions. Surveys allow teachers to check different aspects of their students' learning experience, and enable students to provide regular feedback about what they are doing in a non-threatening way. Moreover, by including students in regular discussion of their vocabulary learning, they may become more engaged in the learning process.

One challenge of teaching large classes is that proficiency levels may vary widely. There are several ways in which teachers can deal with this:

- Place students into sub-groups according to level. In this case, appropriate tasks can be designed for students at each level to enhance vocabulary learning. The advantage of this approach is that completion of a task should indicate some degree of learning.
- Place students in mixed-ability groups to allow more advanced students to provide support for their less advanced peers. In essence, this is a form of cross-proficiency peer teaching: students working at a higher level provide

teaching support to those at lower levels. The advantage of this approach is that more advanced students can take on a larger role in the task and less advanced students can receive individualized support. The disadvantage is that less advanced students may rely on their more capable partners to complete tasks. So teachers need to carefully monitor the progress of all students.

- Include a lot of independent activities that allow students to work at their own level. Reading activities, writing activities, flashcards, presentations, and extensive viewing are all examples of vocabulary learning activities that work well for independent study. A particularly good example is the spoken journal, where students record themselves rather than write; this allows them to use the vocabulary that they know and have recently learned to develop their productive vocabulary knowledge. As students are working on their own, teachers can move around and provide support when it is needed. The disadvantage of independent study is that it may take time for teachers to develop a sufficient number of resources for students at varying levels. Ideally, activities and tasks should be developed and pooled together among all teachers involved in the programme. If a number of teachers are working on developing resources for students at different levels, then it may not be long before there are enough to cater for a range of proficiency levels.

Learning vocabulary at different levels of proficiency

Having looked at a range of learning contexts, let us now consider how vocabulary is learned at different levels of proficiency.

Beginner to Elementary

Helping students to develop a basic foundation of vocabulary knowledge that can be used to scaffold future learning should be the primary lexical aim of any beginner language course. The Essential Word List (Dang & Webb, 2016b) is a key resource for beginners, because it provides a manageable number of words (800) to learn over a proposed two-year period that accounts for up to 75% of the English language. In the initial stages, deliberate learning is likely to account for most of the words learned. Chapter 5 listed a range of useful deliberate learning activities to use with beginners, such as linked skills, information transfer, dictation, flashcards, and word parts.

It is difficult to engage in meaning-focused input and output if you do not have the vocabulary you need to understand and use the language. However, once beginners have developed a basic knowledge of words, interactive reading and repeated reading while listening to simplified texts can be a useful introduction to meaning-focused input. You can create these yourself, or use graded readers. The controlled vocabulary in graded readers allows students to gradually progress from focusing on individual words to sequences of words. Reading to the students or getting them to listen to the text as they read along will further encourage them to process the text in chunks, rather than word by word (Brown, Waring, & Donkaewbua, 2008). It is also useful to include speed-reading in the early stages of learning, to improve students' ability to process words in a more fluent manner.

Intermediate

At the intermediate level, students should be working towards learning the 3,000 most frequent word families. If they are planning to study at an English-medium university, then they should also aim to learn the words included in the Academic Word List (Coxhead, 2000). Lexical growth may be fuelled by reading graded readers, watching L2 television programmes and online videos, and doing various deliberate learning activities. At this level, there is the potential for much lexical development to occur outside the classroom, so it is worth spending time in class promoting strategies for autonomous vocabulary learning. Since the majority of learning should ideally come from encountering and using words in context, finding opportunities to develop productive vocabulary knowledge is particularly important. Activities such as computer-mediated written interaction, ten-minute writing, and task-focused spoken interaction (see Chapter 5) are useful ways of moving from simply understanding words to being able to use them as well. Lexical growth is also likely to be fuelled by reading graded readers, watching L2 television and online videos, and doing various deliberate learning activities which involve guessing from context and intensive reading.

Upper-intermediate to Advanced

At more advanced levels, students should be aiming to understand written texts such as novels and newspapers without the support of teachers and dictionaries. This requires knowledge of the 8–9,000 most frequent word families (Nation, 2006). Mid-frequency graded readers and L2 television programmes and online videos are useful sources of vocabulary growth at this level. Intensive reading of texts about topics that are relevant to students' needs and interests is also useful, and so too is having students learn through narrow reading. Texts that relate to one particular topic tend to use similar words, so the lexical burden of understanding the texts will be lower (Schmitt & Carter, 2000). Moreover, as subsequent texts are read about the same topic, background knowledge will be enhanced and comprehension may become easier. (This is similar to the process of learning through a linked skills activity.)

Advanced learners may also be looking to improve their fluency and accuracy. This is likely to be most important with the productive skills of speaking and writing, because if they have reached a higher proficiency level, they should have accumulated a great deal of experience in processing the language that they encounter. Activities focusing on speed, such as presentations and ten-minute writing, are useful for promoting fluency. Learning formulaic language may help students to improve their lexical accuracy. Multi-word combinations can be learned in the same ways as single words—incidentally through repeated encounters (Webb, Newton, & Chang, 2013) and deliberately in a variety of activities (Boers & Lindstromberg, 2009). Other approaches that are unique to learning word sequences can also contribute to learning, such as focusing on imagery (Boers, Demecheleer, & Eyckmans, 2004) and exploiting sound patterns such as assonance and alliteration (Lindstromberg & Boers, 2009).

ACTIVITY 6.5   Simplifying the vocabulary in a text

The following text is from a mid-frequency reader for learners with knowledge of the 8,000 most frequent word families (approximately advanced level). Look at the underlined words and simplify the text so that it is more appropriate for learners with knowledge of the 3,000 most frequent word families (approximately pre-intermediate level). Then check your ideas at the end of the chapter.

> A man entered who could hardly have been less than six feet six inches in height, with the chest and limbs of a Hercules. His dress was rich with a richness which would, in England, be looked upon as akin to bad taste. Heavy bands of wool fabric were slashed across the sleeves and fronts of his double-breasted coat, while the deep blue cloak which was thrown over his shoulders was lined with flame-coloured silk and secured at the neck with a brooch which consisted of a single flaming beryl. Boots which extended halfway up his calves, and which were trimmed at the tops with rich brown fur, completed the impression of barbaric opulence which was suggested by his whole appearance. He carried a broad-brimmed hat in his hand, while he wore across the upper part of his face, extending down past the cheekbones, a black mask, which he had apparently adjusted that very moment, for his hand was still raised to it as he entered. From the lower part of the face he appeared to be a man of strong character, with a thick, hanging lip, and a long, straight chin suggestive of resolution pushed to the length of obstinacy.

Materials extract 6.1 Adapted from the Project Gutenburg version of Arthur Conan Doyle's The Adventures of Sherlock Holmes, by Sonia Millet

---

Teaching vocabulary when time is limited

To conclude this chapter, let us briefly consider the issue of time. There is often limited time for teaching vocabulary, because classes are typically geared towards covering other aspects of language. This means that there may be insufficient time to focus on all the aspects of vocabulary development discussed in this book, and teachers may have to prioritize certain aspects over others. When time is lacking, the most pressing needs should be dealt with first. In the earliest stages of learning, priority should be given to developing a foundation of vocabulary knowledge that will enable further independent learning. In later stages, learning strategies to become effective and efficient autonomous learners should be prioritized. At all stages, clear vocabulary learning goals should be set which take into consideration the amount of time available for learning and are realistic in scope; there is no point in having unachievable goals, because this may discourage rather than encourage learning.

Summary

It is intuitively logical that we need to adapt how we teach and learn vocabulary to the context of learning. However, there is relatively little information about what we should change. Moreover, it is often difficult to give up using activities and materials that we have found to be effective in one context when we are not sufficiently aware of what may be most useful in another context. In this chapter, we have described how aspects of vocabulary learning may change in different learning contexts and discussed what should be considered when teaching in different types of classrooms, with different types of students. Awareness of the different features and demands of each learning context should help teachers to create a more principled vocabulary learning programme for their own context.

Questions for reflection

1 What do you think are the keys to successful vocabulary learning in the ESL context?

2 How would you change your approach to teaching vocabulary if you moved from an ESL context to an EFL context?

3 Look at some of the activities in Chapter 5. Think about how you might modify these activities to make them more appropriate for 10–12 year olds in the ESL context.

4 Which vocabulary learning activities do you think work best with advanced language learners? Why?

Keys to activities

ACTIVITY 6.2   **Evaluating topics in EFL and ESL contexts**

Some things to bear in mind when considering topics for EFL versus ESL students:

- Is there an immediate need? Both EFL and ESL students may have vocabulary learning priorities. Topics which relate to their needs are more likely to motivate both kinds of learners.
- Will students ever need the vocabulary for specific situations? ESL students may need to use specific vocabulary on a daily basis in common situations such as asking for directions and shopping. EFL students may never need to use English in such situations unless they travel abroad; on the other hand, some EFL students might be intending to visit, live, or study in an English-speaking context in future.
- Will thematic topics motivate students? This depends both on the students' context and their own interests and/or future interests and needs, including examinations.
- Does the topic provide students with exposure to vocabulary and language that is specific to cultural aspects of learning English? An important part of learning ESL involves understanding and adapting to the way in which native speakers of the language typically interact. This may also be relevant for EFL students intending to live or work abroad.

ACTIVITY 6.3   **Which activities work best with children?**

With suitable modifications, most activities and exercises suitable for older learners can be used with younger learners. The following work particularly well with children: asking and answering simple questions, role-play, 'listen and do' activities (for example, listen and draw a picture; listen and complete the actions, such as 'Simon says…'), games, guessing games, singing songs, saying rhymes, reading stories aloud, repeated reading and listening, watching L2 television and online videos, writing lists/captions/cartoons.

ACTIVITY 6.5   **Simplifying the vocabulary in a text**

Suggested simplification:

> A man entered who could hardly have been less than six feet six inches in height, with the chest, **arms, and legs** of a Hercules. His dress was rich with a richness which would, in England, be looked upon as **an example of** bad taste. Heavy bands of wool fabric **covered his arms** and the fronts of

his coat, while the deep blue material which was thrown over his shoulders was lined with red and closed at the neck with a green pin. Short boots with tops of rich brown fur completed the impression of wealth which was suggested by his whole appearance. He carried a wide hat in his hand, while he wore across the upper part of his face […] a black mask, which he had apparently adjusted that very moment, for his hand was still raised to it as he entered. From the lower part of the face he appeared to be a man of strong character, with a thick, hanging lip, and a long, straight face with a stubborn expression.

The highlighted parts show changes. In some cases, it is possible to simplify a text by simply removing a low-frequency word. In other cases, you may need to rephrase. You can check the frequency of the simplified words using a lexical profiler (see Chapter 9).

Suggestions for further reading

Nation, I. S. P. (2013b). *What should every ESL teacher know?* Seoul: Compass Publishing.

Nation provides a useful overview of key issues that ESL teachers need to consider, such as the needs of the learners, the different types of ESL learning situations, and the different approaches to teaching in the ESL context. This book is freely available for download through Compass Publishing (see Website references).

Nation, I. S. P. (2013c). *What should every EFL teacher know?* Seoul: Compass Publishing.

In this companion book to the one above, Nation provides a clear and practical account of the different features of teaching EFL. This includes description of approaches used for teaching the different language skills, as well as some useful resources for teachers.

Boers, F., & **Lindstromberg, S.** (2009). *Optimizing a lexical approach to instructed second language acquisition.* Basingstoke: Palgrave Macmillan.

In this practical and accessible book, Frank Boers and Seth Lindstromberg explain the value of learning formulaic language. They outline the challenges of learning multi-word combinations and also describe different approaches to learning word sequences.

7 DEVELOPING AUTONOMOUS LEARNERS OF VOCABULARY

Introduction

The development of lexical knowledge occurs both inside and outside the classroom. While students may be carefully taught, monitored, and evaluated on their learning within the classroom, there is also a need to ensure that they are successful in their vocabulary learning outside the classroom. Teaching vocabulary learning strategies should enable students to become more effective and efficient autonomous learners. In this chapter, we explain why an important part of a language teacher's job is to help their students to successfully use such strategies, and we describe those which may provide the greatest value for current and future vocabulary learning. By spending time inside the classroom deliberately developing strategies for learning vocabulary independently, students will have a greater chance of further developing their vocabulary knowledge outside the classroom.

Why do vocabulary learning strategies need to be taught?

There are two main reasons why we should teach students strategies for learning vocabulary on their own. First, although lexical development is central to language learning, it is just one of many aspects of language, all competing for attention. While some language courses focus on specific areas, such as improving writing, reading, speaking, grammar, and test scores, vocabulary rarely drives a course; it is normally considered to be a component of all language courses. Without an explicit focus on developing lexical knowledge within a course, the importance of vocabulary learning may not be transparent. Second, in both the second and foreign language learning contexts, a great deal of time is needed to learn the thousands of words necessary to understand spoken and written discourse without support. Teachers and students may focus on the deliberate learning of words in the classroom; however, there is normally insufficient classroom time for students to deliberately learn the 3,000 word families they need to know in order to understand most conversations, let alone the 8–9,000 word families they need to understand most written texts (see Chapter 1). It is therefore essential that we teach our students strategies for effectively and efficiently learning vocabulary autonomously outside the classroom.

Three principles for teaching vocabulary learning strategies

It is a massive task for students to learn thousands of words on their own. Many students are able to learn vocabulary effectively and efficiently outside the classroom, but many others fail to make much progress in their lexical development. Because there is not enough classroom time to develop students' vocabulary to the level that is required to understand the target language without support, it is very important that teachers equip their students with the tools they need to be successful on their own, outside the classroom. The following three principles should be applied to the teaching of vocabulary learning strategies.

Principle 1: Classroom time

Given the importance of developing autonomous vocabulary learners, there is clear merit in spending classroom time on vocabulary learning strategies. Like many things in life, such as driving a car or using an electric drill, vocabulary learning strategies may not seem particularly complex or difficult to learn. Indeed, the strategies described in this chapter could be explained in a matter of minutes. However, understanding a brief explanation is not the same as being able to successfully apply that knowledge to a new task. When there are significant consequences at stake, time and training are generally required. It may be relatively easy to understand the processes involved in driving or using power tools, but it would be dangerous to assume that a brief explanation will enable everyone to successfully apply that knowledge. Similarly, while vocabulary learning strategies may be relatively simple, it is important to ensure that students understand these strategies and are able to use them effectively. The cost of spending classroom time on teaching and training students to use vocabulary learning strategies is likely to be outweighed by the benefit of more effective and efficient autonomous learning.

Principle 2: The value of strategies

The value of many exercises and tasks that are completed in the classroom may not be completely transparent to students. They may consider an exercise or task useful and work to varying degrees to complete it, without fully appreciating how each one contributes to language development. Because vocabulary learning strategies should not only be understood but also applied and used regularly by students outside the classroom, it is important that their value is clear. This makes it worth discussing why vocabulary learning strategies are essential. One way to highlight their value is by asking students how many words they expect to learn inside and outside the classroom. This might be discussed in relation to the number of words that students believe they will learn through classroom study and how far that will take them in achieving their language learning goals.

Principle 3: Training and assessment

Teaching vocabulary learning strategies should include both training and assessment. This means there should not only be sufficient time for students to learn each strategy but also time for teachers to evaluate whether students can successfully apply the strategy. Strategy training should occur over multiple sessions to ensure that students a) understand the importance of using a strategy, b) are able to successfully apply it, and c) are applying the strategy to learning outside the classroom. Evaluation should involve checking whether students can correctly use a strategy, and monitoring the degree to which students are using it. Teachers could monitor strategy use through learning journals. For example, if students are focused on learning word parts, then one component of a learning journal could include making a list of the different words that are encountered which include the target affixes. Similarly, a learning journal might chart students' use of words outside the classroom, as well as the opportunities they had to use the target language.

By spending classroom time teaching, monitoring, and evaluating the use of vocabulary learning strategies, teachers can put their students in a better position to succeed in learning autonomously.

Key strategies for autonomous vocabulary learning

The rest of the chapter presents six key strategies for autonomous vocabulary learning that will provide students in both the second and foreign language learning contexts with all the tools they need to develop their vocabulary effectively.

Strategy 1: Finding ways to encounter the L2 outside the classroom

Finding ways to encounter the target language outside the classroom is arguably the most important vocabulary learning strategy. As discussed in Chapter 3, incidental vocabulary learning is dependent on the amount of language that we encounter, and we learn words incidentally by encountering them again and again in speech and written text. If students encounter the language outside the classroom, then there is the opportunity to consolidate knowledge of taught words when they are encountered, making them less likely to be forgotten. There is also the possibility of incidentally learning new words that are encountered.

In the second language learning context, there should be many opportunities to encounter the target language outside the classroom. However, the degree to which learners choose to engage with the language will vary; some learners may prefer to communicate in L1 because it is easier, while others may relish the chance to learn and immerse themselves in the L2. In the foreign language learning context, although L2 resources may be widely available, the L2 may rarely be encountered unless students are motivated to seek it out. A key role for teachers in both contexts is to help students find sources of L2 input that they can understand outside the classroom. This should encourage learners to encounter the L2 more often. There are many useful online resources for learning English as an L2, such as BBC Learning English, YouTube, and TED Talks (see Website references). However, the most useful sources of English input outside the classroom are graded readers and English language television programmes, because the former are specifically designed to facilitate comprehension and vocabulary learning, and learners tend to be highly motivated to learn with the latter. Both of these resources can be used in an extensive learning programme.

Chapter 3 explained how encountering words inside and outside the classroom provides information about the form, meaning, and use of those words that may help to develop lexical knowledge. We saw how, by encountering words in context, students may be able to increase their knowledge of partially known words, as well as learn new words. Table 7.1 summarizes the aspects of receptive vocabulary knowledge that are most likely to be gained by encountering words repeatedly in meaning-focused input.

Form	recognition of ... the pronunciation of the word the spelling of the word the different inflections and derivations of the word
Meaning	recognition of ... the core meaning that the word signals the different meanings that the word conveys other words that are related in meaning to the word
Use	understanding of ... the grammatical functions of the word the different words that are used together with the word when, where, and how often the word is used

Table 7.1 Aspects of receptive vocabulary knowledge gained from meaning-focused input

Teacher's role

Teachers have two distinct responsibilities in helping their students to encounter a greater amount of the target language outside the classroom. The first is to educate them about the value of encountering large amounts of meaning-focused input outside the classroom. We recommend making students aware of the following points that we have covered in this book so far:

1 It is only possible to learn a relatively small number of words deliberately inside the classroom due to time constraints.
2 In our first language, we learn most vocabulary incidentally through encountering words repeatedly in speech and writing.
3 You need to know at least 8–9,000 words to understand written texts such as novels and newspapers without support (Nation, 2006).
4 You are unlikely to learn everything about a word when you study it deliberately. The other words that are commonly used together with it will remain unknown, and so too will the different meanings that the word can convey, as well as its inflections and derivations. Repeatedly encountering words in speech and text outside class will help to develop this knowledge.

Educating students about the importance of encountering meaning-focused input outside the classroom may help to motivate them to seek out English language resources for autonomous learning. However, without guidance and support, students may find these resources difficult to understand and quickly become discouraged from using them.

The second responsibility teachers have is to reveal to their students that they may be better able to understand and enjoy meaning-focused English language resources if they use them in a principled way. Training students in the classroom about how they might best select and use resources is a key step towards developing learner autonomy; and because developing a native-like vocabulary size is dependent on encountering large amounts of meaning-focused input, it is worth spending considerable classroom time on this. So training students to engage with meaning-focused input outside the classroom begins inside the classroom, through extensive reading and extensive viewing.

Extensive reading

Richard Day and Julian Bamford (2002) proposed the following principles for extensive reading:

1 The reading material is easy.
2 A variety of reading material on a wide range of topics must be available.
3 Learners choose what they want to read.
4 Learners read as much as possible.
5 The purpose of reading is usually related to pleasure, information, and general understanding.
6 Reading is its own reward.
7 Reading speed is usually faster rather than slower.
8 Reading is individual and silent.
9 Teachers orient and guide their students.
10 The teacher is a role model of a reader.

These principles for extensive reading highlight the value of reading texts that are at the appropriate level (i.e. easy to understand without external support) and enjoyable. Extensive reading should be pleasurable, in order to motivate further reading. Including an extensive reading programme in the classroom allows learners to see that there are materials they can understand and enjoy, and that there is much to gain through extensive reading.

Nation (2015) also argues that it is important to focus on reading at a faster rate in extensive reading programmes. This may help learners to process words in a more native-like manner. It may also allow students to move from word-by-word reading to processing the text in meaningful chunks, which can in turn contribute to their knowledge of formulaic language.

Extensive viewing

While teachers, students, and parents may understand the value of extensive reading, they may be sceptical about the value of extensive viewing. The following reasons outline why watching L2 television and online videos has the potential to make a substantial contribution to language learning.

1 L2 television programmes and online videos are widely available.
2 L2 television is a useful source of aural input that may help students learn the spoken forms of words.

3 Research consistently shows that viewers can learn words incidentally through watching videos and television programmes (Neuman &
Koskinen, 1992; Rice & Woodsmall, 1988; Rodgers, 2013) and that
the amount of learning may be similar to that gained through reading
(Neuman & Koskinen, 1992; Rodgers, 2013).

4 People tend to spend a great deal of time watching L1 television. A
survey revealed that the average daily household viewing time across 18
countries ranged from 2.43 hours in Sweden to 8.18 hours in the United
States (OECD, 2007).

5 L2 learners are motivated to learn through watching television programmes (Gieve & Clark, 2005; Sueyoshi & Hardison, 2005).

6 Not all L2 learners will be motivated to learn through extensive reading.
Some students may not read a great deal in their L1, so expecting everyone to read extensively in the L2 may be unrealistic. Providing an alternative
form of extensive learning should increase the potential for more students to
embrace it.

Given the fact that people tend to spend more time watching television
than reading in their L1, it may seem odd that there has been relatively little
discussion of the value of extensive viewing for language learning. A possible reason for this is that watching television is more strongly associated
with entertainment than education. However, the fact that many people
are motivated to watch television for enjoyment should be considered a
key advantage for language learning. If learners can also watch L2 television programmes for enjoyment, then they are more likely to use them as a
source of meaning-focused input.

Extensive viewing is based on the same principles as extensive reading.
The content should be comprehensible and enjoyable in order to motivate
further viewing outside the classroom. If it includes dialogue spoken at a
faster rate than is typically heard in the classroom, this may help students
to move from processing words as individual units of meaning to processing larger chunks of dialogue. And similar to developing fluency through
extensive reading, processing the language encountered through extensive
viewing as sequences may help students to learn formulaic language.

Understanding L2 television programmes and online videos is likely to
be challenging at first, which is why it is important for teachers to train
students in the best ways to use television and videos for learning. Webb
(2015) suggests the following principles for extensive viewing:

• The language learning benefits of extensive viewing must be clear to
everyone involved. It is important that students, parents, teachers, and
administrators are all aware that, although television programmes and
online videos are forms of entertainment, there is great value for lexical

and language development in encountering large amounts of L2 spoken input. For example, Rodgers (2013) found that, by regularly watching L2 television, EFL learners were able to learn words incidentally and their listening comprehension improved.

- Learners should be at the appropriate level. If the content is incomprehensible, students are unlikely to watch it outside the classroom. The high-frequency words should be known before beginning extensive viewing.
- Listening comprehension should be supported. L2 television will initially be challenging to understand. Watching a television series in sequence, beginning with its first episode, will help learners to develop background knowledge that should help them understand subsequent episodes (Rodgers & Webb, 2011). Watching the same episode more than once will also help to build comprehension.
- Precise comprehension should be a goal rather than a requirement. L2 listening comprehension occurs on a continuum from incomprehensible to fully comprehensible. Students should not be expected to have the same level of comprehension as their teachers. Instead, the focus should be on achieving a level of comprehension that allows them to enjoy viewing.
- Classroom-based extensive viewing should guide out-of-class viewing. Extensive viewing in class should demonstrate to students how they can learn with television and online videos autonomously outside the classroom.
- Learners should watch L2 television as much as possible. The purpose of extensive viewing in the classroom is to develop autonomous L2 television viewers. The amount of language they learn through extensive viewing in the classroom will be limited; but if students are then motivated to regularly watch L2 television outside the classroom, the potential vocabulary and language learning gains could be substantial.

In summary, the use of extensive reading and viewing programmes in the classroom can help students to see how and why they might learn with resources that often initially seem too difficult. Simply asking students to read graded readers and watch L2 television programmes in their free time is likely to result in failure. In the same way that students who have never read a graded reader may find it too challenging without some support, students who have never watched an L2 television programme are also likely to find it too difficult to understand without support. Students may end up discouraged, and little if anything may be achieved. To avoid this happening, it is worth discussing all of the different resources that can be used for learning autonomously and spending time workshopping the use of these resources. If students are able to see that they can understand these different resources and enjoy using them, they may be encouraged to engage in meaning-focused learning outside the classroom.

ACTIVITY 7.1   Sources of meaning-focused input

Try to think of at least ten different sources of meaning-focused input that students might access outside the classroom to strengthen their vocabulary knowledge. Then check your ideas at the end of the chapter. Which sources do you think your students have used or would use on their own?

Strategy 2: Finding ways to use the L2 outside the classroom

Students may learn much about a word by deliberately studying it and encountering it in context. However, they may still have difficulty using these words, because producing words when they are required tends to be more difficult and take longer than recognizing and understanding words when they are encountered (Morgan & Oberdeck, 1930; Stoddard, 1929; Waring, 1997a, 1997b). The lexical knowledge required for speech and writing is best gained through activities and experiences that develop productive knowledge of words (Webb, 2009b). But while there are many approaches and materials oriented towards using language, more classroom time tends to be devoted to developing the comprehension of language than to its use. The majority of classroom activities involve encountering language, which certainly helps to develop students' receptive skills but may fail to help them develop the productive skills they need to use words in a fluent manner. Moreover, even in cases where there is sufficient time and opportunities for words to be used in activities, students often avoid using target vocabulary because they lack confidence in their ability to use it correctly. These are some of the reasons why language learners might struggle to use words outside the classroom when the opportunity arises.

As words are used more and more frequently, the amount of time it takes to recall and use them in context is likely to decrease. Through use, knowledge of words is likely to be strengthened, and vocabulary may be used in a more fluent, native-like way. Table 7.1 listed the receptive aspects of lexical knowledge that might be most effectively gained by encountering words repeatedly in meaning-focused input; these aspects may also be gained through repeated use of the words. Table 7.2 lists the productive aspects of lexical knowledge that may be most effectively gained by using words in meaning-focused output.

Form	correct . . . pronunciation of the word spelling of the word production of the different inflections and derivations of the word
Meaning	production of . . . the word to express its meaning the word to convey its different meanings other words that are related in meaning to the word
Use	use of . . . the word with grammatical accuracy the word together with other words that it typically collocates with the word in the correct situations

Table 7.2 Aspects of productive vocabulary knowledge gained through meaning-focused output

Teacher's role

In the second language learning context, there should be opportunities to use recently taught words outside the classroom on a daily basis. However, in the foreign language learning context, there may be few opportunities to use the L2 outside the classroom. The teacher's role in developing this strategy is twofold. First, education is again important. Teachers should raise awareness of the fact that the ability to use words effectively is to a large degree dependent on experience in using these words in speech and writing. Most students are familiar with, and often frustrated by, an inability to produce words in a fluent manner; if we do not know a word well, or have not used it for a long time, it often takes longer to recall that word. Teachers can highlight this in the classroom by demonstrating that words which have not been produced are harder to recall than those which have been produced. This may help students to appreciate the need to use target vocabulary on a regular basis.

The second aspect of the teacher's role is to help students to explore the different opportunities available for using the language outside the classroom. In both the foreign and second language learning contexts, there are various opportunities which involve writing. These include keeping a journal, and writing on blogs, discussion boards, texts, and emails. Familiarizing students with these different forms of writing, and making them feel comfortable with the prospect of using them, may need to begin in the controlled and supportive environment of the classroom. When students are accustomed to writing in the L2, then an emphasis might be placed on completing similar tasks outside the classroom.

The opportunities to use words in speech differ between the second and foreign language learning contexts. As discussed in Chapter 6, while there should be plenty of opportunities to speak in English outside the classroom in the ESL context, there may be very few opportunities to do so in the EFL context. In the ESL context, teachers can guide students towards using English outside the classroom in specific situations (for example, shopping, asking for directions, renewing visas) and to develop functional, conversational, and other more sophisticated language skills, such as those relating to argument and discussion. These opportunities allow teachers to track their students' language and vocabulary use. In the EFL context, however, opportunities to speak in English may need to be manufactured. Within a language course, discussion groups could be created. Social media could be used to create online discussion groups on sites such as Facebook, and videoconferencing tools such as Skype could be used to set up face-to-face video chats. Spoken journals could be included as a daily component of the course and submitted as part of the assessment. Within an institution, English language lounges would provide students with a place to go and speak in English in a non-threatening atmosphere. In both the EFL and ESL contexts, teachers could include tasks that involve students using the target vocabulary in speech. If students are able to find opportunities to use the target vocabulary in their own time, teachers should keep track of their students' progress and highlight the gains that are made. Raising awareness of the progress that students are making in using recently learned words in speech is likely to motivate them to continue to make the effort to do so.

The principles for using words in meaning-focused output should, to a large degree, follow those for encountering words in sources of meaning-focused input through extensive reading and viewing:

1 There should be a focus on using language for pleasure.
2 Learners should be encouraged to speak and write about topics that interest them.
3 Learners should be encouraged to use the vocabulary that they have learned.
4 Learners should be encouraged to speak and write as much as possible.
5 Learners should be encouraged to speak and write at a faster rate.
6 The ability to communicate effectively should be the priority.
7 Precise and accurate use of words should be a goal rather than a requirement.
8 The teacher is a role model of a speaker and writer.

ACTIVITY 7.2   Types of meaning-focused output

Try to think of at least ten different types of meaning-focused output that students might engage with outside the classroom to strengthen their vocabulary knowledge. Then check your ideas at the end of the chapter. Which types would your students have the opportunity or the motivation to use?

Strategy 3: Learning word parts: affixes and stems

Affix frequency

A large proportion of English words include affixes; that is, word parts (**morphemes**) which mark the derivations and inflections of headwords. The 2,000 most frequent word families have 13,205 derived and inflected forms (Nation, 2013a). The number of derivations and inflections is substantial at all frequency levels, though it tends to decrease as word frequency decreases. For example, the 5,001–7,000 most frequent word families have 7,776 derived and inflected forms, whereas the 10,001–12,000 most frequent word families have 5,924 derived and inflected forms (Nation, 2013a). Table 7.3 shows the different forms of just six headwords from the 1,000 most frequent word families (the headwords are shown first in bold).

danger	**deep**	**difficult**	**discover**	**door**	**doubt**
dangerous	deepen	difficulty	discovered	doors	doubted
dangerously	deepened	difficulties	discoverer	indoor	doubter
dangers	deepening		discoverers	indoors	doubters
endanger	deepens		discoveries	outdoor	doubtful
endangered	deeper		discovering	outdoors	doubtfully
endangering	deepest		discovers		doubting
endangerment	deeply		discovery		doubtless
endangerments	depth		rediscover		doubts
endangers	depths		rediscovered		doubtable
			rediscoveries		undoubtable
			rediscovering		undoubtably
			rediscovers		undoubted
			rediscovery		undoubtedly
			undiscovered		

Table 7.3 Derived and inflected forms of headwords from the 1,000 most frequent word families

As discussed in Chapter 2, learning affixes has great value, because if the affix found in an unknown word is known, this increases the chances of the meaning of the word being successfully inferred (White, Power, & White, 1989). For example, if a learner has never encountered the words 'booklet' and 'droplet' but is familiar with the headwords 'book' and 'drop' and knows that the affix -*let* means 'small', then they may be able to recognize that these derivations mean 'small book' and 'small drop'.

The frequency of different affixes varies. Some affixes, such as *un-*, *non-*, -*less*, and -*ly* are very frequent, while others such as *arch-* ('arch-rival'), *be-* ('belittle'), -*dom* ('boredom'), and -*et* ('packet') are much less frequent. This means that some affixes have greater value to learners than others. Sasao (2013) examined all of the derived and inflected forms of the 10,000 most frequent word families in the British National Corpus (BNC) lists (Nation, 2006) and found that there were 118 affixes which featured in more than one word. Sasao and Webb (2017) classified the affixes into three levels according to their learning difficulty: beginner, intermediate, and advanced. Each level includes around 40 affixes. Table 7.4 lists examples of affixes at each of these levels.

Beginner-level affixes		
Affix	**Meaning**	**Examples**
dis-	not	disappear	disorder
mis-	wrongly	misuse	misconduct
inter-	between	international	interface
-ant-	person	consultant	servant
-er	person	manager	leader
Intermediate-level affixes		
Affix	**Meaning**	**Examples**
il-	not	illegal	illogical
super-	beyond	supernatural	superhuman
de-	opposite	decompose	decode
-en	made of	wooden	golden
-ism	theory of	socialism	nationalism
-ible	can be	accessible	convertible
Advanced-level affixes		
Affix	**Meaning**	**Examples**
a-	towards	ahead	aside
mal-	bad	malfunction	malnutrition
sur-	over	surpass	surreal
-ette	small	kitchenette	cigarette
-let	small	booklet	droplet
-ite	person	urbanite	socialite

Table 7.4 Affixes at three levels of learning difficulty (adapted from Sasao & Webb, 2017)

Affix form, meaning, and use

Affix knowledge is multidimensional, and 'knowing' an affix involves learning all of its three dimensions: form, meaning, and use.

- Learning the form involves being able to recognize and produce affixes in speech and writing. Recognition of affix form is particularly important for comprehension, because if the form of an affix is unknown, this most certainly reduces the potential for learners to recognize known words that include the affix. For example, if the word 'accept' is known but the affix *-able* is unknown, then 'acceptable' may not be recognized as being a word that is related in meaning to 'accept'.
- Learning affixes typically involves learning their meanings. For example, *un-* ('unnatural') = 'not', *multi-* ('multicultural') = 'many', *-ess* ('waitress') = 'female', and *-ist* ('specialist') = 'person'.
- Learning the use of an affix involves learning how its inclusion may change the part of speech of a word. For example, adding the suffix *-ee* to 'train' and 'employ' changes these verbs to nouns. Similarly, adding the suffix *-ish* to 'child' and 'self' changes these nouns to adjectives.

Measuring affix knowledge

A useful tool for measuring knowledge of affixes is the Word Part Levels Test (Sasao & Webb, 2017), which measures knowledge of all three of the dimensions described above. The test has three levels of about 40 items each (beginner, intermediate, and advanced) so that a teachable number of affixes may be learned in a course. The test may also have the positive effect of raising awareness of the three different dimensions of affix knowledge.

Table 7.5 shows examples of test questions designed to measure knowledge of form. Test takers must indicate which item is an affix in each set of four options. Here, they would need to select *fore-* and *-ful*.

I	(1) yogh-	(2) shee-	(3) brea-	(4) fore-
2	(1) -rse	(2) -ack	(3) -ful	(4) -uin

Table 7.5 Examples of form-testing questions from the Word Part Levels Test (Sasao & Webb, 2017)

Similarly, in the section of the test focusing on meaning, test takers must select the correct affix from four options. Table 7.6 shows examples of test questions designed to measure knowledge of the meanings of *de-* ('opposite') and *-less* ('without').

1 de- (decompose; decode)	2 -less (endless; useless)
(1) opposite	(1) before
(2) person/thing	(2) without
(3) together	(3) the furthest
(4) small	(4) person

Table 7.6 Examples of meaning-testing questions from the Word Part Levels Test (Sasao & Webb, 2017)

Knowledge of the use of affixes is also measured in a similar way. Test takers must look at two words that include a target affix that has changed the part of speech of a word stem and choose the correct part of speech. For example, adding *en-* to 'sure' and 'able' changes these words from adjectives to verbs. Table 7.7 shows two examples from this section of the test.

9 en- (ensure; enable)	11 -al (personal; traditional)
(1) Noun	(1) Noun
(2) Verb	(2) Verb
(3) Adjective	(3) Adjective
(4) Adverb	(4) Adverb

Table 7.7 Examples of use-testing questions from the Word Part Levels Test (Sasao & Webb, 2017)

Teachers can use the Word Part Levels Test to determine which affixes their students should be trying to learn, as well as which dimensions of affix knowledge they may be struggling with. (The Word Part Levels Test is discussed in more detail in Chapter 9, and the Intermediate level is provided in Appendix 4.)

Teacher's role: affixes

Once teachers have determined where attention should be focused on learning affixes, it is worth spending classroom time helping students to further develop their knowledge of word parts.

Focusing on form

Here are two common approaches to learning the forms of word parts.

1 Breaking down words into parts: Give students a list of derivations and ask them to separate the items into word stems and affixes. For example:

disappearance   impossible   international
irregular   multicultural   transformer

dis / appear / ance   im / possible   inter / nation / al
ir / regular   multi / cultur / al trans / form / er

This exercise focuses learners on recognizing word stems ('appear', 'nation', etc.), affixes (*dis-*, *-ance*, etc.), and derivations. To make the exercise easier, focus on different words that include the same affix (for example, 'transform', 'transplant', 'transport'), or focus on the same stem with different affixes (for example, 'believable', 'believer', 'unbelievable').

2 Word building: Provide students with a word stem and affixes and ask them to create as many different words as they can with the parts. For example:

> word stem: 'help'   affixes: *un-, -er, -ful, -less*

To make the exercise more challenging, provide multiple stems, or withhold the affixes.

Focusing on meaning

Breaking down words into parts and word building can also focus attention on meaning. Teachers could ask students to explain the meanings of the affixes in the exercise on breaking down words into parts. Similarly, students could be asked to explain the meanings of the words they create in the word building exercise. Flashcards with the form of each affix on one side of a card and its meaning on the other can also be used to learn the meanings of affixes. Perhaps the most common approach to learning the meanings of word parts involves filling in word part tables like the one shown in Table 7.8. These typically provide the form of an affix together with some example words and a blank column for the meaning of the affix to be added by the students.

Affix	Example words	Affix meaning
co-	co-worker, co-pilot	
dis-	disappear, disagree	
mis-	misunderstand, misleading	
multi-	multinational, multicultural	
re-	rebuild, redo	
-less	restless, careless	
-ful	careful, beautiful	
-able	breakable, enjoyable	

Table 7.8 A word part table

Focusing on use

Because the function of affixes is not often transparent during language learning, it is best to deliberately learn this aspect of affix knowledge. The Word Part Levels Test (Sasao & Webb, 2017) is a useful resource in this respect, because it provides clear examples of how word parts may change the part of speech of words. Word part tables can be created around these examples to help students learn the function of affixes (see Table 7.9).

Word stems	Part of speech	Affix	Derivations	Affix function
train, employ	verb	-ee	trainee, employee	
child, self	noun	-ish	childish, selfish	
manage, lead	verb	-er	manager, leader	
accept, predict	verb	-able	acceptable, predictable	
aware, ill	adjective	-ness	awareness, illness	
luck, health	noun	-y	lucky, healthy	

Table 7.9 A word part table for learning affix use

Students might then be asked to find other examples of derivations where these affixes have the same function. It is important to note that not all occurrences of affixes have the same function, so not all words that include the target affixes will be altered in the same way. For example, the function of the affix -al in 'personal' and 'traditional' is to change a noun to an adjective, whereas the function of -al in 'approval' and 'proposal' is to change a verb to a noun. Moreover, because this exercise requires knowledge of grammatical terms, it is more appropriate for older learners.

Teacher's role: stems

A second aspect of learning word parts is being able to recognize the word stems that are found in different words. There are around 2,000 mid-frequency words which include word stems that are also found among the 2,000 most frequent word families. If learners are able to recognize that an unknown word includes a word stem found in a higher-frequency word, it may help them to guess the meaning of the unknown word. For example, the word stem -scrib(e)- is found in words like 'describe', 'scribble', and 'prescribe'. If students can recognize the word stem and understand that its meaning ('write') is conveyed in each case, it may help them to understand words such as 'subscribe', 'inscribe', 'scribe', and 'transcribe'. There are a great number of English word stems, but not all word stems are worth learning; the most useful ones are those which are easily recognized and found in a large number of words. Wei and Nation (2013) compiled a list of the most useful English word stems (for example, -ceive-, -graph-, -duce-). A version of this list can be found in Appendix 3.

Wei and Nation (2013) describe a useful technique for learning word stems. A version of this is shown in Figure 7.1 (Wei, 2015).

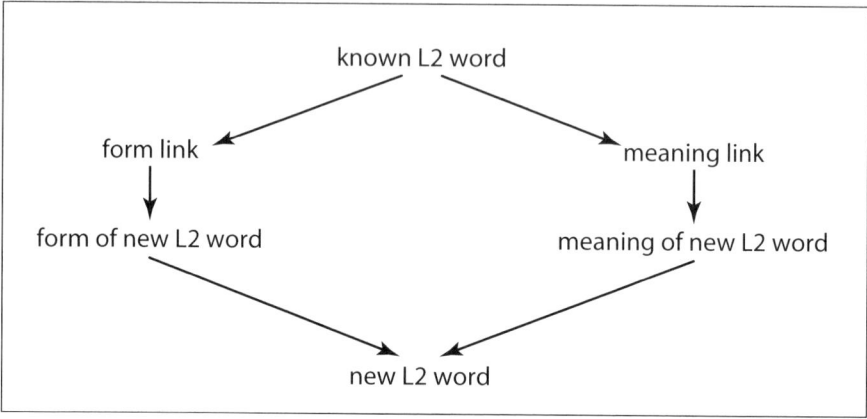

Figure 7.1 The word part technique (adapted from Wei, 2015)

In this technique, the teacher's role is to teach the meaning of word stems and explain their connection to other words. It involves the following steps:

1 Learn the meaning of a word stem; for example, *-super-* (= 'above') or *-mit-* (= 'send').
2 Make the connection between known and unknown words which include the word stem; for example, *super-* in the noun 'superior', and *-mit* in the verb 'transmit'. Understanding that 'superior' means 'a person who is above someone else professionally' may help students to understand related words such as 'supervisor' and 'superintendent'; and knowing that 'transmit' means 'to send out electrical signals' may help students to understand 'permit', 'emit', and 'submit'.

The word part technique may be challenging to begin with, but with practice it will become easier.

ACTIVITY 7.3   Word Part Levels Test

To what extent do you teach word parts? Think about your students and answer the questions.

1 At what point in a course might you focus on word parts? Can you think of an example?

2 Do you teach all three dimensions of affix knowledge: form, meaning, and use? What kinds of activities do you use?

3 Turn to Appendix 4 and complete the Intermediate Word Part Levels Test. Did you find it useful?

Strategy 4: Guessing from context

The guessing from context strategy involves making a deliberate attempt to learn words when they are encountered in context, following a specific procedure. It is a particularly important strategy for language learners, because it can be used to learn any unknown words that are encountered and so has the potential to have a large impact on lexical development. There are several different versions of the strategy. The following steps were included in Clarke and Nation's version (1980):

1 Determine the part of speech of the unknown word.
2 Analyse the immediate context to try to determine the meaning of the unknown word.
3 Analyse the wider context to try to determine the meaning of the unknown word.
4 Guess the meaning of the unknown word.
5 Check the guess against the information that was found in the first four steps.

The first step is focused on determining the part of speech of the unknown word. If the part of speech of the word is known, then it immediately rules out a large number of words and guides learners to guesses that have the same grammatical function. The second step involves examining the sentence in which the unknown word is found and looking to see if there is any information that can be used to determine the meaning. Typically, most clues about the meaning of an unknown word are found in the immediate context. The third step involves considering the wider context to see if there is any further information that might be used to determine or confirm the meaning of the word. The fourth step is to guess the meaning. The fifth and final step is to check the guess against the criteria in steps 1–3: Does the guess conform to the part of speech determined in Step 1? Does the guess fit with the information provided in the immediate context that was examined in Step 2? Is the guess supported by the wider context that was considered in Step 3?

Teacher's role

The teacher should train learners in following a principled approach to guessing from context so that they may become more effective in gaining knowledge of unknown words when they are encountered. This does not mean, however, that students are likely to successfully guess all unknown words they encounter. It is important to make learners aware that the immediate and wider contexts in which unknown words are encountered may contain little information that can be used to infer the meaning, and sometimes the information provided may be misleading. For the most part, students are likely to only make small gains in their knowledge of the form–meaning connection through guessing from context. However, this does not mean that the strategy lacks value. Even if the students' guesses are wrong, they may still gain knowledge of the part of speech of the word by completing the first step. They are also likely to gain some degree of knowledge of the spelling of the word as a result of paying specific attention to it. Moreover, the focus on the immediate and wider contexts in Steps 2 and 3 may help them to develop knowledge of the words that might collocate with the unknown word, as well as words that have related meanings. Together, this represents useful gains in knowledge that should help learners to better understand the unknown word when it is next encountered.

Learning unknown words as they are encountered in context is a slow process; it takes a long time to develop comprehensive knowledge of words through repeated encounters in context. However, the gains made by using the guessing from context strategy may help to speed up the process. Teachers can evaluate their students' ability to use the guessing from context strategy using Sasao's Guessing from Context Test (2013). (For a detailed overview of the guessing from context strategy, see Chapter 5; the Guessing from Context Test will be discussed in Chapter 9.)

ACTIVITY 7.4   **Guessing from context**

Apply the guessing from context strategy, following the five steps outlined above, to the word 'ancient' in the following passage. Then check your answers at the end of the chapter.

> Why do people move to new places? Long ago, ancient people wanted to inhabit places with plenty of food and other resources. These people got food in the same ways we do now: farming, hunting or herding animals, or fishing if they lived near water.
>
> Because of competition for food, over-crowding was one reason early people moved. They sometimes walked very long distances or rode on animals, but they had to sail across water.
>
> Nowadays, modern people may move in search of employment or a better climate. The migration of large groups of people may occur because of economic problems or a lack of food or water. Political problems can also cause people to migrate.

Materials extract 7.1 Excerpt from Milner, Johannsen, and Chase, World English 3 with Student CD-ROM (US) (1st ed.), © 2010 Heinle/ELT, a part of Cengage Learning, Inc., reprinted by permission. www.cengage.com/permissions.

Strategy 5: Using dictionaries effectively

Dictionaries are perhaps the most widely used resource for deliberate vocabulary learning. Most students have their own dictionary (hard-copy or digital), and most classrooms provide access to dictionaries. There are three different types of dictionary: monolingual, bilingual, and **bilingualized**.

- Monolingual dictionaries are typically addressed to advanced native speakers. However, there are a number of excellent monolingual learners' dictionaries, such as the *Oxford Advanced Learner's Dictionary*, the *Cambridge Learner's Dictionary*, the *Longman Dictionary of Contemporary English*, and the *Collins COBUILD Primary Learner's Dictionary*. These dictionaries have been written with language learners in mind, and they use a more basic vocabulary to help readers understand the information provided. Despite this, they may still prove to be difficult to use for beginners.
- Bilingual dictionaries are most widely used by language learners (Atkins & Knowles, 1990), perhaps because they are appropriate for learners at all proficiency levels.
- Bilingualized dictionaries include the information found in monolingual and bilingual dictionaries and may be the most effective of the three types (Laufer & Hadar, 1997), but they are far less common.

As discussed earlier in the book, despite the popularity of dictionaries, students often have difficulty in using them effectively and require training (Laufer & Hadar, 1997). Dictionary entries provide a lot of information that students may not know how to use. For example:

- spelling
- pronunciation of the word provided using phonetic transcriptions
- grammatical function/part of speech
- derivations and inflections
- definitions for each sense
- synonyms
- antonyms
- collocations
- example sentences
- frequency in language.

Figure 7.2 shows an example of a dictionary definition for the adjective 'ineffective'.

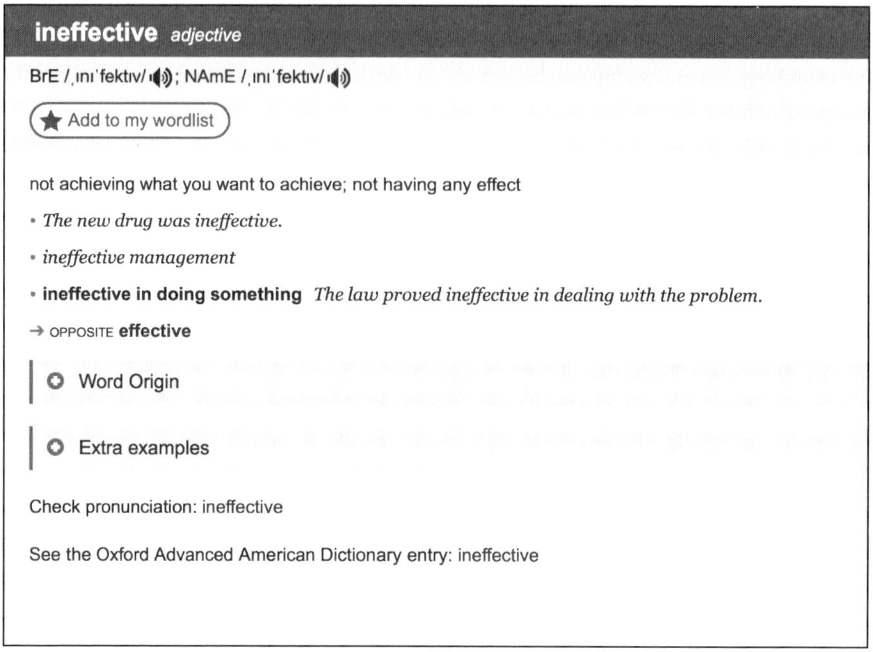

ineffective *adjective*

BrE /ˌɪnɪˈfektɪv/; NAmE /ˌɪnɪˈfektɪv/

Add to my wordlist

not achieving what you want to achieve; not having any effect

- *The new drug was ineffective.*
- *ineffective management*
- **ineffective in doing something** *The law proved ineffective in dealing with the problem.*

→ OPPOSITE **effective**

Word Origin

Extra examples

Check pronunciation: ineffective

See the Oxford Advanced American Dictionary entry: ineffective

Figure 7.2 Definition of 'ineffective' from the online Oxford Advanced Learner's Dictionary (www.oxfordlearnersdictionaries.com)

If teachers do not show students how to make use of each type of information, they may ignore much of the information provided in dictionary entries and struggle to find the information they are looking for. Another reason why students often have trouble using dictionaries is that they may not know all of the words that are used in monolingual definitions, or in the example sentences. The vocabulary included in monolingual learners' dictionaries typically falls within the levels of the 3,000 most frequent words. So if a student has yet to master these levels, they may have trouble making sense of the entries. Another potential problem is the fact that many words are **polysemous**, and users may have difficulty identifying the meaning that they are searching for.

Teacher's role

Training students to use dictionaries has great value, because effective dictionary use is likely to contribute to vocabulary learning gains throughout the language learning process. It is therefore worth spending class time training students to make the best use of their dictionaries. Teachers should check whether students are comfortable with the following common uses of the dictionary.

During reading and listening:

- find the unknown words encountered
- establish the meanings of words encountered
- confirm the meanings of partially known words
- look up the frequency of words encountered.

For speaking and writing:

- look up the unknown words needed
- look up how the word might be used in a sentence.

In relation to partially known words, look up:

- the spellings
- the pronunciation
- the meanings
- the grammatical function
- the derivations and inflections
- common collocations
- synonyms.

Tasks can be created around a set of dictionary entries to ensure that students are able to find and use the information provided in dictionary entries effectively.

Strategy 6: Using flashcards

Flashcards are a popular tool for autonomous vocabulary learning. They are an effective and efficient method of learning form–meaning connections and can be used almost anywhere when there are a few minutes to spare: at home, in the classroom, on a bus or train, while waiting for someone or something, etc.

Teacher's role

There are a number of ways in which flashcards can be used, so in teaching this strategy, the teacher's focus should be on making learners aware of the principles that facilitate the most effective approach.

1 Retrieval from memory increases learning. By looking at one side of a card and trying to recall the information on the other side, students are likely to learn more than by looking at the two together, as they would with a list of words (Landauer & Bjork, 1978).

2 The number of repetitions with each card affects learning. The more the L2 word is successfully recalled, the easier it becomes. Within a single study period, seven repetitions have been found to be sufficient (Crothers & Suppes, 1967).

3 Spacing between encounters improves learning. It is better to have an interval between encounters with each card than to see the same card repeatedly (Nakata, 2015).

4 The direction of learning affects what is gained. Learning can occur in two ways: the L1 meaning of the word is seen, and students try to recall the L2 form; or the L2 form of the word is seen, and students try to recall the L1 meaning. It may be more effective to use the L1 meaning to recall the word form, because this increases the potential for students to produce the L2 form of the word, which is essential for speaking and writing (Webb, 2009a, 2009b).

5 Students should say the target word aloud as they study each card. Saying the word aloud increases the chance that the word will be remembered for a longer period of time (Ellis, 1997).

6 Students should avoid learning words with related meanings together. As we have seen in Chapter 2, learning **semantically related** words together can lead to cross-association; the forms and meanings of the words may be learned, but the link from the different L2 forms is confused with different semantically related meanings. Studying semantically related words together in any learning method is likely to result in interference and reduce the potential for vocabulary learning (Nation, 2000).

Research suggests that using flashcards can lead to durable learning (de Groot, 2006). However, it is also important to make students aware that while this strategy is very useful, it is limited; flashcards may help to strengthen knowledge of form–meaning connections, but other aspects of knowledge may not be fully learned. While one meaning of a word will be learned, other peripheral meanings will not. For example, if students link 'run' with the meaning 'moving quickly on foot', they are unlikely to understand its meaning in 'run for office' or 'run a bath'. Similarly, derivations and collocations of a word will not be learned. Encounters with words in meaning-focused input will help to further develop knowledge of form, meaning, and use, such as the different derivations and inflections, the different meanings of a word, and the ways in which words are used in context. Using words in speech and writing is also necessary, to develop the ability to use the target vocabulary effectively. Learning words using flashcards certainly contributes to growth in vocabulary knowledge, but this knowledge needs to be further expanded through meaning-focused learning approaches.

Summary

Because there are thousands of words to learn and there is only so much classroom time that can be used for vocabulary learning, it is essential that students become effective and efficient autonomous learners of vocabulary. Some students are very successful in their autonomous vocabulary learning while others are not. There are many different ways in which words can be learned outside the classroom. Teaching the vocabulary learning strategies that are most likely to contribute to greater current and future learning will increase students' potential to learn words both inside and outside the classroom. Successful use of these strategies necessitates the deliberate learning of each strategy over multiple sessions, and should involve training, monitoring, and evaluation.

Questions for reflection

1 What are the challenges of improving autonomous vocabulary learning in your context?

2 List the strategies that you have used to learn vocabulary in an L2. Which ones did you find most effective?

3 How much classroom time do you think you would need to teach, train, and evaluate your students' use of each of the strategies discussed in this chapter?

Keys to activities

ACTIVITY 7.1   Sources of meaning-focused input

There are many potential sources of meaning-focused input that students can learn from outside the classroom. We recommend the following:

Reading:

- graded readers
- online blogs, including those written by students
- online resources that are created specifically for L2 learners, such as BBC Learning English
- online shopping at English language sites
- changing the language of software on phones, computers, and apps

Watching:

- L2 television programmes
- L2 films

- L2 YouTube videos
- open lectures
- TED Talks

Listening:

- L2 songs (and reading their lyrics online)
- audio books
- L2 radio and podcasts
- online resources that are created specifically for L2 learners, such as BBC Learning English

---

ACTIVITY 7.2   Types of meaning-focused output

There are many types of meaning-focused output that can help to strengthen vocabulary knowledge outside the classroom. We recommend the following:

Writing:

- L2 blogs and microblogs
- L2 journals
- exchanging postcards from people around the world using services such as www.postcrossing.com
- commenting on online sites such as YouTube
- participating in online communities
- participating in online virtual worlds such as Second Life

Speaking:

- recording spoken journals
- recording video journals
- recording podcasts
- participating in English language clubs
- singing L2 songs
- calling the customer service department of international companies (several Chinese students have told us they have done this)

ACTIVITY 7.4   Guessing from context

Step 1: 'ancient' is an adjective.

Step 2: 'ancient' refers to a type of people. It could refer to people from a certain place or it could refer to people from long ago.

Step 3: In the first sentence of the second paragraph, the adjective 'early' is used with 'people'; this may have a similar meaning to 'ancient'. In the first sentence of the third paragraph, there is a similar but contrasting sentence ('Long ago' versus 'Nowadays') to the one in which 'ancient' is used. In this sentence, the adjective that refers to people is 'modern'.

Step 4: Perhaps the most likely meaning of 'ancient' is 'from long ago'.

Step 5: The guess fits with the criteria in Steps 1–3 and is therefore reasonable.

Suggestions for further reading

Gu, P. Y. (2003). Fine brush and freehand: the vocabulary-learning art of two successful Chinese EFL learners. *TESOL Quarterly, 37(1)*, 73–104.

This study looks at the differences in vocabulary learning strategies that two Chinese EFL students used during and after reading.

Sasao, Y., & **Webb, S.** (2017). The Word Part Levels Test. *Language Teaching Research. 21(1)*, 12–30.

This study describes the development and validation of the Word Part Levels Test. A list of 118 word parts at three levels of difficulty, as well as a test used to measure knowledge of these affixes, is included with the study.

Schmitt, N. (1997). Vocabulary learning strategies. In N. Schmitt & M. McCarthy (Eds.), *Vocabulary: description, acquisition and pedagogy* (pp. 199–227). Cambridge: Cambridge University Press.

This chapter sheds light on the various ways in which students might learn words. Schmitt surveyed Japanese EFL learners to create a taxonomy of vocabulary learning strategies.

8 DEVELOPING AN EFFECTIVE VOCABULARY LEARNING PROGRAMME

Introduction

There is not a big distinction between planning a language course and planning a vocabulary learning programme. At least three quarters of the time spent on both needs to have a communicative focus encompassing the four skills of listening, speaking, reading, and writing. The activities that make up a vocabulary learning programme need to provide a good balance of opportunities for learning, drawing on a wide enough range of activities and making sure that there are sufficient opportunities for incidental learning as well as deliberate learning, and sufficient opportunities for receptive learning as well as productive learning. One way in which this balance can be achieved is by following the principle of the four strands. We have already introduced the principle in relation to analysing vocabulary learning activities in Chapter 5. We will now explore how this principle can be applied and look at its advantages and disadvantages.

Defining the four strands

As we saw in Chapter 5, the principle of the four strands states that, for a vocabulary learning programme to be well balanced, the time spent both inside and outside the classroom should be divided equally between the strands of meaning-focused input, meaning-focused output, language-focused learning, and fluency development. Deliberate learning occurs in the language-focused learning strand, while incidental learning occurs through the other three strands.

Strand 1: Meaning-focused input

This involves learning through listening and reading—that is, receptive learning. Because learning through meaning-focused input is largely incidental, large quantities of input are required to ensure that enough vocabulary is covered, with sufficient repetition. The basic requirement of meaning-focused input is that it should be comprehensible; that is, it should be at the right level for each particular learner and contain a sufficient number of unknown words and partially known words to provide opportunities for new vocabulary learning to occur, without overwhelming the learner and causing comprehension to suffer. The general rule is that around one word in every 50 running words can be completely or substantially unfamiliar. While there is some research to support this, it ought not to be taken too literally, because a range of other factors besides the density of unknown vocabulary also have a strong influence on comprehension. These factors include the medium of the input (listening or reading), the speed at which it is dealt with, the familiarity of the content covered in the input, the learners' skill and fluency in comprehending it, the importance of the unknown vocabulary to the overall message of the input, and the learning burden of the unknown vocabulary.

Strand 2: Meaning-focused output

This involves learning through speaking and writing—that is, productive learning. Productive learning is more difficult than receptive learning, mainly because it requires more precise knowledge of aspects of the form, meaning, and use of words than receptive learning. It also requires the learners to give attention to aspects of vocabulary knowledge that are not so critical for receptive use.

Strand 3: Language-focused learning

This goes by a variety of names but basically involves giving deliberate attention to language features. The role of deliberate attention has always been a matter of debate in the field of language education, but recent research involving the measurement of **implicit knowledge** provides strong support for the deliberate learning of vocabulary (Elgort, 2011), including multi-word combinations. One strength of the principle of the four strands is that it provides a rationale for both including deliberate learning within a vocabulary learning programme and limiting its application to around a quarter of the total time. In any comparison between deliberate and incidental learning, the former will always prove to be more efficient. However, we have seen that this kind of comparison does not make much sense, because both kinds of learning are required: deliberate learning quickly establishes strong item knowledge, while incidental learning puts knowledge to use, enriching it, reinforcing it, and making it fluently available for use.

Strand 4: Fluency development

Fluency involves making the best use of what is already known. The fluency development strand of a vocabulary learning programme is characterized by two important features: 1) the ease and familiarity of the material, and 2) the pressure to process the material as quickly as possible. This means that fluency development activities should not involve unfamiliar vocabulary and should deal with largely familiar content. Moreover, they should be underpinned by the aim to make existing knowledge fluently available. Although there is likely to be a great deal of overlap and transfer of knowledge within a vocabulary learning programme, it is important to ensure that each of the four skills of listening, speaking, reading, and writing receive attention in the fluency development strand. So if we accept the basic premise of the principle of the four strands, which is that of balance, we could estimate that around one 16th of the time available (i.e. a quarter of one quarter) should be spent on developing fluency in each of the four skills.

Flexibility of the four strands principle

While there may be no research to directly justify the equal division of time between the four strands, there is plenty of research showing the value of each strand. The principle of the four strands provides a curriculum-based rationale for balancing the inclusion of the four different areas of learning, rather than a research-based justification. Here are some characteristics of the four strands principle:

- It provides a broad view of how learning occurs; indeed, its greatest strength is its inclusiveness. It allows for a balance between receptive and productive learning, between incidental and deliberate learning, and between acquiring new knowledge and becoming more skilled in using existing knowledge. Achieving a balance between each of these factors is important, because doing so not only reflects the different ways in which we learn languages but also the kinds of knowledge required.
- It works at the programme level rather than at the lesson level. So while there needs to be a balance between the four strands over the duration of the programme, it is not necessary to strike a balance in each lesson.
- There is no set order for the strands. Although readers may be familiar with successful teaching practices where receptive learning precedes productive learning, or where deliberate or incidental learning of new items precedes fluency development, there is no need to lock the four strands into a set sequence. Deliberate learning can occur before, during, or after incidental learning. Fluency development of a particular item can occur immediately after it is introduced, particularly if that item is immediately required for language use. Similarly, productive learning of an item can occur before any substantial receptive learning of it has taken place, for example if it is immediately needed for productive use, or if, as in the case of learning the letters of the alphabet, it is more effective and efficient to go straight to productive learning.

- It provides a rationale for allocating a certain proportion of the time available to particular language activities, and for deciding whether to include a particular type of activity or not. (We will look at this in more detail later in this chapter.)

ACTIVITY 8.1   Balancing the four strands

Here is an example of a one-week lesson plan using activities from Chapter 5.

Lesson 1	Lesson 2	Lesson 3	Lesson 4
speed-reading (5 min)	speed-reading (5 min)	speed-reading (5 min)	dictation (15 min)
extensive reading (20 min)	intensive reading (35 min)	extensive reading (20 min)	4/3/2 (10 min)
task-focused spoken interaction (25 min)	ten-minute writing (10 min)	task-focused spoken interaction (25 min)	writing with feedback (25 min)
Homework flashcards (20 min), extensive reading (20 min), linked skills (20 min), extensive listening (30 min), writing with feedback (30 min)			

Classify the activities into the four strands and see if the balance of time between them is even or not. What are your conclusions? Check your answers at the end of the chapter.

Contributions of the four strands to vocabulary learning

Let us look at each of the four strands in more detail to understand how each can positively influence the effectiveness of a vocabulary learning programme.

Key features of meaning-focused input

Perhaps the best-known advocate of the importance of meaning-focused input in language learning is the linguist and educational researcher Stephen Krashen. His advocacy of **comprehensible input** has had the very positive effect of encouraging the growth of extensive reading and extensive listening; however, this advocacy has also had the negative effect of making language-focused learning seem undesirable. In contrast to Krashen's characterization of comprehensible input as the major component of a language course (Krashen, 1981, 1985), the principle of the four strands sees meaning-focused input as one of four major components. While many courses do indeed spend far too much time on language-focused learning and not enough on learning through meaning-focused input, there is no need to eliminate the former entirely in favour of the latter; both kinds of learning are useful, particularly when they complement each other.

The meaning-focused input strand is of pivotal importance, because without substantial input there are fewer resources for output and fluency development work. The major sources of meaning-focused input are extensive reading, extensive listening (including the listening involved in conversations), and extensive viewing. About half the time spent on meaning-focused input should be on extensive reading, and the other half on extensive listening and viewing. Extensive reading helps to develop knowledge of the written forms of words, while extensive listening and viewing helps to develop knowledge of the spoken forms.

Meaning-focused input through reading
In terms of reading, if comprehensible input is accepted as being integral to vocabulary learning, it follows that we should make use of specially prepared reading texts such as graded readers, which provide learners at every level of proficiency with input that they can comprehend. An extensive reading component involving substantial numbers of graded readers at the right level for the range of learners within the class is an essential part of a well-balanced vocabulary learning programme. In fact, simply adding an extensive reading component to a programme may well be the best thing that a teacher could do to bring about growth in language proficiency; the studies conducted by Warwick Elley and Francis Mangubhai (1981a, 1981b) and numerous other studies involving graded readers have shown that such a programme is likely to deliver substantial results.

There are those who find it difficult to accept the idea of using graded readers because they are not 'authentic'. However, this is based on a particular view of authenticity. A text may be considered authentic because it was written for native speakers of the language, but authenticity can also relate to the experience that readers have with the text, rather than to the text in and of itself. When readers have an authentic reading experience, they respond to the text in a way that is similar to the way in which an experienced reader or a native speaker would respond. For example, the reader may read the text and enjoy or dislike the story; both would be authentic reading experiences. In this case, authenticity comes not from the text itself but from the relationship between the reader and the text. It is this kind of authenticity that gives graded readers legitimacy and value.

In their 'book flood' study in Fiji, which looked at the positive effects of extensive reading on second language learning, Elley and Mangubhai

(1981a) did not use graded readers; instead, they used story books written for young native speakers. Similarly, Krashen (2004) preferred to recommend the Sweet Valley High books (a series written for native-English-speaking teenage girls) for extensive reading, rather than graded readers. As we saw in Chapter 1 in relation to Zipf's law, around half of the different words will occur only once in the text. The problem with books written for native speakers is that many of these words will be well beyond L2 learners' vocabulary levels. Not only will there be a high density of unknown words in the text, there will also be a large number of low-frequency words which are not nearly as valuable to the learner as other words of higher frequency (Webb & Macalister, 2013). While graded readers are also bound by Zipf's law, every word will be worth learning for learners at the corresponding level.

Meaning-focused input through listening and viewing
In the early stages of language learning, there is likely to be little difference between reading speed and listening speed, and this appears to apply to both L1 and L2 learners. But while L1 learners gain most of their high-frequency and mid-frequency vocabulary growth through listening, many L2 learners rely on deliberate learning or incidental learning through reading, largely because of a lack of comprehensible spoken input in foreign language learning environments.

The research on vocabulary learning through listening has been inconsistent. Brown, Waring, and Donkaewbua (2008) found that the number of individual words learned through listening was less substantial than through reading, or reading while listening. In contrast, Webb and Chang (under review) found that EFL students learned collocations at a similar rate through reading and listening but that this was less than through reading while listening. In relation to extensive viewing, Rodgers (2013) found that vocabulary learning from watching L2 television may occur at a similar rate to reading. A positive contribution of spoken input to vocabulary learning is that pauses and hesitations in speech often signal the boundaries between formulaic sequences, such as 'on the other hand', 'of course', and 'going to'. When learning from reading, these boundaries (and sequences) are less apparent.

One of the obstacles to learning through meaning-focused spoken input has been the difficulty of finding comprehensible input. In recent years, however, audio versions of graded readers have become widely available, making it easier for teachers to find level-appropriate listening material. Finding comprehensible extensive viewing input for beginners is likely to be more difficult, because television programmes tend to be made for native speakers who have a larger vocabulary size than most L2 learners. However, as we saw in Chapter 1, research suggests that L2 learners may be able to understand spoken discourse when a smaller proportion of words are known (95%) than is necessary with written discourse (98%) (van Zeeland & Schmitt, 2013). Because the vocabulary size required to understand common forms of spoken discourse such as television and conversation is only 3,000 word families, these sources of input are appropriate for learners at an intermediate level, and it may even be the case that providing these learners with large amounts of meaning-focused spoken input is key to raising their vocabularies from the intermediate to the advanced level.

Key features of meaning-focused output

Meaning-focused output occurs when learners are involved in speaking and writing which at least in some small way stretches their language proficiency. Merrill Swain (1985) referred to this as o+1 (output with a little more to stretch current proficiency), to parallel Krashen's use of the symbol i+1 (input just beyond the current level of proficiency). For example, the linked skills activity (see Chapter 5) can be a useful contributor to the meaning-focused output strand of a vocabulary learning programme: because it provides opportunities to prepare for speaking and writing, the output is likely to be at the level of o+1, rather than staying within what is already known and comfortable.

A language teacher needs to develop skill in promoting meaning-focused spoken output through both monologue and dialogue, across a wide range of degrees of formality and topics. In addition, both meaning-focused input and meaning-focused output need to be truly message-focused. The learners' focus should be on receiving and producing meaningful messages as part of genuine communication. There is a growing body of research which shows that spoken and written interaction can result in significant vocabulary growth (Newton, 2013; McDonough & Sunitham, 2009), and the greatest opportunities for vocabulary learning through interaction are likely to come from small group work (Dobao, 2014a). In collaborative group work, the two strands of meaning-focused input and meaning-focused output are well balanced, with one person's output becoming another person's input. A crucial element of a vocabulary learning programme is thus the inclusion of opportunities for rich and varied communication.

Key features of language-focused learning

As mentioned earlier in this chapter, many second and foreign language learning courses spend too much time on language-focused learning. Moreover, it is often not done efficiently or effectively. This is because the teacher tends to dominate in this strand, relying on direct teaching to promote vocabulary growth. If we look at the outcomes of direct vocabulary teaching, including doing written vocabulary exercises, we find that for every ten words taught, learners are likely to remember five or less if we measure their receptive knowledge, and three or less if we measure their productive knowledge. Direct vocabulary teaching can also take up a considerable amount of time. The most striking example of this is in a study by María Carlo et al. (2004), where 140 words were taught over a total teaching time of 60 hours (with a teaching rate of around two words per hour). Only half of these were successfully recalled in subsequent tests, which gives a learning rate of around one word per hour—not a very good return for the considerable amount of time invested.

While some direct vocabulary teaching is worthwhile, particularly as part of intensive reading and vocabulary learning strategy development, it is far more efficient for learners to be trained and encouraged to lead their own deliberate vocabulary learning. For example, learners should be taught the flashcard strategy and encouraged to make or select their own flashcards. Such individualized deliberate vocabulary study has been thoroughly researched and shown to be highly effective (Nation, 2013a). Other significant strategies include guessing from context, using word parts to relate unfamiliar words to known words, and dictionary use (see Chapter 7).

In light of the above, the language-focused learning strand of a vocabulary learning programme can be usefully divided into:

- vocabulary teaching
- vocabulary strategy training.

It should also contain opportunities for feedback on written work and spoken production. The teacher plays a significant role in certain parts of the strand, but the eventual goal is for learners to become autonomous in their deliberate vocabulary learning, largely taking over responsibility for aspects of their vocabulary development from the teacher. Finally, to reiterate a point made earlier in the chapter, while language-focused learning can result in rapid vocabulary growth, it is likely to need the knowledge that comes from receptive and productive language use to enrich this growth and make vocabulary truly usable.

Key features of fluency development

The fluency development strand shares features of the meaning-focused input and meaning-focused output strands, because the focus of all three is on the meaningful use of the language across the four skills of listening, speaking, reading, and writing. The major difference is that the fluency development strand involves doing activities which are intentionally easy for the learner, involving the use of vocabulary and grammar that is well within their current knowledge. Adapting the symbols used by Krashen and Swain, input and output for fluency development might be represented by i–1 (input minus 1) and o–1 (output minus 1). These symbols encapsulate the goal of the fluency development strand, which is not to learn new vocabulary or grammar but to gain quicker access to what is already known. Fluency development activities are nonetheless highly likely to strengthen and enrich knowledge of partially known vocabulary, as well as enhance the development of knowledge of multi-word combinations. This is due to the substantial amount of input and output involved in fluency development, and because the pressure to perform faster encourages the reformulation of single words into multi-word combinations (McLaughlin, 1990).

As mentioned earlier in this chapter, although there is likely to be some transfer of fluency between different language skills, there is value in focusing on each of the four skills in the fluency development strand of a vocabulary learning programme in equal measure. Useful activities for fluency development include repeated listening and viewing, listening to stories, 4/3/2 speaking, easy extensive reading, speed-reading activities with timed readings and comprehension questions, and ten-minute writing (see Chapter 5). These activities all share the following criteria that typify a fluency development activity, ranked in order of importance:

1 The language and content used in the activity is easy and very familiar to the learners.
2 There is pressure to perform at a faster rate than usual.
3 There is quantity of practice.
4 The activity is meaning-focused.

These criteria can be used to check if an activity can be used to develop fluency or not.

Fluency development should occur at every stage of a vocabulary learning programme. Even in the very first lesson, greetings and expressions of politeness should be practised to gain fluency in producing them. Similarly, numbers should be practised to a high degree of fluency, especially for listening.

In summary, the purpose of designing a vocabulary learning programme on the basis of the principle of the four strands is to create a good balance of opportunities for learning so that the language learned is available for both receptive and productive use across the four skills of listening, speaking, reading, and writing. The most significant features of a vocabulary learning programme include, in this order: a substantial extensive reading, listening, and viewing component; a fluency development strand spanning the four skills; and a rich and varied communicative speaking component.

ACTIVITY 8.2   Analysing a fluency development activity

Apply the four fluency development criteria listed above to the following activity. The 4/3/2 activity has already been analysed for you, as an example. Then check your answers at the end of the chapter.

Speed-reading

This activity consists of 20 500-word passages, each with ten comprehension questions. Students take a passage and begin reading when the teacher says 'go'. As soon as each person finishes reading, they look at their time and note it down. They then answer the comprehension questions and mark them themselves using an answer sheet. They record their reading speed and their comprehension score on their individual graphs. Their goal is to keep increasing reading speed while maintaining their comprehension score at around seven out of ten.

Fluency criteria	4/3/2	Speed-reading
Easy	The talk is repeated three times. A very familiar topic is chosen.	
Pressure to go faster	The time available for each delivery of the talk is reduced from 4 to 3 to 2 minutes.	
Quantity of practice	Total talking time is 9 minutes.	
Meaning-focused	There is a new partner for each delivery of the talk so that each delivery is focused on meaning.	

Deciding what vocabulary to focus on

Word frequency

Because the relative value of words depends on their frequency in a language, an important part of developing an effective vocabulary learning programme is selecting target vocabulary that provides the greatest benefits to the learners. It is worth recapping the key information about word frequency that we have covered in this book so far.

High-frequency words

As discussed in Chapter 1, words vary in their frequency of occurrence in a language. Some words occur very frequently and thus make up a large proportion of any given spoken or written text. The 800 items in the Essential Word List represent 75% of English if their inflections are also known. They include function words (for example, 'the', 'in', 'he', 'because'), but by far the largest number of them are content words (for example, 'make', 'time', 'slowly', 'happy'). These words should be learned very early on in a language course to provide a lexical foundation that will support further lexical and language development. There are also 2–3,000 word families which are common enough across spoken and written English to be considered high-frequency. If these word families are known, learners should know about 95% of the spoken words that they encounter. They are therefore words which should represent a key vocabulary learning goal and be learned by the end of a vocabulary learning programme. Where English is taught as a foreign language, or to adults as a second language, we would expect these words to be learned in three to four years, although research shows that learners often fail to fully learn the high-frequency words after many years of study (Webb & Chang, 2012a). This is in contrast to young native speakers of English, who normally know all of these high-frequency words before they begin school.

Mid-frequency words

The next most frequent group of words are called mid-frequency words, and there are around 6,000 of them. Knowing these words in addition to the high-frequency words (for a total of around 9,000 words) gives around 98% coverage of most texts. Native speakers can be expected to know these words by the time they are 11 or 12 years old. ESL learners, on the other hand, take years to learn these words, and many never achieve a vocabulary size this large. A 9,000-word vocabulary allows learners to read unsimplified texts such as novels and newspapers without encountering high densities of unknown words. Learners with this vocabulary size can also readily cope with university-level study, having only to master the technical vocabulary of the subjects that they are studying.

Low-frequency words

Beyond the 9,000 most frequent words of the language, there are tens of thousands of other words, some of which are frequent in specialized areas of discourse, but infrequent in general use of the language. The words in this very large group are considered low frequency.

Teacher's role

When planning a vocabulary learning programme, directing learners towards the high-frequency words should be the first priority, because these words will be needed no matter what use is made of the language. They should be the focus of both incidental and deliberate learning.

Once these high-frequency words are known, it is then important to consider the specific needs and goals of the learners. Learners studying a language for academic purposes (in preparation for studying specialist subjects through the medium of English) should move on to learning the general academic vocabulary of the language. The most useful list of academic words is the Academic Word List (Coxhead, 2000). The 570 word families in the AWL (for example, 'theory', 'environment', 'empirical', 'administer', 'flexible', 'formula', 'forthcoming') cover around 10% of the running words in a wide range of academic subjects. In other words, there is on average one word from the AWL in every line of an academic text.

Learners studying a language for academic purposes should also learn the technical vocabulary of the subjects they wish to study. Technical vocabulary is often ordered by frequency in the lists. (For technical word lists, see Chapter 1.) The vocabulary needs to be learned while studying the specific subject area, because the meanings of the words will be closely related to the content of the subject. Technical vocabulary can vary in size, from around 2,000 words in subject areas such as applied linguistics or economics to tens of thousands of words in subject areas such as botany and medicine.

Different types of vocabulary require different treatment from the teacher. High-frequency vocabulary deserves a great deal of attention and needs to be encountered many times across the four strands of the vocabulary learning programme. The teacher can play a very active role in helping learners to expand their knowledge of high-frequency words. Because these are a relatively small group of words, it is feasible for the teacher to give each word some degree of attention. Mid-frequency vocabulary, however, is a much larger group, so learners should be encouraged to take responsibility for learning these words by doing large amounts of reading, listening, and viewing, and by systematically learning unknown words using flashcards. The teacher's main role regarding mid-frequency and low-frequency vocabulary is to train the learners in the strategies of guessing from context, using flashcards, analysing word parts, using dictionaries, etc., and to spend time supporting students' use of resources for autonomous learning (see Chapters 5 and 7). Learners need to keep expanding their vocabulary, because the skills of listening, speaking, reading, and writing all depend on vocabulary size.

Measuring vocabulary knowledge

To develop a truly effective vocabulary learning programme, teachers should be aware of the vocabulary knowledge of their learners, as this will allow them to decide whether to focus on essential vocabulary, high-frequency words, mid-frequency words, or low-frequency words. Vocabulary tests allow teachers to find out where their learners are in their vocabulary development, and to use the test results to help them plan materials and activities more effectively. (See Chapter 9 for a more in-depth discussion of the vocabulary tests outlined below.)

Vocabulary Levels Test

Webb, Sasao, and Ballance's (2017) updated version of this test (see Chapter 1 and Appendix 2) focuses on the 5,000 most frequent words. Table 8.1 shows how the levels in the Vocabulary Levels Test correlate with the different types of vocabulary.

1,000 level	
2,000 level	high-frequency words
3,000 level	
4,000 level	mid-frequency words
5,000 level	

Table 8.1 Types of words measured by the Vocabulary Levels Test

At best, the Vocabulary Levels Test gives a rough indication of knowledge of the mid-frequency words; however, it does not enable us to work out how many of the mid-frequency words a learner still needs to learn.

Vocabulary Size Test

Several versions of this test are available, including some bilingual versions where the choices are written in the test takers' L1. This test attempts to give a measure of total receptive vocabulary size. The word lists that it is based on use a consistent definition of a word family, so we can be sure what the sample of words in the Vocabulary Size Test represents. A weakness of the Vocabulary Size Test is that it uses a multiple-choice format which allows learners to draw on a wide range of knowledge when answering an item, as well as guess from context.

Picture Vocabulary Size Test

This test is aimed at young pre-literate learners and measures knowledge of the 6,000 most frequent word families. It uses a multiple-choice format where the stem is spoken for the test taker, and the choices are pictures.

Summary

A well-balanced vocabulary learning programme is composed of the four strands of meaning-focused input, meaning-focused output, language-focused learning, and fluency development—each of which should be given roughly the same amount of time. These four strands provide different opportunities for learning: the meaning-focused input strand involves listening and reading, and depends on the learners getting input which is at the right level for them, i.e. where only a small proportion of the vocabulary is unknown; the meaning-focused output strand involves speaking and writing, and helps to convert learners' receptive knowledge into productive use; the language-focused learning strand involves deliberate learning, including the development of vocabulary learning strategies; the fluency development strand pushes learners to make the best use of what they already know, through the use of activities characterized by the absence of any unfamiliar language items and some pressure to perform at speed. Vocabulary can be classified as essential, high frequency, mid frequency, and low frequency; and words should generally be learned in this order of classification. Vocabulary tests can be used to find out what vocabulary needs to be learned next.

Questions for reflection

1 According to the principle of the four strands, fluency development should take up around a quarter of the time available on a vocabulary learning programme, at all levels of proficiency. Do you agree? Think of arguments for and against this allocation of time. For example, some argue that fluency development is best carried out only once learners have acquired substantial knowledge of the language.

2 How could you apply the principle of the four strands to a programme where the priority is predominantly on one skill area, for example academic reading?

3 Word frequency lists provide a source of information for sequencing the introduction of vocabulary in a programme. In your experience, what other sources of information could guide the choice and order of vocabulary covered in a programme?

Keys to activities

ACTIVITY 8.1   Balancing the four strands

Meaning-focused input	Meaning-focused output	Language-focused learning	Fluency development
extensive reading (60 min)	task-focused spoken interaction (50 min)	intensive reading (35 min)	speed-reading (15 min)
extensive listening (30 min)	writing with feedback (55 min)	dictation (15 min)	ten-minute writing (10 min)
		flashcards (20 min)	
	linked skills (20 min)		4/3/2 (10 min)
90 minutes	125 minutes	70 minutes	35 minutes

The key above shows that each strand is well represented, but that fluency development deserves more attention. To more effectively balance the four strands, it would be useful to reduce the amount of time devoted to the meaning-focused output strand by about 35 minutes and use that time to add another fluency development activity such as repeated viewing. The balance would still be slightly off, so language-focused learning and fluency development could receive slightly more attention in the following week.

ACTIVITY 8.2   **Analysing a fluency development activity**

Fluency criteria	Speed-reading
Easy	The reading texts and questions are written using a strictly controlled vocabulary that students already know.
Pressure to go faster	The reading is timed and the speed entered on a personal graph. Students know that the goal is to read faster.
Quantity of practice	Students read a 500-word text each time and read a total of 20 texts.
Meaning-focused	The comprehension questions ensure that comprehension is not sacrificed to speed. The questions are easy enough for students not to need to slow down to read for details.

Suggestions for further reading

Nation, I. S. P. (2007). The four strands. *Innovation in Language Learning and Teaching, 1(1)*, 1–12.

> This article introduces the four strands and presents arguments for including them in a course. These arguments are based on both research and common sense.

Nation, I. S. P., & Yamamoto, A. (2012). Applying the four strands to language learning. *International Journal of Innovation in English Language Teaching and Research, 1(2)*, 167–181.

> The four strands apply not only to classroom learning but also to self-directed learning, and this article explores how this can be done, using the example of a learner of Spanish as a foreign language. The article also shows how the four strands can be used to answer such basic curriculum design questions as: 'How much writing should learners do in a course?' 'Is it worth including grammar translation in a course?'

Nation, I. S. P. (2013a). *Learning vocabulary in another language, second edition.* Cambridge: Cambridge University Press.

Chapter 14 of this book looks in detail at the different ways in which vocabulary learning programmes might be developed.

9 RESOURCES FOR VOCABULARY LEARNING

Introduction

There are many resources available for vocabulary learning. The challenge for teachers and learners is identifying which resources are most useful. For example, if we search online for word lists, vocabulary tests, or digital flash-cards, we will come across many instances of each. Distinguishing between those that are based on sound research and those based on intuition is often difficult. The aim of this chapter is to highlight and give examples of key resources for vocabulary learning that are supported by research findings, expanding on information about resources that have been touched on earlier in this book, and providing guidelines for how these resources might best be selected and used.

Word lists

Perhaps the most useful resources for beginners and students who are learning a language for specific purposes are word lists. The value of word lists derives from the fact that they reveal the words which are most useful to learn. For example, lists of high-frequency words show the vocabulary that is most likely to be encountered, lists of technical words show the vocabulary that is frequent and unique to a specific area, and lists of academic vocabulary reveal the words that are common across academic disciplines. In essence, word lists provide a shortcut to improving performance in all skill areas, as learning a large proportion of the words that we are likely to encounter increases the potential for comprehension. Similarly, if we know the vocabulary that is most widely used in communication, then we are more likely to succeed in making ourselves understood. Word lists thus provide an efficient way to develop vocabulary knowledge and in turn improve the potential to understand and use the target language.

Criteria for selection

Word lists often do not provide much information about how they are best used. There are a couple of points that teachers and learners should bear in mind when using word lists.

Levels of frequency

Word lists are often made up of a very large number of items, so it is important to check whether there is any information available about how best to select items from a list for learning. For example, both the Essential Word List (Dang & Webb, 2016b), and the Academic Word List (Coxhead, 2000) include sets of words that are ordered according to their frequency. Learning the higher-frequency sets of words within the lists may provide the greatest benefit to learners.

Interference

Users should avoid selecting semantically related items such as synonyms or antonyms and lexical sets (for example, 'north', 'south', 'east', 'west'; days of the week; names of animals) to learn at the same time. This may seem counter-intuitive and contrary to how learners may be accustomed to encountering words in language materials. It may also be easier to teach semantically related words together. But ease of learning should be prioritized over ease of teaching. Learning semantically related words together increases the level of interference between words, making them more difficult to learn. The best way to avoid interference is to learn semantically related words separately at different times. If this is not an option, then it is best to learn semantically related words in sentences that help to distinguish between their meanings (Nation, 2000). For example, when learning the words 'hot' and 'cold', sentences such as 'Summer is hot.' and 'Winter is cold.' may help learners to link the word forms to the correct meanings. In contrast, learning words in sentences such as 'It is hot.', 'The room is hot.', 'He had a cold drink.' and 'I feel cold.' are unlikely to reduce the potential for interference, because in each of these examples, the words 'hot' and 'cold' could be substituted for each other.

ACTIVITY 9.1   **Examining interference**

1 Work with a partner to do a vocabulary learning experiment. Use the two sets of words below. Set A consists of pseudo-words with unrelated English meanings. Set B consists of pseudo-words with related English meanings.

Set A: kilme – lamp   ifpa – peach   blaikel – rain
       uchen – trumpet   nalo – camera   kawvas– sheet

Set B: ijos – lion   denga – beaver   esmek – giraffe
       pairnya – horse   uldon – possum   nakew – sheep

a Create two sets of flashcards with each pseudo-word on the front of a card and the meaning on the back.

b Use Set A. Show your partner the pseudo-words one by one and tell them the English meaning on the back. Then show them each English meaning one by one and ask them to say the pseudo-word. See how many times they need to go through all of the cards before they can correctly tell you all the pseudo-words when you present the English meanings in order.

c Repeat the process with Set B.

d Which set took longer to learn?

2 Consider your own language learning experiences. Can you think of any examples of words that you had difficulty learning due to interference between the forms and meanings of semantically related words? Make a list.

Lists of high-frequency words

There are tens of thousands of words to learn, and thousands of these may seem useful. Deciding which words to learn first is a challenging task that can end up simply being based on the words that are used in course materials. Lists of high-frequency or 'general service' vocabulary provide a principled starting point for vocabulary learning. They direct teachers and learners to the words that are used most often and have the greatest impact on language development. Table 9.1 summarizes information about four high-frequency word lists for English (Dang & Webb, 2016a, 2016b). (For more background on these word lists, see Chapter 1.)

Word list	Author(s)	Size	Coverage	Available from
The Essential Word List (EWL)	Dang & Webb (2016b)	800 most frequent lemmas broken down into 624 content words and one list of 176 function words	about 75% of spoken and written English	Stuart Webb's website (see Website references)

The British National Corpus and Corpus of Contemporary American English (BNC/ COCA) first and second 1,000 frequency level word lists	Nation (2012a)	2,000 most frequent word families broken down into two lists of 1,000 word families	about 87% of spoken English and 82% of written English	Paul Nation's website (see Website references)
The new-GSL	Brezina & Gablasova (2015)	2,494 most frequent lemmas	about 86% of spoken English and 81% of written English	provided as supplementary material for the article that describes its development in the journal *Applied Linguistics*
The General Service List (GSL)	West (1953)	2,168 most frequent word families broken down into two lists of around 1,000 word families	about 86% of spoken English and 81% of written English (= mean percentages)	Paul Nation's website (see Website references) and several other online sites

Table 9.1 Four lists of high-frequency words

Vocabulary targets for beginners

The most useful word list for beginners is the Essential Word List (see Appendix 1). The reason for differentiating between content and function words in this list is that, while many function words are particularly high in frequency, it is not easy to effectively teach these words before a reasonable number of content words are known. The list of content words is broken down into 12 sub-lists of 50 words and one sub-list of 24 words that are ordered according to their frequency within the list. Items in the first sub-list (for example, 'know', 'like', 'well') are more frequent than those in the second sub-list (for example, 'again', 'own', 'quite'), and these are more frequent than those in the third sub-list (for example, 'problem', 'love', 'name'), and so on.

Vocabulary targets for intermediate learners

If learners have mastered the words in the EWL, then the next vocabulary learning target should be to master the first and second 1,000 word frequency levels of the BNC/COCA lists or the new-GSL. As the BNC/COCA lists are made up of word families, with the underlying assumption being that users may be able to recognize word stems, their inflected forms, and their derived forms (for example, 'accept' – 'accepts', 'accepted', 'accepting' – 'acceptance', 'acceptable', 'unacceptable'), these lists are likely to be more suitable for intermediate and advanced learners than beginners. The most influential word list has been the GSL; however, some of the words in this list are out of date, and some modern words are not included, so its value is limited in comparison to the other more recent lists in Table 9.1.

Lists of academic words

Academic words are those which are high in frequency across a range of academic disciplines. A lack of knowledge of these terms may lead to comprehension problems for students engaging in academic discourse, and also the inappropriate use of colloquial language in academic speech and writing. Table 9.2 summarizes information about two useful lists of academic vocabulary. (For more background on these word lists, see Chapter 1.)

Word list	Author(s)	Size	Coverage	Available from
The Academic Word List (AWL)	Coxhead (2000)	570 most frequent academic word families broken down into ten sub-lists	about 10% of academic written text	Averil Coxhead's website (see Website references)
The Academic Vocabulary List (AVL)	Gardner & Davies (2014)	3,000 most frequent academic word families ordered according to their frequency	about 14% of academic written text	Mark Davies's Academic Vocabulary List website (see Website references)

Table 9.2 Two lists of academic words

Vocabulary targets for English for Academic Purposes (EAP) students
The AWL consists of words that are relatively low frequency in general English, but are high frequency in academic written text. The greatest value of this list comes from the fact that it is made up of teachable sets of academic words that are often unknown to non-native speakers of English planning to study at English-medium universities. The AVL is a much more comprehensive inventory of academic vocabulary than Coxhead's list. It accounts for a larger proportion of academic text (14%) than the AWL (10%). However, it is made up of 3,000 words, a proportion of which are higher-frequency words (for example, 'need', 'study', 'understand') that students are likely to already know before entering English-medium universities. Ordering the words in this list by frequency gives a useful indication of their relative values. Gardner and Davies provide two different versions of the lists and a great deal of information about each word, including its frequency in academic text and its degree of occurrence across academic disciplines. They also display the part of speech of the different members of each word family. One potential limitation of the AVL is that it may require some effort on the part of teachers and students in deciding which words to select for learning.

Lists of multi-word combinations

Lists of multi-word combinations highlight vocabulary that language learners often have difficulty using correctly in speech and writing and are useful supplements to lists of single-word items. Because most vocabulary is taught as individual words, these lists also raise awareness of frequently occurring sequences of words that deserve attention in language courses.

There are two such lists that are freely available. The **Phrasal Expressions List** (Martinez & Schmitt, 2012) identifies 505 frequently occurring multi-word combinations that have meanings which may not be transparent to language learners (for example, 'as well as', 'in fact', 'carry out'). It can be downloaded from Norbert Schmitt's homepage (see Website references).

The Academic Formulas List (Simpson-Vlach & Ellis, 2010) identifies common sequences of words in academic spoken text (for example, 'does that make sense', 'trying to figure out'), academic written text (for example, 'on the other hand', 'due to the fact that', 'it should be noted'), and both academic spoken and written text (for example, 'in terms of', 'at the same time', 'from the point of view'). Because one of the biggest challenges for language learners studying in English-medium universities is using words correctly in writing, lists of academic multi-word combinations are of great value for EAP programmes. The Academic Formulas List is available in the appendix of the article describing the creation of the list, which can be downloaded from Nick Ellis's website (see Website references).

Tests

Tests of vocabulary are an important resource for teachers and learners. They have four key functions:

1 Tests can be used as diagnostic tools to identify which words are unknown to learners, as well as how skilful learners are at learning vocabulary. This is particularly important because in a language course, students should both be learning the words with the greatest value and improving their vocabulary learning skills.
2 Tests show where learners are in their vocabulary learning progress.
3 Tests have the potential to motivate learning, because they demonstrate the importance that is placed on vocabulary in a language course.
4 Tests allow teachers to measure the amount of vocabulary that is learned over a period of time, and this in turn helps them to evaluate the effectiveness of the programme for vocabulary learning.

In this section, we will compare several established tests that are typically used to fulfil the first and second functions noted above.

Vocabulary Levels Test

In Chapters 1 and 8, we looked at how vocabulary knowledge can be measured using the Vocabulary Levels Test (Nation, 1983; Schmitt, Schmitt, & Clapham, 2001; Webb, Sasao, & Ballance, 2017). Earlier versions of the Vocabulary Levels Test developed by Nation (1983) and Schmitt, Schmitt, and Clapham (2001) were based on word lists created in pre-computer days that are not as good as those now available. Webb, Sasao, and Balance's recent version is based on the BNC/COCA lists (Nation, 2012a), and is therefore more likely to reflect knowledge of current vocabulary. The Vocabulary Levels Test is the most important type of vocabulary test, providing a reliable measure of knowledge of the 5,000 most frequent words. It measures knowledge by level, using 30 items in ten sets of three questions (see Table 9.3 for an example). The test taker's task is to match words with short definitions by ticking the correct box.

	game	island	mouth	film	song	yard
land with water all around it		✓				
part of your body used for eating and talking			✓			
piece of music					✓	

Table 9.3 Example of a question set from the Vocabulary Levels Test

A key point to note is that the Vocabulary Levels Test does not measure knowledge of any words beyond the fifth 1,000 word frequency level, which means it is unlikely to accurately assess vocabulary size, as some words from levels containing less frequent words are often known, even by beginners. Nevertheless, the test does have a sufficient number of items at each level to provide a valid and reliable evaluation for each part of the test, so individual levels can be used on their own. Most importantly, the test reveals to teachers and learners which words should be focused on during learning.

See Appendix 2 for Webb, Sasao, and Ballance's (2017) updated version of the test. This version is also freely available for download on Stuart Webb's website. Earlier versions of the test are available on Norbert Schmitt's website and Tom Cobb's Compleat Lexical Tutor website (see Website references).

ACTIVITY 9.2   Vocabulary Levels Test

Go to Appendix 2 and take the Vocabulary Levels Test to become familiar with it. What are the strengths and weaknesses of the test, in your opinion?

Vocabulary Size Test

The purpose of the Vocabulary Size Test (Nation & Beglar, 2007; Coxhead, Nation, & Sim, 2015) is different from that of the Vocabulary Levels Test. While the latter was designed to determine the extent of knowledge of particular sets of words, the Vocabulary Size Test provides a measurement that may indicate the extent of L1 and L2 lexical development, as well as the extent to which L2 learners have progressed in relation to their L1 vocabulary size. The two tests should not be confused, because neither one provides a valid and reliable measurement beyond its intended purpose.

In its original form (Nation & Beglar, 2007), the Vocabulary Size Test was designed to measure knowledge of the 14,000 most frequent word families in English. Because native speakers of English tend to have larger vocabulary sizes than this, it was solely intended to measure the vocabulary size of non-native speakers of English. The test has 14 ten-item sections, with a total of 140 questions. Each of the sections is made up of items that evaluate knowledge of words at each 1,000 word frequency level (i.e. 1,000, 2,000, 3,000, etc.). However, in contrast to the 30-item level-by-level testing which characterizes the Vocabulary Levels Test (Schmitt, Schmitt, & Clapham, 2001), the Vocabulary Size Test does not provide a valid and reliable measurement for each level but, rather, for the 14,000 most frequent word families as a whole. As such, the complete test should be administered and the overall score used, rather than scores for any individual sections. Table 9.4 shows examples from Section 1 of the test. Test takers circle the letter (a–d) with the closest meaning to the key word in the question.

1 see: They <saw> it.	2 time: They have a lot of <time>.	3 period: It was a difficult <period>.
a money b time c looked at it d friends	a question b waited for it c hours d book	a closed it tightly b food c thing to do d started it up

Table 9.4 Example of questions from Section 1 of the Vocabulary Size Test

In an updated version (Coxhead, Nation, & Sim, 2015), the Vocabulary Size Test was expanded to measure knowledge of the 20,000 most frequent word families. This version is made up of 100 randomly sequenced items, five of which are from each of the 20 1,000 word frequency levels. The updated version of the test may provide an accurate measure of both L1 and L2 vocabulary size.

Both the original and the updated versions of the test use a monolingual format—that is, the target words and definitions are both in English. However, there are also several bilingual versions of the original test where the target words are in English and the definitions are in the test taker's L1. Bilingual versions of the test are currently freely available in a number of languages, including Gujarati, Korean, Japanese, Mandarin, Russian, and Vietnamese. The different versions of the test, as well as an explanation of the process for creating the tests, instructions, and answer sheets for the updated version, are available on Paul Nation's website. A version of the original Vocabulary Size Test is also available on the Compleat Lexical Tutor website and at vocabularysize.com. (See Website references.)

Picture Vocabulary Size Test

Most tests of vocabulary knowledge require test takers to have reached a certain level of vocabulary knowledge that allows them to understand the written forms of the words in the questions and answers. This makes them inappropriate for children. The Picture Vocabulary Size Test (Nation & Anthony, 2016) is designed specifically for pre-literate children, who may lack knowledge of the written form of words but have knowledge of their spoken form. The test measures receptive knowledge of the 6,000 most frequent word families. Figure 9.1 shows an example question from the test.

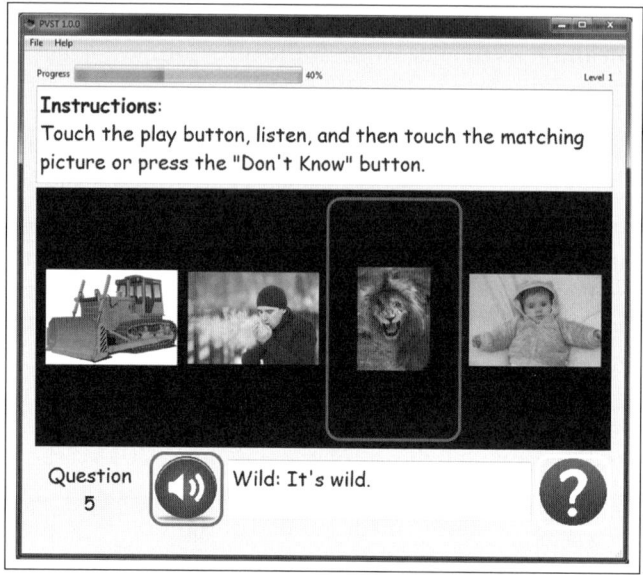

Figure 9.1 Example of a question from the Picture Vocabulary Size Test

As Figure 9.1 shows, test takers are presented with four pictures. They hear a target word by itself and in a short sentence, then select the picture that conveys the closest meaning. The complete test is made up of 96 items and takes about 15–20 minutes to complete. The test is administered one to one to ensure that the test format and items are clearly understood and that learners remain on-task during the whole test. The total scores are multiplied by 62.5 to calculate knowledge of the 6,000 word families.

The test is available for download from Laurence Anthony's website (see Website references).

Guessing from Context Test

The Guessing from Context Test (Sasao, 2013) measures the ability to successfully infer the meanings of unknown words encountered in context. This is very useful, because guessing from context is the most common strategy used in autonomous vocabulary learning (de Bot, Paribakht, & Wesche, 1997; Hulstijn, 1992; Paribakht & Wesche, 1999). The test measures learners' skill in using three different aspects of the strategy:

1 Can they recognize the parts of speech of unknown words?
2 Can they identify the contextual information that can be used to successfully infer the meanings of unknown words?
3 Can they successfully recognize the correct meanings of unknown words?

By isolating these different aspects of the guessing from context strategy, the test provides a clearer picture of where learners need to improve.

The test is made up of three sections. In each section, test takers read 20 short passages and answer 20 questions. The target words in all sections of the test are substituted by pseudo-words, to ensure that even advanced learners will need to use the guessing from context strategy. The first section measures whether or not test takers can recognize the part of speech of a target word in a sentence. Table 9.5 shows an example. Test takers circle the part of speech of the pseudo-word 'turmilted'. The correct response is (2).

17 He was brought back to the building on June 9th, but the following day he **turmilted** again and this time was away for 94 days. (1) noun (2) verb (3) adjective (4) adverb

Table 9.5 Example of a question from Section 1 of the Guessing from Context Test

The second section measures whether test takers can identify the contextual clue that may help them to successfully guess the meaning of the target word. Table 9.6 shows an example. Test takers circle the word or phrase that helps them to work out the meaning of the pseudo-word 'turmilted'. The correct response is (1).

[Passage 17] He was locked up for having injured her. On May 23rd, he ran away for 17 days. He was found and caught when he was in a car taken from another person. He was brought back to the building on June 9th, but the following day he **turmilted** again and this time was away for 94 days. (1) ran away (2) car (3) for 94 days

Table 9.6 Example of a question from Section 2 of the Guessing from Context Test

The final section of the test involves reading the same passages as those in Section 2 and selecting the meanings of the unknown words. Table 9.7 shows an example. Test takers circle the closest meaning of the word. The correct response is (1), because it is closest in meaning to the target word (substituted by the pseudo-word 'turmilted' in previous sections of the test).

[Passage 17] (1) escape (2) travel (3) pay

Table 9.7 Example of a question from Section 3 of the Guessing from Context Test

The scores for each section are more important than the score for the test as a whole, because the section scores indicate how effective test takers are in each aspect of the guessing from context strategy. Test takers can then focus their efforts on the aspect(s) of the strategy that they need to improve on. This may help learners to develop their ability to successfully infer unknown words that are encountered in future. The Guessing from Context Test is freely available for download on Yosuke Sasao's website, together with information about the test, instructions, and an answer key (see Website references).

Word Part Levels Test

As we saw in Chapter 7, the Word Part Levels Test provides a valid and reliable measurement of affix knowledge at three levels of difficulty: beginner, intermediate, and advanced (Sasao & Webb, 2017). It is very useful to measure knowledge of affixes, because they feature in a large number of words, so determining how well affixes are known may provide some indication of the ease or difficulty that learners will have in inferring the meaning of unknown words they encounter. The test also provides a logical sequence in which to learn affixes: it covers 118 common affixes and presents them according to their difficulty in the three levels. Each level covers a teachable number of affixes for a course (about 40), and there is no need for learners to take subsequent levels of the text if they have not yet mastered the lower levels.

The Word Part Levels Test measures three components of affix knowledge (form, meaning, and use) in separate sections. We looked at some examples in Chapter 7; here we examine a few more. Section 1 of the test measures whether or not the written form of an affix is known. Four options are presented to test takers, and their task is to select the only one that is an affix. Table 9.8 shows an example. The answers are *dis-* and *micro-* (prefixes); *-ful* and *-ness* (suffixes).

1	(1)	sal-	(2)	cau-	(3)	lin-	(4)	dis-
2	(1)	micro-	(2)	cerem-	(3)	sheph-	(4)	pecul-
3	(1)	-rse	(2)	-ack	(3)	-ful	(4)	-uin
4	(1)	-onse	(2)	-inge	(3)	-ound	(4)	-ness

Table 9.8 Example of prefix and suffix questions from Section 1 of the Word Part Levels Test

Section 2 measures whether or not the meaning of an affix is known. Test takers are presented with an affix, two words containing that affix, and four options. Their task is to select the option that conveys the meaning of the affix. Table 9.9 shows an example. The answers are *mono-*: one, *dis-*: not, *-ess*: female, and *-able*: can be.

1 mono- (<u>mono</u>tone; <u>mono</u>culture)	3 -ess (act<u>ress</u>; princ<u>ess</u>)
(1) person/thing	(1) female
(2) not	(2) small
(3) one	(3) not
(4) into another state/place	(4) many
2 dis- (<u>dis</u>appear; <u>dis</u>order)	4 -able (accept<u>able</u>; predict<u>able</u>)
(1) not	(1) person
(2) person	(2) not
(3) new	(3) can be
(4) main	(4) one

Table 9.9 Example of questions from Section 2 of the Word Part Levels Test

Adding certain affixes to words has the function of changing their part of speech. Section 3 measures whether or not test takers can recognize the grammatical function of an affix. Test takers are presented with an affix, two example words, and four options: noun, verb, adjective, and adverb. The test taker's task is to select the part of speech of the example words. Table 9.10 shows an example. The answers are that 'development' and 'manage-ment' are nouns, and that 'awareness' and 'illness' are also nouns.

1 -ment (develop<u>ment</u>; manage<u>ment</u>)	2 -ness (aware<u>ness</u>; ill<u>ness</u>)
(1) Noun	(1) Noun
(2) Verb	(2) Verb
(3) Adjective	(3) Adjective
(4) Adverb	(4) Adverb

Table 9.10 Example of questions from Section 3 of the Word Part Levels Test

The scores for each section are more important than the scores for the test as a whole, because learners may have varying degrees of knowledge for each of the three components. If test takers have strong knowledge of one component but are weak in others, then they can adjust the focus of their learning accordingly. Improving knowledge of affixes can help learn-ers to more effectively learn unknown words that contain these affixes in future. The Word Part Levels Test is freely available for download on Yosuke Sasao's website, together with instructions, an explanation of the test, and answer keys (see Website references). The Intermediate level is provided in Appendix 4.

Flashcards

A very effective and efficient method of learning the form–meaning connection of words is using flashcards (see Chapter 5 for an explanation of using flashcards and the key features that contribute to learning). In the most basic use of flashcards, learners make a set of flashcards by writing a target word on one side of each card and the definition or translation on the other side. Sets of as many as 100 flashcards take up little space and can be carried around and used whenever the opportunity arises.

The popularity of computers and mobile devices has led to the development of a wide range of flashcard software. Although the quality varies considerably (Nakata, 2011), such software has the following advantages over using traditional flashcards:

1 Flashcard software usually comes with existing sets of target vocabulary, as well as the option to create your own flashcards.
2 Target vocabulary often includes both individual words and multi-word combinations.
3 The software is usually designed around sound research findings, and some applications include discussion of key criteria for learning.
4 Flashcards may include audio support that helps users to recognize both the spoken and written forms of the target vocabulary.
5 The software can schedule study sessions to space learning effectively.
6 The software can keep track of learning, making users more aware of their progress.
7 Flashcard software often supports the learning of more than one language.

With regular improvements in the functionality, availability, and cost of flashcard software, it is difficult to recommend one in particular. At present, two free applications, *Anki* and *Flashcards+*, appear to be quite promising. *Anki* can be used on most desktop and mobile operating systems, and the flashcards can be synchronized across computers and mobile devices. Sets of flashcards can be created and shared among users, and the application includes many of the useful features listed above. *Flashcards+* has similar features to *Anki*. It also allows users to share their flashcards, providing a large inventory of existing flashcards, and includes many useful features to help make learning more efficient.

The disadvantages of digital flashcards are few. However, learners should be aware of the following:

1 The target vocabulary may not necessarily be presented according to the relative value of words or the needs of the user. However, the option to create flashcards, which is a common feature, does allow users to select and sequence words from established word lists.

2 The cost varies, and the price does not necessarily indicate a better quality application. Of the nine applications that Tatsuya Nakata (2011) evaluated, the one with the best evaluation at that time was free.

It is also important to remember that learning with flashcards is only one step in the vocabulary learning process. The objective of the activity is to link the form of a word to its meaning. Although there is potential to transfer other aspects of word knowledge (grammatical functions, collocations) to newly learned target words when there is overlap in knowledge between L1 and L2 words (Webb, 2007b), learners are likely to be limited in the degree to which they can effectively use these target words (Webb, 2009b). Flashcards should be supplemented with plenty of meaning-focused input that includes the target words to provide models for how these words are used, and meaning-focused output that provides opportunities to use them.

ACTIVITY 9.3   Assessing a flashcard app

Download a freely available flashcard application on your computer or mobile device and select a set of flashcards for a language that you do not know. Spend 15 minutes each day for two weeks learning your flashcards. How many words did you learn? What was your success rate? What was your learning rate (number of words per hour)?

Corpora and concordancers

As we saw in Chapter 1, a corpus is a collection of texts that is created to be representative of an aspect of a language. For example, there are corpora that are based on British English (for example, the BNC: the British National Corpus), American English (for example, the COCA: the **Corpus of Contemporary American English**), academic written English (for example, the academic sections of the BNC and COCA), academic spoken English (for example, BASE: British Academic Spoken English Corpus), international English (for example, ICE: International Corpus of English), and learner English. (A list of the many different learner corpora is available at the Center for English Corpus Linguistics at Université Catholique de Louvain website; see Website references.) A large number of corpora have also been created to represent the language of academic disciplines (for example, engineering, medicine, science) and discourse types such as films, television, and graded readers. However, these more narrowly defined corpora are not normally freely available.

A concordancer is a type of software that generates a concordance of a text or corpus—that is, it produces a list of all the occurrences of keywords (or key phrases) in the text. It might best be described as a search engine that presents the results of the search in a format that reveals a range of information about how the keyword is used. Typically, users type in the keyword and select how they want the concordance to be presented. Figure 9.2 (see pages 212–213) shows two examples in the most common format, where the key word is presented in context and aligned in a column down the middle of the screen.

The order of occurrences is usually alphabetical and sorted according to the words on the left or right of the keyword; so in Figure 9.2, for example, the concordance is sorted according to the first (bold) word to the left of the keyword 'effect'. (It could alternatively be sorted according to the second or third word to the left or right, etc.) This allows users to see which words are commonly used before or after the keyword. Only a small portion of the surrounding text is shown in the concordance, but clicking on the keyword usually presents users with an expanded context.

The information from concordancers is most appropriate to use with intermediate and advanced learners, to reveal how words are used in speech and writing. Comparisons between keywords may raise awareness of differences in how words are used. The centred alignment of keywords in a column and the emboldening or underlining of neighbouring words also makes concordancers particularly useful for helping users to notice collocations. In the two examples in Figure 9.2, we can see that the article 'an' and adjectives such as 'adverse' and 'apparent' are particularly common before 'effect', while 'can', 'could', and adverbs such as 'adversely' and 'immediately' are more likely to be used immediately before 'affect'. The full list of 251 occurrences for 'effect' reveals that the three most common words preceding it are 'the' (61 occurrences), 'in' (14 occurrences), and 'no' (seven occurrences). In contrast, the most frequently used words before the 52 occurrences of 'affect' are 'not' (six occurrences), 'which' (six occurrences), and 'adversely' (five occurrences). Looking at the words further to the left of the keywords, as well as those further to the right, provides additional useful information.

Concordancers provide a useful indication of keyword frequency, because they list all occurrences of the word in a particular text or corpus. In our comparison of 'effect' and 'affect', we have seen that 'effect' is about five times more frequent in that corpus. Of course, it is important to be aware that results from concordances vary according to the corpora from which the concordance is derived. For example, 'effect' and 'affect' are far less frequent in a million-word spoken section of the British National Corpus (72 and 28 occurrences, respectively) than they are in a million-word written section of that corpus.

Several sites provide online concordancers that are free and easy to use. Three in particular are worth noting (see Website references):

- Tom Cobb's Compleat Lexical Tutor site includes a concordancer that allows users to search for the occurrences of keywords in many different corpora.
- Mark Davies's Brigham Young University corpus site allows users to generate concordances of keywords in many different corpora.
- The *Word Neighbors* concordancer has a slightly different format from the others. It was developed at The Hong Kong University of Science and Technology, and lists the frequency of different forms of the keyword in the corpus (for example, 'effect': 49,916 occurrences, 'effective': 15,717 occurrences, 'effectively': 6,744 occurrences, 'effected': 2,316 occurrences), or the keyword plus words to the right or left (for example, 'the effect of': 14,095 occurrences, 'adverse effect on': 8,173 occurrences, 'the effect that': 1,393 occurrences). It also links all of these forms to an online dictionary.

ACTIVITY 9.4   Concordancers

Using one of the concordancers listed above, look up three words that your students have difficulty using in speech or writing. Do multiple searches for each keyword and sort the results according to the words on either side of the keyword. What did you learn about how each word is used that might be useful for your students to know?

Lexical profilers

A **lexical profiler** is a piece of software used to reveal information about the words in a text. These are most often used to determine the frequency levels of words that are found within a text, or a range of texts, and to evaluate the suitability of language learning materials. They are quite easy to use, and within a few seconds provide three types of useful information:

1 the proportion of words at each frequency level in a text
2 a list of all the words in the text that occur at each frequency level
3 the number of occurrences of each word in the text.

There are several freely available lexical profilers. Nation and Heatley's RANGE software (2002) and Laurence Anthony's *AntWordProfiler* are the best tools for analysing large amounts of text. Perhaps the easiest lexical profiler to use for teaching and learning purposes is *VocabProfile*, which can be found on Tom Cobb's Compleat Lexical Tutor site. (See Website references for links to these lexical profilers.)

ng stress on stimulates treats stimulation as an **additional** effect of hunger, strong stress on man treats man as an addi

th forces inherent in our economy but rather to the **adverse** effect of inappropriate economic policies combined with retr

ce of obscurity than in the breach. This creates an **amusing** effect because its position in a sentence seems to make it a

ghettos, but only to assert that these horrors have had **an** effect on the nerves of people who did not experience them,

agician's gesture, with a piquant turn of harmony giving **an** effect of strangeness. Another theme, sinuously chromatic, a

a bleak motif with barren octaves creating a rather **ancient** effect: @ An imaginative storyteller, Pimen takes on the cha

re certain tax attributes of a corporation whose nature **and** effect might depend on the facts of the particular reorganiz

s a situation in which he can perceive no visible cause **and** effect sequence, he should be alert to intuition and unconsc

ore than unity in the nitrogen dissociation region. **Another** effect discovered is the large coefficient of thermal diffus

wly. Bisque fire to cone 08 with lid on jar. For an **antique** effect on jars, brush Creek-Turn brown toner on bisque ware

e who are merely paid employees, is, therefore, the **baneful** effect on the caliber of the teaching itself. This is a prob

by those immediately affected. This will have a **beneficial** effect by expediting public business; it will also correct s

lism, this disc displays London's new technique to the **best** effect. All of the jackets carry a fairly technical and deta

iology and medicine stated: "The question of the **biological** effect ... of [radiation] doses is not considered" herein. O

n old William Billings tune with rousing woodwind and **brass** effect. #@ All these- potboilers or no- provided a welcome

ptions that man can master the principles of this **cause-and-** effect universe and that such mastery will necessarily bette

and pungent as it might in a cave deprived of the **cleansing** effect of the sun's rays. She had the feeling that, under th

s material does he tamper with it to improve its **commercial** effect or does he leave it pure? Is the writer propagandisti

makers qualified persons who are cognizant of the **corrosive** effect of crisis upon personal relationships and are also ab

as a tightly knit quality that makes for maximum **cumulative** effect. The Presto ma non assai of the first trio of the sch

```
ample caused Krim and his friends to put on "Englishy airs, affect all sorts of impressive scholarship and social-regist
e drop conforms to the force field, it does not appreciably affect the distribution of forces in the fluid. These are re
n place", explains Dr. Brodie. "Moving one or two teeth can affect the whole system, and an ill-conceived plan of treatm
ree hours. TO WHAT extent and in what ways did Christianity affect the United States of America in the nineteenth centur
ade up her mind to do. She couldn't see how her death could affect Maude. She couldn't see any reason why Maude would at
was scoffed at; now we know that family characteristics do  affect tooth formation to a large extent", he says. "Fortuna
: the Thank-Heaven-We're-not-Involved viewpoint, It Doesn't affect Us! Southern Liberals (there are a good many) - especi
t water"? He looked piously to heaven and said, "Beer don't affect the tissues none", and the ingenious hypocrisy of thi
Prize in medicine and physiology for discovering how genes  affect heredity by controlling cell chemistry (TIME, Cover,
are well separated and so the position of one could hardly  affect the position of another, and also since ordered "up"
ociated? Considered as an independent variable, how does it affect behavior in various sectors of life? Until such work
projection. American and free-world policies can marginally affect the pace of transition; but basically that pace depen
nnected with justice or morality save as these values might affect international relations. No longer did the sovereign
slight cellular core that would reduce costs yet would not  affect physical properties of the end product to any great e
were only this the story would be banal. Why does the story affect us? How does the rocking exert its uncanny effect upo
rly enter commerce or the operations of which substantially affect commerce, for the purpose of gathering data and infor
iodide concentration in the thyroid. It does not appear to  affect the iodinating mechanism as such. The other group of
do not still exist? that the Court order does not unequally affect the Southern region? Who will deny that in a vast por
m and a general exchange of views on the major issues which affect the relationships between the two countries". @ #THE
ed this regrettable action". The reduction in expenses will affect employees in the thirteen states in which the B. + O.
```

Figure 9.2 Concordances for keywords 'effect' and 'affect' in a one million-word written section of the British National Corpus using the online concordancer at Compleat Lexical Tutor

Let us consider the benefits of using a lexical profiler by analysing the short text about eating habits in Materials extract 9.1. This is from a coursebook in the series *Issues for Today*, which is designed to improve L2 reading skills. The analysis was carried out using *VocabProfile* and the BNC/COCA-25 lists (Nation, 2012a).

Changing lifestyles and new eating habits

Americans today have different eating habits than they had in the past. There is a wide selection of food available. They have a broader knowledge of nutrition, so they buy more fresh fruit and vegetables than ever before. At the same time, Americans purchase increasing quantities of sweets, snacks, and sodas.

Statistics show that the way people live determines the way they eat. American lifestyles have changed. They now include growing numbers of people who live alone, single parents and children, and double-income families. These changing lifestyles are responsible for the increasing number of people who must rush meals or sometimes skip them altogether. Many Americans have less time than ever before to spend preparing food. Partly as a consequence of this limited time, more than 90% of all American homes now have microwave ovens. Moreover, Americans eat out nearly four times a week on the average.

It is easy to study the amounts and kinds of food that people consume. The United States Department of Agriculture (USDA) and the food industry—growers, processors, marketers, and restaurateurs—compile sales statistics and keep accurate records. This information not only tells us what people are eating, but also tells us about the changes in attitudes and tastes. Red meat, which used to be the most popular choice for dinner, is no longer an American favorite. Instead, chicken, turkey, and fish have become more popular. Sales of these foods have greatly increased in recent years. This is probably a result of the awareness of the dangers of eating food that contains high levels of cholesterol, or animal fat. Doctors believe that cholesterol is a threat to human health.

According to a recent survey, Americans also change their eating patterns to meet the needs of different situations. They have certain ideas about which foods will increase their athletic ability, help them lose weight, make them alert for business meetings, or feel more romantic. For example, Americans choose pasta, fruit, and vegetables, which supply them with carbohydrates, to give them strength for physical activity, such as sports. Adults choose foods rich in fiber, such as bread and cereal, for breakfast, and salads for lunch to prepare them for business appointments. For romantic dinners, however, Americans choose shrimp and lobster. While many of these ideas are based on nutritional facts, some are not.

Americans' awareness of nutrition, along with their changing tastes and needs, leads them to consume a wide variety of foods—foods for health, for fun, and simply for good taste.

Materials extract 9.1 Excerpt from L. C. Smith and N. N. Mare, *Reading for Today 3: Issues for Today* (4th ed.), © 2011, 2004, 1995 Heinle/ELT, a part of Cengage Learning, Inc., reprinted by permission. www.cengage.com/permissions.

Identifying the level of difficulty of a text

By analysing different texts, teachers can identify which ones might be more difficult for learners to understand. Profiling a text against a particular word list enables you to find out how many words in a text also appear in that list. Table 9.11 shows the lexical profile of the above text. The 'Tokens (%)' column indicates that 77.14% of the words are the 1,000 most frequent words (K–1 Words) in the BNC/COCA lists, and 11.67% the second 1,000 most frequent (K–2 Words). The 'Cumul. token %' column (= cumulative coverage of tokens) tells us that, if learners know the 5,000 most frequent words, they will understand more than 95% of the words in the text.

Freq. Level	Families (%)	Types (%)	Tokens (%)	Cumul. token %
K–1 Words :	140 (67.31)	159 (67.66)	324 (77.14)	77.14
K–2 Words :	41 (19.71)	43 (18.30)	49 (11.67)	88.81
K–3 Words :	13 (6.25)	13 (5.53)	15 (3.57)	92.38
K–4 Words :	5 (2.40)	6 (2.55)	8 (1.90)	94.28
K–5 Words :	5 (2.40)	5 (2.13)	5 (1.19)	95.47
K–6 Words :	2 (0.96)	2 (0.85)	2 (0.48)	95.95
K–7 Words :				
K–8 Words :				
K–9 Words :				
K–10 Words :				
K–11 Words :	1 (0.48)	1 (0.43)	1 (0.24)	96.19
K–12 Words :				
K–13 Words :				
K–14 Words :				
K–15 Words :	1 (0.48)	1 (0.43)	1 (0.24)	96.43
...				
K–25 Words :				
Off-List:	??	5 (2.13)	15 (3.57)	100.00
Total (unrounded)	208+?	235 (100)	420 (100)	≈100.00

Table 9.11 Lexical profile of 'Changing lifestyles and new eating habits' (Smith & Mare, 2011)

Identifying challenging vocabulary in a text

Lexical profiling can identify which words in a text learners may find challenging, based on their vocabulary level. For example, if the Vocabulary Levels Test scores indicate that learners have only mastered the 3,000 most frequent words, then identifying words in the text beyond this level may help to focus the vocabulary teaching. In the example text above, scrolling down to additional colour-coded information in the *VocabProfile* output reveals that certain words fall outside the 3,000 most frequent word families; this makes them lower-frequency words which might be unknown to the learners (for example, 'cholesterol', 'nutrition', 'carbohydrates', 'shrimp', 'lifestyles', 'turkey').

Identifying words that are important for understanding a text

Lexical profiling can also be used to identify the number of occurrences of word types or word families in a text. This information is useful for a number of reasons:

- It signals the importance of the word for understanding the text; words that occur more often are likely to be of greater value for comprehension than those which occur only once. For example, the numbers in square brackets beside the lower-frequency words identified above indicate the number of times each of these words is found in the text: 'cholesterol' [2], 'nutrition' [2], 'carbohydrates' [1], 'shrimp' [1], 'lifestyles' [3], 'turkey' [1].
- It may indicate whether the words might be learned incidentally through reading or listening to the text, as words which occur more often are more likely to be learned to some degree than those which are only encountered once.
- It can help teachers to adapt texts to make them more suitable for their students. For example, teachers could identify low-frequency words which occur only once and replace them with known words to simplify the text and improve comprehensibility.
- It can help teachers to select or discard potential materials. To teach vocabulary effectively, we should aim to provide repeated encounters with the target words in speech and written text over an extended period of time. It can be very challenging to find multiple texts that include target vocabulary. But some lexical profilers allow us to quickly analyse as many as 32 texts at one time and see the extent to which target words occur between the texts.

Identifying the value of individual words

Knowing the frequency level of words is useful for learners, because it reveals the relative value of the words that they encounter. Because learners may not be able to recognize the relative value of unknown words, they may spend as much time trying to learn low-frequency words as high-frequency words. Lexical profilers can be used by the teacher to quickly identify the frequency level of individual words, and learners can be trained to do the same, to support autonomous learning.

ACTIVITY 9.5   **Using a lexical profiler**

Investigate the frequency levels of the following words using the online lexical profiler *VocabProfile* and the BNC-COCA-25 word lists (see Website references):

> abroad   adult   aerobics   afraid   aggressor   ambience
> ambiguous   antagonize   appetite   asteroid

What is the frequency level of each word? Check your answers at the end of the chapter.

Resources for increasing incidental vocabulary learning

As this book has argued in earlier chapters, receiving large amounts of L2 input is vital for lexical development. There is much to be learned about each word, and only a fraction of that knowledge is likely to be gained through a single deliberate learning exercise. Besides, there is insufficient classroom time available for students to develop the vocabulary knowledge necessary to understand more challenging sources of input such as newspapers and novels without support. Encountering taught words in speech and writing helps to consolidate vocabulary knowledge and expand on earlier gains. Moreover, learning unknown words incidentally through reading and listening is considered to be the greatest source of L1 vocabulary growth. If learners are to attain a native-like vocabulary size, then incidental vocabulary learning through encountering large amounts of meaning-focused input is likely to play a large role in getting there. In the sections that follow, we examine a range of resources which can be used to increase incidental vocabulary learning.

Written input

There is a vast quantity of English language written input available online. Most of this has been written for native speakers of English, but while it might be at an inappropriate level for extensive reading tasks, it may be appropriate for intensive reading. Selection of texts should be based on learners' needs, interests, and goals. Lexical profilers can help teachers to select texts and indicate how they might best be modified for students' use.

Useful sites for selecting glossed and simplified digital texts for intensive reading purposes are the BBC Learning English website and the Voice of America Learning English website (see Website references).

Extensive reading serves as a means of allowing learners to encounter a greater amount of input than through intensive reading. Graded extensive reading materials are written using a controlled vocabulary, with the number of words increasing level by level, allowing learners to select appropriate texts that they can read quickly without support. By reading such texts, there is greater potential for learners to re-encounter vocabulary (Webb & Macalister, 2013) and further develop their lexical knowledge.

Many websites provide written materials for English language learners of varying levels. However, the extent to which these materials are appropriate for extensive reading is open to question, as they are often based on intuition rather than any methodological framework. There are vast collections of graded readers available from commercial ELT publishers, in both print and digital format. There are also a small number of digital readers that are freely available online. The Compleat Lexical Tutor website includes 11 graded readers, under the resource-assisted reading link, and Paul Nation's website also includes a number of graded readers (see Website references). There are two graded readers that are at a beginner and an intermediate level, and 12 mid-frequency readers that were written for learners at three stages of vocabulary development and designed to help bridge the gap between graded reading series and texts written for native speakers. They are simplified adaptations of classic novels such as *Wuthering Heights* and *A Christmas Carol*, with many of the lowest-frequency words replaced with higher-frequency alternatives. Each book has three versions, and readers can select the one that is at the most appropriate level. For the first level, 98% of the text is made up of words from the 4,000 most frequent word families. For the second and third levels, a similar proportion of the text is made up of words from the 6,000 and 8,000 most frequent word families respectively.

The Extensive Reading Foundation provides a list of the many graded readers on their website, as well as information on award-winning texts (see Website references). It includes a list of resources for extensive reading, and a guide to extensive reading that explains its value and offers guidance on how to incorporate it into a learning programme.

Spoken input

Spoken input is necessary to develop knowledge of the spoken forms of words and model how words are used in speech. As we discussed in Chapter 6, spoken input is often lacking in the foreign language learning context, so it is particularly important to know what resources are available to help facilitate incidental learning through spoken input. There are several useful sources of spoken input: television programmes, films, aural versions of graded readers, and online videos. These are suitable to use for extensive listening and viewing both inside and outside the classroom.

Television

The benefits of incidental learning via television have been explained in detail earlier in the book (see Chapter 7). Research has consistently shown that it is possible to learn vocabulary incidentally through watching television and online videos (Koolstra & Beentjes, 1999; Neuman & Koskinen, 1992; Rice & Woodsmall, 1988). Unknown words can be learned by watching television, knowledge of partially known words is likely to be enhanced, and learners may improve their recognition of the spoken forms of words. Moreover, regular L2 television viewing has been shown to contribute to incidental vocabulary learning at a rate that may be similar to that of extensive reading, and may lead to improved listening comprehension (Rodgers, 2013).

Teaching using television as a resource for language learning has several challenges. The following points summarize what teachers can do to overcome these challenges:

- If fellow teachers, students, programme directors, or parents are sceptical about the value of television for language learning, try to educate them. Watching L2 television over a substantial period of time can contribute to vocabulary growth, improved listening comprehension, and gains in other aspects of L2 development. Although there may be resistance to learning with television regularly in the classroom, the long-term benefits of increasing the amount of L2 meaning-focused input should be taken into consideration.
- If a television programme is too difficult for beginners, try to delay watching it until students have reached the appropriate level. If students are at a level where they cannot understand and enjoy watching television, then using it for learning may have the negative effect of discouraging rather than encouraging further viewing.
- If the speed of the dialogue, the amount of connected speech, and a lack of familiarity with the spoken forms of words in a television programme limit comprehension, try to provide support. Comprehension should gradually increase until students reach the point where they can understand and enjoy television viewing without support.
- If there is only time to watch an occasional episode of a television programme in class, try to raise awareness of the long-term benefits of watching L2 television and encourage regular extensive viewing outside the classroom.

There are several ways in which comprehension can be supported in the classroom. First, teachers might employ a **narrow viewing** approach, where the episodes of one television programme are watched in sequence (Rodgers & Webb, 2011). Narrow viewing allows learners to gradually develop background knowledge of the characters and storyline that may facilitate greater comprehension of subsequent episodes. With greater background knowledge of a television programme, students can then focus greater attention on understanding the language that they encounter. Second, teachers could provide glossaries of difficult words used in the programme, or pre-teach frequently used words that are likely to be unfamiliar. Increasing the amount of known vocabulary in a programme reduces the lexical demands and may improve comprehension (Webb, 2010a, 2010b). Third, it may be useful for students to watch an episode of a programme more than once, because comprehension and vocabulary learning are likely to increase through repeated viewings. Fourth, foreign language learners have reported that watching television with L2 captions improved their comprehension (Rodgers, 2013), and there is some evidence to support this (Winke, Gass, & Sydorenko, 2010).

Films

Films have similar lexical features to television. Research also indicates that learners are motivated to learn English through watching films (Chapple & Curtis, 2000; King, 2002). This makes them a valuable source of L2 spoken input and a useful resource for vocabulary learning. However, L2 films do have two disadvantages in comparison to television. The first is that they can rarely be used in a narrow viewing approach, because each film is typically an original story with new characters, so viewers have the additional burden of trying to understand the content while coping with the language demands of the film. Second, because of their length, films are rarely appropriate for classroom use. Moreover, television programmes may give a slightly better return for the amount of input provided. In their study of television programmes, Rodgers and Webb (2011) found that, on average, one 43-minute episode consisted of 4,684 words, compared with an average of 8,937 words in a film (based on the average number of words in 318 films analysed in a study by Webb and Rodgers (2009b)).

TED Talks

TED Talks are freely available online presentations that cover topics on technology, entertainment, and design (hence the acronym TED). The talks are often given by well-known figures in their fields, and they attract considerable interest. Several studies have examined the value of TED Talks for language learning purposes. They have found that the lexical demands of reaching the 95% coverage figure associated with the comprehension of spoken texts is higher for TED Talks (5,000 word families) than it is for other sources of spoken input such as conversation, television, and films (3,000 word families) (Coxhead & Walls, 2012), but similar to that of academic spoken discourse (Nurmukhamedov & Sadler, 2011). This similarity to academic spoken discourse has contributed to the use of TED Talks as material in English for Academic Purposes programmes (Coxhead & Walls, 2012). Authentic, adapted, or simulated TED Talks are also a popular resource for listening activities in many contemporary general English language coursebooks.

For learners who are not as far along in their lexical development, TED Talks may be more appropriate for intensive listening exercises than for extensive viewing. One advantage of using TED Talks for language learning is that they are relatively short, so learners may be willing to view one talk multiple times to enhance comprehension and increase the potential for incidental vocabulary learning. An additional positive feature of TED Talks is that transcripts of the presentations are readily available. This is quite a useful feature which may help viewers to link the spoken forms of words to their written forms. Moreover, research indicates that reading while listening contributes to greater incidental vocabulary learning than reading alone (Brown, Waring, & Donkaewbua, 2008; Webb & Chang, 2012b), so viewing TED Talks with captions, or listening while reading the transcript, could increase the potential for vocabulary learning. The transcripts can also be run through a lexical profiler to help teachers identify presentations that are at an appropriate level for their students. One limitation of using TED Talks in comparison to television programmes is that the language is likely to vary considerably between presentations, so viewers will need to develop background knowledge for each topic, as well as cope with the language demands.

Summary

There are many ways in which vocabulary can be learned and many resources that can be used for learning. In this chapter, we have provided an overview of the resources that we believe are most useful for teaching vocabulary today. With frequent advances in technology, this list is quite different from what it would have been ten years ago, and it will undoubtedly need to be updated again in the relatively near future. Having access to resources and taking the trouble to access them in a principled way can have a significant impact on what we can and cannot do in our classes. Ideally, teachers will work together within their institutions and create a repository of useful vocabulary learning resources that can be drawn on and gradually expanded as more and more resources are found or created.

Questions for reflection

1 Think about the resources discussed in this chapter and complete the chart. Then decide on reasons for your answers.

	Have used	Have not used	Reluctant to use
Word lists			
Levels Test			
Size Test			
Guessing from Context Test			
Word Part Levels Test			
Flashcards			
Concordancers			
Lexical profilers			
Extensive reading texts			
Extensive viewing materials			

2 What are the advantages and disadvantages of using a word list with your students?

3 Think of three ways in which digital text analysis such as concordancing and lexical profiling could benefit your students. Which of the two do you think would make the most significant impact on your students' vocabulary learning?

Keys to activities

ACTIVITY 9.5   Using a lexical profiler

abroad	3,000 word frequency level
adult	2,000 word frequency level
aerobics	6,000 word frequency level
afraid	1,000 word frequency level
aggressor	9,000 word frequency level
ambience	7,000 word frequency level
ambiguous	4,000 word frequency level
antagonize	10,000 word frequency level
appetite	5,000 word frequency level
asteroid	8,000 word frequency level

Note that the frequency level of the words will depend on the word lists that are used in the analysis.

Suggestions for further reading

Cobb, T. (2007). Computing the vocabulary demands of L2 reading. *Language Learning & Technology*, *11(3)*, 38–63.

This study looks at the potential for lexical development through reading different types of material. The research suggests a need for learners to encounter greater amounts of L2 input in order to further develop their vocabulary. A discussion of some of the useful resources available on the Compleat Lexical Tutor website is also included.

Nakata, T. (2011). Computer-assisted second language vocabulary learning in a paired-associate paradigm: a critical investigation of flashcard software. *Computer Assisted Language Learning*, *24(1)*, 17–38

Nakata provides a review of computer-assisted vocabulary learning with flashcards. He discusses the justification for learning with flashcards and lists useful criteria for evaluating flashcard software.

Webb, S. (2015). Extensive viewing: language learning through watching television. In D. Nunan & J. C. Richards (Eds.), *Language learning beyond the classroom* (pp. 159–168). New York, NY: Routledge.

This chapter outlines a classroom-based extensive viewing approach designed to encourage L2 television viewing outside the classroom. Webb discusses the need for language learners to encounter greater amounts of L2 input and suggests that L2 television has great potential as an extensive learning resource, because language learners are motivated to use it for learning. He differentiates between intensive and extensive viewing and describes a principled approach to L2 television viewing.

Webb, S., & **Nation, I. S. P.** (2008). Evaluating the vocabulary load of written text. *TESOLANZ Journal*, *16*, 1–10.

This article discusses how vocabulary tests can be used together with lexical profilers to evaluate the suitability of digital texts for classroom use. Webb and Nation also suggest steps that teachers may take to support learning with digital texts.

10 KEY QUESTIONS ABOUT VOCABULARY LEARNING

Introduction

In this final chapter, we revisit key topics discussed in this book and address some common questions that were first presented in the Introduction about how vocabulary is learned. We hope this chapter will lead the reader back into the classroom in possession of greater awareness of the issues surrounding vocabulary learning, an enhanced knowledge of key research, and, above all, with many practical ideas for maximizing students' vocabulary learning.

Question 1: *What is the teacher's role?*

As we have seen, there are many things that teachers need to consider in order to help their students make meaningful progress in lexical development, and a great deal of planning and preparation needs to occur before teachers enter the classroom. Without careful planning, many students may make minimal progress. There is much to be learned about words; and without a principled approach to teaching vocabulary, many words are likely to be studied only to be forgotten. It might be assumed that the teacher's primary role in vocabulary learning is to teach words. However, direct teaching is only one of several important methods that should be used to facilitate the lexical development of students (Nation, 2008). There are thousands of words to learn and only enough classroom time to teach a relatively small number of words; so if students are to make significant progress in their lexical development, the direct teaching of vocabulary in the classroom is likely to account for only a small proportion of the words that are learned. Teachers need to help their students to further develop knowledge of partially known words and to become more effective and efficient learners so that they can make progress outside the classroom. We have identified nine key aspects of the teacher's role in supporting and enhancing lexical development.

1 Select the words to be learned

Words should be carefully selected according to their relative value. If students are at a beginner level, words should be from the Essential Word List (Dang & Webb, 2016b). If students are at an intermediate level, then words should be from the second and third 1,000 word frequency levels. If students are at a more advanced level, then words should be selected according to need. At the start of the course, teachers should have a set of words that they expect their students to learn and be ready to sequence and evaluate the learning of these words throughout the course, in order to assess vocabulary learning progress. The number of words to be learned should be sufficiently large to make a meaningful contribution to lexical development. It should also represent a vocabulary learning goal that is achievable for the majority of students in a class, as having a goal that is too large may discourage rather than encourage learning.

2 Raise awareness of the vocabulary learning programme

If we expect our students to buy into our vocabulary learning programme, then it is important that they understand what is involved. For example, students may not understand why they are learning certain target vocabulary rather than other words that they consider to be more important, or why encountering words in meaning-focused input is useful. If students are at an appropriate cognitive level to understand the programme, explaining the different aspects of it may help students to become more engaged and motivate them to work towards reaching vocabulary learning targets within and between courses.

3 Teach words deliberately

Teachers should spend time helping their students to learn high-frequency target vocabulary. These words will have the greatest impact on language development, because they will be encountered regularly in materials and needed for communication. Lower-frequency words should receive minimal attention in class (Nation, 2001, 2013a). With insufficient time to teach a large number of words, teachers should quickly define or translate words of lesser value when necessary and instead prioritize time for the deliberate learning of target vocabulary. However, as we saw in Chapter 8, the deliberate teaching of vocabulary contributes to only one of four strands of a well-balanced vocabulary learning programme. Deliberate teaching may result in students learning the form–meaning connection of target vocabulary, but the other three strands are necessary to consolidate and expand on the gains made through deliberate teaching.

4 Choose materials containing target vocabulary

Teachers should set up regular encounters with target words in meaning-focused input throughout the course, to consolidate knowledge of the words and model how they can be used in speech or writing. Finding or modifying materials so that there are regular encounters with words is probably the most challenging aspect of the teacher's role. Extensive reading materials are useful, because they are designed to promote repetition and deeper learning of the vocabulary found in the texts. Selecting different materials that are related by topic is another way to increase the potential for repetition of target vocabulary—for example, watching multiple episodes of a television series, beginning with the first episode (narrow viewing). In this example, topic-related vocabulary is likely to be encountered both within and between different episodes, increasing the chances of learning (Rodgers & Webb, 2011). Lexical profilers (see Chapter 9) are useful tools that can also be used to help teachers choose appropriate materials.

5 Design activities to create opportunities for vocabulary use

Without opportunities to use target words in speech or writing, it may be difficult for students to develop sufficient productive knowledge to use the words outside the classroom. Designing activities which ensure that students use words repeatedly throughout a programme represents a major challenge for teachers. Deciding on a set of target vocabulary at the start of the programme and using materials that include the target vocabulary throughout its duration should help teachers to more easily design relevant activities.

6 Include fluency development activities

A key element of vocabulary development involves being able to process words at a faster rate and in a more native-like way. Activities that contribute to fluency development, such as speed-reading, ten-minute writing, and repeated listening/viewing, will help students to enrich their knowledge of partially known words. The effect is cumulative: if students can process words more quickly, they should be able to communicate more naturally, and this should also allow them to devote more attention to the less familiar words they encounter, which in turn should increase the potential for vocabulary learning.

7 Measure progress

The testing of target vocabulary to evaluate learning progress has several functions. First, it raises awareness of the importance of vocabulary learning. Many students will allocate study time according to what is tested, so if there is testing of vocabulary, students are more likely to prioritize the learning of vocabulary. Second, tests reveal vocabulary learning progress. If students are making good progress, this may encourage further learning. If students are doing poorly, teachers can modify their plan to try to improve learning. Third, tests can be used to raise awareness of what should be learned about words (Nation & Webb, 2011; Webb, 2013). Tests may focus on different aspects of vocabulary knowledge: some test questions may ask for the meaning of words, others might ask for the derivations, while others might ask for collocations of target vocabulary. Raising awareness of the different aspects of vocabulary knowledge may help students to develop a more comprehensive understanding of taught words.

8 Train students in learning strategies

As we saw in Chapter 7, if students are to reach the target vocabulary sizes necessary to understand spoken and written discourse, they need to become effective and efficient learners both inside and outside the classroom. It is particularly important to help students to find and make use of available sources of the target language outside the classroom that may increase the potential for learning through meaning-focused input. Other strategies that can impact current and future learning, such as learning word parts and guessing words from context, should also be prioritized. Because students need to make meaningful progress in lexical development on their own, it is important that teachers take the time to ensure that vocabulary learning strategies are understood and used correctly.

9 Evaluate and modify

Teachers may evaluate the effectiveness of the vocabulary learning programme by examining the extent to which the target vocabulary was learned, as well as the depth of vocabulary developed, and adapt the programme accordingly. For example, if students cannot use the words in speech or writing, then there may need to be an increase in the opportunities to use the target vocabulary in subsequent versions of the programme. Evaluation might also include a sample of student feedback to gauge the level of engagement with vocabulary learning. If students lack engagement, then it may be useful to spend more time on raising awareness of the principles behind the key components of the vocabulary learning programme.

ACTIVITY 10.1   Selecting and sequencing target vocabulary

Decide on a vocabulary learning target for a programme that you are teaching or are familiar with. How will the target vocabulary be introduced in the programme? How many words will students learn each week? How many words will be learned by the end of the programme? Justify your answers.

Question 2: What is the student's role?

Learning enough words to understand spoken and written discourse without support is a goal that many students fail to reach. Perhaps one reason for this is that many students are unaware not only of how many words they need to learn but also of the amount of learning that needs to occur outside the classroom in order for them to achieve this target. It is therefore important that students understand what they need to do to optimize their lexical development and become autonomous vocabulary learners. Students need to take responsibility in three key areas.

1 Deliberately learn words inside and outside the classroom

Since students will only be able to learn in class a small proportion of the 3,000 most frequent word families that are needed to understand spoken discourse (Webb & Rodgers, 2009a, 2009b; van Zeeland & Schmitt, 2013) and the 9,000 word families that are needed to understand written discourse (Nation, 2006), they must spend some time learning words on their own in order to reach these goals. Teachers can guide students towards becoming effective and efficient autonomous vocabulary learners by raising awareness of strategies and approaches to vocabulary learning that are likely to be successful (see Chapter 7).

2 Encounter the target language outside the classroom

The greater the amount of input, the more often unknown and partially known words will be encountered. These repeated encounters will help to develop and strengthen knowledge of words, particularly if words are learned according to their frequency in the language. At the beginner level, reading graded readers provides the greatest potential to develop lexical knowledge, because they are specifically designed to provide repeated encounters with the high-frequency words that are found in them. At the intermediate level, watching L2 television programmes and reading mid-frequency readers may provide the greatest potential for further increasing vocabulary knowledge. At the advanced level, reading newspapers, novels, and online content, as well as watching L2 television programmes and films, is likely to further improve vocabulary knowledge.

3 Use the target language

As we discussed in Chapter 6, one of the major differences between the foreign and second language learning contexts is the number of opportunities learners have to use the target language. In the ESL context, for example, it should be possible to use English on a daily basis. For many learners in this context, the difference between learning English successfully and remaining at a relatively low level is directly related to the amount of effort made to use the target language. The lack of opportunities to use English in many EFL contexts is why these learners often lag far behind their ESL counterparts. Learners may need to be creative to find ways to use English outside the classroom, but the pay-off is clear.

Question 3: Why do some students make greater progress than others?

One issue that needs to be examined further in studies of vocabulary learning is the degree to which individuals differ in their ability to learn words.

Research often suggests that one approach to learning vocabulary is superior to another, but there is little discussion of the variation among students themselves. There are often large differences in the number of words that are learned by students. For example, we have seen in Chapter 3 that in a study of the vocabulary growth of EFL students in Greece, Milton (2006a) found that some students learned very few words, while others were able to learn more than 1,000 lemmas in a year. Research in other contexts has also indicated that there is likely to be considerable variation among students in the number of words that they learn (Orosz, 2009; Webb & Chang, 2012a). Some students might work harder than others (by finding more opportunities to encounter and use the language, and by doing more deliberate learning), and this may account for differences in vocabulary learning progress. Aptitude may also account for some of this variation; some learners might simply be better at learning and remembering new vocabulary than others. For example, in a study investigating aptitude for learning word pairs, W. B. Webb (1962) found that over a period of six hours, one student was able to learn as many as 166 words per hour while another learned 33 words per hour.

Aptitude may not account for all of the differences, however. Another reason why some students are able to accumulate more words than others is that they have a larger vocabulary size. This phenomenon, known as the Matthew effect, highlights the importance of developing lexical knowledge. Students who have a smaller vocabulary size may make relatively small gains in lexical growth in comparison to those who have a larger vocabulary size. Monitoring vocabulary size and helping students to improve their lexical knowledge is therefore extremely important, because students who struggle to keep up are likely to fall further and further behind those with greater lexical knowledge. Administering a test such as the Vocabulary Levels Test (Nation, 1983; Schmitt, Schmitt, & Clapham, 2001; Webb, Sasao, & Ballance, 2017) at the start of a course is a quick and easy way of determining which students may require additional support.

Question 4:   How much classroom time should be spent teaching vocabulary?

In a well-balanced vocabulary learning programme, deliberate learning of vocabulary should represent about one quarter of the time spent developing lexical knowledge (see Chapter 8). Class activities which teach the form–meaning connection of words will help students to recognize and understand words when they are re-encountered. However, if this is the only method of vocabulary learning, students' knowledge of taught words is likely to decay. In the classroom, vocabulary learning should also occur in the following ways:

- Knowledge of taught words should be further developed through encounters in both spoken and written texts which contain target vocabulary.
- Many students know words but are unable to use them. Tasks that involve using taught words in speech and writing will help students to more effectively develop productive vocabulary knowledge.
- Fluency development activities further develop knowledge of taught words by forcing students to process these words more quickly and understand and use them more fluently.

Question 5: How many words should students learn at a time, and how often?

It is important to consider how many words should be learned at one time. For instance, is it more effective to learn one large set of 200 words, four sets of 50 words, ten sets of 20 words, or 20 sets of ten words? Research examining this question has looked at whether it is better to learn something as a whole or in parts. Some researchers have suggested that it is better to learn smaller sets of words than larger sets (Joseph, Watanabe, Shiung, Choi, & Robbins, 2009; Salisbury & Klein, 1988). A survey of American university students also suggested that the majority of students believe that learning a small number of words at one time is more effective than learning a large number (Wissman, Rawson, & Pyc, 2012).

Research suggests that there may be little difference in the efficacy of learning smaller and larger sets of words. In a carefully controlled study that examined whether it is better to learn 20 words together, or to break them up into smaller sets of ten or four items, Nakata and Webb (2016) found no difference in learning gains. Instead, they found that students learned most effectively when there was greater spacing between each encounter with the same words. From a practical perspective, this suggests that learning a larger number of words may be more effective than learning a smaller number, because if the words are studied in sequence, there is likely to be a greater amount of time between each word being encountered and studied. Nakata and Webb found that there is one caveat to learning larger sets of words: while the eventual learning outcome may be better, the larger spacing between learning each word actually results in a decline in study performance (the number of correct answers in a study session). There is then the danger that students may be discouraged by their study performance when learning larger sets of words.

It may be useful for teachers to point out that, although it may initially be more difficult to learn words when there is greater spacing between study sessions, these words are likely to be better retained. A useful example that many older students may be able to relate to is the effectiveness of 'cramming' (learning a large amount of information at one time); in the long term, we retain more information when we learn over many spaced study sessions than when we cram. Research on vocabulary learning clearly supports this. Harry Bahrick, Lorraine Bahrick, Audrey Bahrick, and Phyllis Bahrick (1993) found that when there were long intervals (56 days) between studying a set of words, although performance in each study session was not as high as it was when there were shorter intervals, a larger proportion of the words could be recalled five years later.

The spacing effect also highlights the importance of incorporating repeated encounters with target vocabulary throughout a vocabulary learning programme. Encountering target vocabulary over a short period of time in one unit of a coursebook is similar to cramming; we may initially learn the words, but they are unlikely to be remembered in the long term. Instead, we need to provide opportunities for students to encounter and use the target vocabulary at different points in the programme in order to increase the likelihood of long-term retention.

Question 6: How much vocabulary should students learn per year?

In the L1 learning context, it is estimated that we learn about 1,000 word families per year from the time we start reading until we reach university age (Goulden, Nation, & Read, 1990). Unfortunately, in the L2 learning context, there is no clear answer to this question. Some students may learn as many as 1,000 lemmas in a year, while others in the same programme appear to make no progress in their learning (Milton, 2006a). On a more general level, we have also seen in Chapter 6 that vocabulary growth varies between second and foreign language learning contexts, with the relative lack of exposure to L2 input outside the classroom in the latter making it more difficult for learners in that context to make as much progress. Webb and Chang (2012) suggested that in a principled vocabulary learning programme in the EFL context, learning 400 word families per year may be a realistic goal for all learners. This would involve developing a relatively comprehensive knowledge of these words through repeated encounters in spoken and written discourse, as well as frequent opportunities to use them. If the focus is simply on learning the form–meaning connections of target vocabulary, it may be possible to learn considerably more words. For example, a reasonable target may be to learn 1,000 words per year. This might involve learning 25 words per week over 40 weeks. With so many words to learn in a limited amount of time, it may be difficult to move beyond learning the form–meaning connections. This does not mean learners cannot exceed expectations, of course; there may be some very successful learners who make meaningful progress in their lexical development through hard work and by seeking out contact with the target language on their own. But these cases are likely to be exceptions rather than the norm.

Initially, it may be best for learners to have an achievable goal to work towards that is meaningful in their context. A vocabulary learning programme could perhaps start with the aim of developing comprehensive knowledge of 400 words in a year. If this goal is achieved, then, in order to maximize lexical development, it might be worth gradually increasing the number of words to be learned in a year to the point where the majority of students can cope with the challenge. Students should also be encouraged to study independently outside the classroom to optimize their lexical development. If the goal set at the start of the programme cannot be achieved, then the programme should be evaluated to see if any aspects can be improved. If not, then the vocabulary learning target could be gradually reduced to identify the number of words that can be successfully learned. This would be a very useful topic for future research.

Question 7: What is the best way to group vocabulary for learning?

In Chapter 1, we highlighted the value of learning the highest-frequency words before lower-frequency words. We have also just discussed the importance of having a vocabulary goal for a programme which involves learning a pre-determined set of words. With these in place, teachers then need to decide how to group the target vocabulary into smaller sets of words to be learned at different points in the programme. The easiest and perhaps the most intuitively logical way to do this is to group semantically related words into lexical sets (for example, a 'nature' set or a 'family' set). Indeed, this is often the way in which target vocabulary is introduced in language learning materials.

Research clearly shows that the relationships between the words that are learned together have an impact on learning. If a target vocabulary set consists of words that often appear together in sequence, this might have a positive effect on learning (Tinkham, 1997). For example, it may be easier to learn words such as 'sunny', 'beach', and 'swim' than to learn unrelated words, because words that appear in sequence are linked in meaning, while the fact that they are different parts of speech helps learners to distinguish between them. In contrast, learning semantically related words that have the same parts of speech together can be difficult. In earlier chapters, we looked at the issue of interference—that is, how we often confuse the meanings of semantically related words and cross-associate the meaning of one word with the form of another. For example, if we learn the different types of fruit at one time, we may manage to learn the different word forms ('apple', 'orange', 'peach'…) and remember that each of these word forms represents a type of fruit. But the similarity in meaning may generate interference, leaving us uncertain as to which word form should be linked to which type of fruit.

As we have seen, the main solution to the problem of interference is to introduce unrelated words together and semantically related words at different times. Here is a reminder of the most effective ways of reducing the potential for interference.

Use sets of unrelated words

Organize the introduction of sets of target vocabulary so that the words in each set are unrelated. This is perhaps the best way of reducing interference and thus increasing the potential for small sets of words to be learned.

Raise awareness of interference

Explain to students why it is best to learn words with very different meanings together, if they are old enough to understand. Discussing examples is perhaps the best way to do this. Many students have had the experience of cross-associating semantically related words that have been learned at the same time, such as 'left' and 'right'. Raising awareness of interference is useful, because some students may have difficulty understanding why they are not finding it easy to learn related words together. Moreover, we want our students to learn effectively outside the classroom, so awareness of interference should help to optimize autonomous learning.

Use differentiating sentences

Introduce words in sentences that help learners to differentiate between words with similar meanings. For example, rather than introducing the words 'right' and 'left' in sentences where the words are interchangeable, such as 'Turn right at the corner.', introduce them in sentences that capture their distinct meanings, such as 'Most people write with their right hand.'.

ACTIVITY 10.2   Practising avoiding interference

Write a sentence for each of the words below that may help students to differentiate between the meanings of the semantically related words in each pair. Then compare your ideas with the examples at the end of the chapter.

increase / decrease (nouns)   long / wide   sweet / sour   bored / tired

---

Question 8: How should teachers select vocabulary activities?

As Chapter 5 revealed, there are many ways of learning vocabulary, and different approaches contribute to learning in different ways. Some activities are more effective than others. There are several issues that teachers might want to consider when choosing activities for vocabulary learning.

The target vocabulary

Ideally, teachers would choose and create activities and exercises that involve learning pre-selected target vocabulary. However, teachers often have to follow a prescribed curriculum that involves learning with a particular coursebook. In coursebooks, the target vocabulary included in the activities is decided by the author and publisher. These words will have particular value for learners in completing that unit of the coursebook, but it is important to assess whether the vocabulary is really worth spending time learning. For example, if students are still in the process of learning words from the first 1,000 word frequency level, then it would be of less value to spend class time learning topic-related words encountered in a unit on, say, restaurants, that are unlikely to be encountered regularly outside that unit (the following examples are taken from such a unit: 'appetizer', 'bland', 'crunchy', 'doggie bag', 'entrée'). Instead, these words could be briefly translated, defined, or glossed so that class time can be spent on activities focusing on words of higher value to the learners.

Time

Some activities take much longer to complete than others. The amount of learning to be gained by doing an activity should be considered in relation to the time it will take to complete it. If an activity takes more time, this does not mean that it should not be used; the benefits might outweigh the additional time required. However, as this is not always the case, it is useful to consider whether longer activities result in greater learning or not.

The vocabulary learning focus

When choosing activities, it is worth identifying what might be gained by completing an activity. Some cover many different aspects of vocabulary knowledge, while others have a primary focus on one or two specific aspects, such as form, meaning, or use. For example, learning with flashcards involves linking the form of a word to its meaning; the primary aim here is to develop knowledge of the form–meaning connection. Although this represents an important gain in knowledge, it is quite different from what might be gained by encountering the same word repeatedly in meaning-focused input, which is likely to develop more aspects of vocabulary knowledge.

Evaluating activities

In this book, we have looked in depth at how learning conditions relate to the effectiveness of different activities. Frameworks such as the Involvement Load Hypothesis (Hulstijn & Laufer, 2001; Laufer & Hulstijn, 2001) and Technique Feature Analysis (Nation & Webb, 2011) can be used to evaluate the efficacy of different learning conditions. Research indicates that, of the two methods, Technique Feature Analysis is more effective for evaluating the effectiveness of activities (Hu & Nassaji, 2016). Awareness of the conditions that affect learning can help teachers to select the most effective activities and exercises, and modify them when necessary to optimize vocabulary learning (see Chapters 4 and 5). Table 10.1 shows the evaluation criteria included in Technique Feature Analysis.

	Criteria	Flashcards	Writing sentences
	Motivation		
1	Is there a clear vocabulary learning goal?	1	1
2	Does the activity motivate learning?	1	0
3	Do learners select the words?	1	1
	Noticing		
4	Does the activity focus attention on the target words?	1	1
5	Does the activity raise awareness of new vocabulary learning?	1	1
6	Does the activity involve negotiation?	0	0
	Retrieval		
7	Does the activity involve retrieval of the word?	1	1
8	Is it productive retrieval?	1	0
9	Is it recall?	1	1
10	Are there multiple retrievals of each word?	1	0
11	Is there spacing between retrievals?	1	0
	Varied encounters and varied use		
12	Does the activity involve varied encounters and use?	0	1
13	Is it productive?	0	1
14	Is there a marked change that involves the use of other words?	0	1
	Retention		
15	Does the activity ensure successful linking of form and meaning?	1	0
16	Does the activity involve instantiation?	0	0
17	Does the activity involve **imaging**?	0	0
18	Does the activity avoid interference?	1	1
	Total score	12	10

Table 10.1 Example of Technique Feature Analysis

Teachers analyse the effectiveness of an activity by answering 18 questions about it. The higher the score for an activity, the more effective it is. Table 10.1 shows a comparison between two vocabulary activities: learning with flashcards and writing sentences. In both activities, the students choose the words that they want to study. The table shows that although both activities contribute to learning in many ways, the former (12 points) may be slightly more effective than the latter (10 points). One of the strengths of Technique Feature Analysis is that it highlights the complex nature of the criteria that contribute to vocabulary learning. In particular, being aware of the conditions that affect learning can help teachers to select the most effective activities and exercises, and modify them when necessary to optimize vocabulary learning (see Chapters 4 and 5).

Question 9: When is meaning-focused input appropriate inside the classroom?

In Chapter 8, we discussed the need to balance vocabulary learning between the four strands of meaning-focused input, meaning-focused output, language-focused learning, and fluency development. However, teachers may not be confident about whether learning in each strand should occur inside or outside the classroom. For example, the meaning-focused input strand includes activities such as extensive reading and viewing that involve reading and listening for pleasure. We have considered how some teachers may feel uncomfortable about simply having their students read or watch television for long periods of time, and may instead feel pressured to focus more on the language-focused learning strand inside the classroom because it represents a more conventional form of teaching. Extensive learning with meaning-focused input might then be assigned as homework. However, as we have seen, problems may arise if this type of input is not also included within the classroom (Webb, 2015):

- Students may find it too difficult. The task of reading a graded reader, listening to a longer spoken text, or watching an L2 television programme is likely to be challenging initially. For example, some students may not enjoy reading in their L1 and therefore lack the motivation to engage in extensive reading. Others may find the speech rate of spoken input too fast and feel discouraged from engaging further beyond the assigned tasks. In the classroom, teachers can provide support and help students to understand and hopefully enjoy the extensive learning approach. This may in turn motivate further learning outside the classroom.
- Students may not recognize the value. The real value of extensive learning stems from the engagement students have with meaning-focused input on their own. If little emphasis is placed on meaning-focused input in the classroom, students may simply view extensive learning tasks as

mandatory assignments that need to be completed as homework. Lexical development beyond the high-frequency words is likely to be dependent on how much L2 input is encountered, so there is a need for students to be encouraged to encounter as much language on their own as possible. If they are not aware of the value of extensive learning, then they are unlikely to be encouraged to do this.

The key reasons for including meaning-focused input in the classroom as well as beyond are as follows:

- There may not be sufficient classroom time to deliberately learn enough words to become fluent in the target language. Incidental vocabulary learning through encountering large amounts of meaning-focused input fuels L1 vocabulary growth and has the potential to do the same for L2 vocabulary growth.
- Meaning-focused input reveals a great deal about vocabulary that is unlikely to be learned through deliberate learning. With large amounts of meaning-focused input, the different meanings, derivations, and collocations of a word are likely to be encountered again and again and may eventually be learned.
- Because meaning-focused input is so important for lexical development, it is essential that students are familiar with what it is and feel confident in learning with it in the classroom. This may then encourage autonomous learning with meaning-focused input outside the classroom.
- Including meaning-focused input in a language course raises awareness of its importance for language learning. Excluding meaning-focused input from the classroom may suggest to students that it is less important than language-focused learning and reduce the likelihood that students will seek out opportunities to learn with meaning-focused input in their own time.

Question 10: Is there value in language-focused learning?

As much of L1 vocabulary growth is the result of repeated encounters with words in context, we should perhaps question the value of language-focused methods of vocabulary learning, particularly the use of decontextualized exercises that do not reveal how words are used in context. However, there are several good reasons why decontextualized vocabulary learning exercises are useful:

- Decontextualized exercises are often very effective at enabling learners to link form to meaning. Exercises such as those involving the use of flashcards and the keyword technique tend to result in fast and efficient gains in knowledge of the form–meaning connection of words, so they might provide a useful starting point for the development of lexical knowledge that could then be expanded through encounters with the words during listening and reading activities.

- They provide a quick way of developing a lexical foundation that can be used to make learning with meaning-focused input easier. A big part of the process of learning to read in L1 involves learning the spellings of known words and linking the written forms of these words to their spoken forms. Deliberate L2 vocabulary learning in decontextualized (and contextualized) exercises may provide a relatively quick way to develop a basic knowledge of vocabulary. Without direct instruction, students are likely to struggle to reach the lexical thresholds necessary to understand and start learning with meaning-focused input.

- They may contribute to vocabulary knowledge to a larger degree than might be expected. There might be the perception that the only way to gain knowledge of the use of an L2 word is by encountering it in context. However, if there is overlap between the meanings of L1 and L2 words, then there is also likely to be overlap between other aspects of vocabulary. For example, if we learn the L2 word 'hospital', we may be able to identify certain similarities in how it is used in the L1 and L2, such as the fact that 'hospital' is likely to be used with words that mean 'doctor', 'nurse', 'ambulance', 'emergency', 'heart', 'bone', and 'blood' in both languages. Learners may be able to take advantage of such similarities between L1 and L2 words and use their L1 vocabulary knowledge as a model for how they might use L2 words (Webb, 2007b). This will not always work, as there will be some words that are not found in the L1, some that are not well known in the L1, and some that have many differences between the L1 and L2. However, any overlap between L1 and L2 vocabulary knowledge may help students to learn more about words through decontextualized exercises than just their form and meaning, and even enable them to successfully use the words.

We hope we have shown in this book that there are many different ways of learning words, and that different approaches have different benefits. The principle of the four strands we have recommended for developing a well-balanced vocabulary learning programme involves learning words in a variety of ways which may include deliberate learning through the use of decontextualized exercises, as well as incidental learning through meaning-focused input.

Question 11: Is it useful to provide students with the L1 translations of unknown words?

Research suggests that providing learners with L1 translations can be a more effective way of learning the form–meaning connection of words than providing them with L2 definitions (Lado, Baldwin, & Lobo, 1967; Laufer & Shmueli, 1997). The reason for this is that L1 translations convey existing L1 knowledge, whereas understanding L2 definitions hinges on the learner's L2 knowledge, as well as the quality of the definition. Translations also provide perhaps the quickest method of conveying meaning, and the time saved can then be used for other learning tasks. One potential issue with using L1 translations is that there may be little overlap between the L2 and L1. In such cases, using other approaches to convey meaning may be more useful—for example, providing learners with synonyms, showing them pictures or real objects, or through gestures.

Question 12: To what extent are words which are taught by teachers ever really known by students?

Learning is often understood in terms of a dichotomy between what is 'known' and what is 'unknown'. Thus, researchers may make the assumption that the words found to be correct on a post-test in a study on vocabulary learning have been learned and are known. Teachers and students may make the same assumption about words found to be correct in a vocabulary test. The results of such tests are, however, somewhat misleading. As we discussed in Chapter 2, there is much to be learned about each word. The amount of vocabulary knowledge that is measured in an isolated study or test is typically a small fraction of what could potentially be learned about words. Table 10.2 shows three test formats that might be used to measure knowledge of the word 'accept'.

I	Circle the correct meaning of 'accept'. (a) speak to someone (b) take something given to you (c) go back again
2	Write different derivations of the word 'accept'. ————————————————————————
3	Use 'accept' in a sentence. ————————————————————————

Table 10.2 Three test formats

In each of these examples, if test takers answered correctly, they would have demonstrated that they knew the word 'accept' to some degree. However, their responses would indicate only a degree of partial knowledge. Choosing the correct option in the first example does not demonstrate that the test taker knows that 'accept' also means 'to make a favourable response' (for example, 'accept an offer') and 'to give admittance or approval' ('accept him as one of the team'). Similarly, providing the correct responses 'acceptable' and 'acceptance' in the second example does not mean that other derivations such as 'acceptably' and 'unacceptable' are known. A response for the third example such as 'He accepted the gift from her, even though he did not deserve it.' demonstrates that the test taker understands the core meaning of 'accept' and is able to use it correctly. However, it represents but one example of use, and using a word correctly in one sentence does not prove that it can be used correctly in another.

This does not mean that vocabulary tests are not useful; rather, it highlights the inherent limitations of testing. Tests can indicate that some learning has occurred, but they cannot indicate the extent to which further learning is still required. It is important that both teachers and students are aware of this. Similarly, it is essential that they are aware of the gradual nature of vocabulary learning and the need for both further encounters with recently learned words and opportunities to use these words in speech and writing.

ACTIVITY 10.3   How well do we 'know' words?

1 To what extent do you feel you 'know' each of these three words?

| attract   bridle   auspicious |

Quickly write down what you know about the form, meaning, and use of each word.

2 Think about the different inflections and derivations, meanings, and collocations of each word. Can you add more information?

3 Now use a good dictionary. Can you find any other information about each word?

Summary

Learning vocabulary is not a simple process. There are too many words to be learned through formal language instruction alone, so choices about the vocabulary that is to be learned need to be made. Moreover, there is much to be learned about each word, and there are many different ways in which vocabulary can be learned. There are thus many approaches to dealing with vocabulary in the classroom, and many strategies that learners should be encouraged to use outside the classroom. We hope that this book has provided some insight into key issues related to vocabulary learning, as well as a range of practical solutions. Because lexical development is likely to impact performance in all aspects of language development, it is worth taking the time to carefully consider how vocabulary learning might be optimized within a vocabulary learning programme and beyond.

Questions for reflection

1 Look again at your answers to the activity in the Introduction. What points did you find particularly useful in this chapter?

2 Based on your reading of this book, how might you adapt your own approach to teaching vocabulary in future? What challenges do you face?

Keys to activities

Activity 10.2   Practising avoiding interference

- increase / decrease (nouns):

  She loved her new job even more after she got an increase in her salary.

  In winter, there is a decrease in temperature, and it often snows.

- long / wide:

  Motorways are usually long.

  Oceans are wide.

- sweet / sour:

  Ice cream, cake, and chocolate are sweet.

  Lemons are sour.

- bored / tired:

  The kids are bored because they have nothing to do.

  People often feel tired after they exercise or get up early.

Note: It is easier to write differentiating sentences for some words than it is for others. In the examples above, 'long' and 'wide' may still present challenges for students: 'motorways' can be other things besides 'long', and students may not make an accurate association between 'ocean' and 'wide'. More precise examples giving measurement would support meaning here.

Suggestions for further reading

Laufer, B. (2001). Reading, word-focused activities and incidental vocabulary acquisition in a second language. *Prospect, 16(3)*, 44–54.

Laufer provides a useful discussion of the contributions that direct teaching and incidental vocabulary learning make towards lexical development. Although many researchers stress the gains that can be made through meaning-focused input, Laufer reveals that direct learning may also account for a great deal of learning in the EFL context.

Laufer, B., & **Shmueli, K.** (1997). Memorizing new words: does teaching have anything to do with it? *RELC Journal, 28(1)*, 89–108.

This study looks at some common questions that teachers have about vocabulary learning, which activities are most effective, and whether it is better to learn with L1 translations or L2 definitions. The practical focus of the study makes it a useful introduction to how research on vocabulary might be conducted in the classroom.

Nation, I. S. P. (2000). Learning vocabulary in lexical sets: dangers and guidelines. *TESOL Journal, 9(2)*, 6–10.

This study presents a useful overview of the research on interference. It includes discussion of the different types of semantic relationships that inhibit learning and also provides practical suggestions for how teachers might reduce the negative effects that interference can have on lexical development.

Nation, I. S. P., & **Webb, S.** (2011). *Researching and analysing vocabulary*. Boston: Heinle Cengage Learning.

Chapter 1 of this book discusses Technique Feature Analysis, explaining in detail each of the conditions that contributes to learning, along with examples of activities that meet each criterion.

APPENDIX 1   Essential Word List

The Essential Word List was developed by Thi Ngoc Yen Dang and Stuart Webb (2016b). There are 624 content words grouped into 12 sub-lists of 50 words and one sub-list of 24 words. This is followed by a list of 176 function words. (For an editable version of this list, see www.oup.com/elt/teacher/hvil.)

Content words

Sub-list 1

know	go	mean	take	long
like	yes	come	make	need
well	very	also	year	Mr
just	see	okay	look	thought
think	people	want	thing	lot
right	here	way	man	same
then	good	even	put	old
now	only	new	let	word
get	really	too	day	course
time	say	work	never	life

Sub-list 2

again	kind	point	night	side
own	actually	number	left	god
quite	sort	school	found	week
give	government	end	high	family
home	house	money	help	ever
tell	find	better	maybe	talk
world	place	big	far	state
use	different	probably	case	set
always	part	fact	whole	system
great	sure	bit	today	keep

Sub-list 3

problem	real	later	sorry	try
love	best	hand	show	change
name	laugh	already	able	general
percent	room	mind	together	area
call	remember	thank	order	believe
water	nice	job	head	young
important	rather	business	least	power
country	public	else	read	almost
small	mother	group	morning	start
feel	less	question	car	person

Sub-list 4

company	care	open	city	become
perhaps	ask	pretty	possible	local
ago	social	matter	cause	run
hard	national	information	present	anyway
form	book	hey	leave	full
party	father	face	service	office
means	bad	early	stuff	live
often	war	please	idea	development
example	large	pay	line	level
play	true	woman	guess	understand

Sub-list 5

fine	food	wrong	reason	boy
certain	moment	further	black	research
turn	sense	move	human	light
control	law	guy	university	data
sometimes	programme	girl	body	wait
political	free	wife	act	road
top	front	education	hope	particular
story	language	close	child	paper
door	study	stop	interest	view
hear	white	class	air	major

Sub-list 6

thinking	late	short	Mrs	deal
stay	cut	community	living	news
market	south	cost	difficult	future
age	report	friend	town	death
support	soon	economic	music	figure
clear	usually	position	health	land
police	bring	period	buy	process
department	society	policy	certainly	meeting
table	history	special	type	seem
experience	couple	center	street	interesting

Sub-list 7

situation	available	low	effect	private
alright	mum	meet	subject	easy
court	church	west	college	month
exactly	rate	art	red	evidence
main	council	century	hour	total
rest	answer	dead	provide	indeed
son	common	particularly	watch	strong
miss	north	hi	staff	stage
hold	happy	result	board	committee
especially	building	plan	husband	tax

Sub-list 8

thanks	instead	ready	individual	listen
middle	action	sound	similar	likely
suppose	personal	international	doctor	sit
field	write	necessary	yesterday	feeling
game	team	training	nature	voice
test	heart	ok	increase	poor
dad	value	according	Dr	self
section	issue	single	bed	chance
industry	various	term	fire	speak
sir	alone	stand	baby	earlier

Sub-list 9

finally	letter	hair	cold	evening
quality	range	bank	central	hello
happen	ground	obviously	throat	hospital
amount	reading	east	eat	simply
role	tomorrow	writing	learn	walk
force	due	return	price	hit
difference	knowledge	break	foreign	recent
phone	brother	project	lead	final
forward	decision	minute	analysis	beginning
member	beautiful	check	post	attention

Sub-list 10

president	standard	wish	fun	security
production	record	serious	financial	send
trouble	ball	minister	ahead	dog
management	piece	growth	tonight	degree
account	interested	blood	lower	dear
size	natural	bill	current	date
hot	agree	trade	recently	normal
worth	modern	list	model	blue
simple	student	basis	population	material
hell	summer	floor	funny	choice

Sub-list 11

approach	pressure	island	fish	cover
computer	picture	sign	clearly	afternoon
straight	relationship	basic	share	science
space	dark	military	doubt	movement
colour	drive	press	wide	expect
fall	visit	spend	step	capital
performance	green	consider	income	economy
culture	teaching	sea	drink	Christmas
pick	hotel	complete	authority	fast
river	truth	bye	film	continue

Sub-list 12

kill	design	theory	completely	earth
follow	wonder	shot	worry	organisation
function	dinner	energy	generally	wall
practice	medical	offer	page	property
former	fair	patients	average	activity
sister	radio	significant	respect	note
absolutely	legal	deep	structure	treatment
somewhere	pass	begin	club	station
include	nearly	quickly	purpose	teacher
Sunday	daughter	charge	specific	forget

Sub-list 13

television	born	trust	environment	original
western	park	window	cool	dollar
opportunity	response	carry	sex	square
key	style	rights	eye	direct
series	hall	fight	region	

Function words

the	all	where	around	although	everyone
and	she	over	while	past	near
of	no	back	each	himself	inside
to	his	first	under	seven	nineteen
a	do	much	away	eight	yourself
I	can	down	every	along	fifty
in	if	its	next	round	whose
you	about	should	anything	several	anyone
that	my	after	few	someone	per
it	her	those	though	whatever	except
for	which	may	since	among	forty
he	up	something	against	across	nobody
on	out	three	second	behind	unless
we	would	little	nothing	million	mine
they	when	many	without	outside	anybody
be	your	why	during	nine	till
with	will	before	six	thousand	herself
this	their	such	enough	shall	twelve
have	who	off	once	myself	fifteen
but	some	through	however	themselves	beyond
as	two	still	half	itself	whom
not	because	last	yet	somebody	below
at	how	being	whether	upon	none
what	other	must	everything	thirty	nor
so	could	another	until	third	more
there	our	between	hundred	above	most
or	into	might	within	therefore	
one	these	both	ten	everybody	
by	than	five	twenty	towards	
from	any	four	either	thus	

APPENDIX 2 Vocabulary Levels Test (Version B)

The updated Vocabulary Levels Test (2017) was created by Stuart Webb, Yosuke Sasao, and Oliver Ballance. It looks at how well you know useful English words. Version B of this test is provided here. (For a version with answers, see www.oup.com/elt/teacher/hvil.)

Put a tick under the word that goes with each meaning. Here is an example:

	game	island	mouth	film	song	yard
land with water all around it						
part of your body used for eating and talking						
piece of music						

It should be answered in the following way:

	game	island	mouth	film	song	yard
land with water all around it		✓				
part of your body used for eating and talking			✓			
piece of music					✓	

1,000 word level

	choice	computer	garden	photograph	price	week
cost						
picture						
place where things grow outside						

	eye	father	night	van	voice	year
body part that sees						
parent who is a man						
part of the day with no sun						

	center	note	state	tomorrow	uncle	winter
brother of your mother or father						
middle						
short piece of writing						

	box	brother	horse	hour	house	plan
family member						
sixty minutes						
way of doing things						

	animal	bath	crime	grass	law	shoulder
green leaves that cover the ground						
place to wash						
top end of your arm						

	drink	educate	forget	laugh	prepare	suit
get ready						
make a happy sound						
not remember						

	check	fight	return	tell	work	write
do things to get money						
go back again						
make sure						

	bring	can	reply	stare	understand	wish
say or write an answer to somebody						
carry to another place						
look at for a long time						

	alone	bad	cold	green	loud	main
most important						
not good						
not hot						

	awful	definite	exciting	general	mad	sweet
certain						
usual						
very bad						

2,000 word level

	coach	customer	feature	pie	vehicle	weed
important part of something						
person who trains members of sports teams						
unwanted plant						

	average	discipline	knowledge	pocket	trap	vegetable
food grown in gardens						
information which a person has						
middle number						

	circle	justice	knife	onion	partner	pension
round shape						
something used to cut food						
using laws fairly						

	cable	section	sheet	site	staff	tank
part						
place						
something to cover a bed						

	apartment	cap	envelope	lawyer	speed	union
cover for letters						
kind of hat						
place to live inside a tall building						

	argue	contribute	quit	seek	vote	wrap
cover tightly and completely						
give to						
look for						

	avoid	contain	murder	search	switch	trade
have something inside						
look for						
try not to do						

	bump	complicate	include	organize	receive	warn
get something						
hit gently						
have as part of something						

	available	constant	electrical	medical	proud	super
feeling good about what you have done						
great						
happening all the time						

	environmental	junior	pure	rotten	smooth	wise
bad						
not rough						
younger in position						

3,000 word level

	angle	apology	behavior	bible	celebration	portion
actions						
happy occasion						
statement saying you are sorry						

	anxiety	athlete	counsel	foundation	phrase	wealth
combination of words						
guidance						
large amount of money						

	agriculture	conference	frequency	liquid	regime	volunteer
farming						
government						
person who helps without payment						

	asset	heritage	novel	poverty	prosecution	suburb
having little money						
history						
useful thing						

	audience	crystal	intelligence	outcome	pit	welfare
ability to learn						
deep place						
people who watch and listen						

	consent	enforce	exhibit	retain	specify	target
agree						
say clearly						
show in public						

	accomplish	capture	debate	impose	proceed	prohibit
catch						
go on						
talk about what is correct						

	absorb	decline	exceed	link	nod	persist
continue to happen						
goes beyond the limit						
take in						

	approximate	frequent	graphic	pale	prior	vital
almost exact						
earlier						
happening often						

	consistent	enthusiastic	former	logical	marginal	mutual
not changing						
occurring earlier in time						
shared						

4,000 word level

	cave	scenario	sergeant	stitch	vitamin	wax
healthy supplement						
opening in the ground or in the side of a hill						
situation						

	candle	diamond	gulf	salmon	soap	tutor
something used for cleaning						
teacher						
valuable stone						

	agony	kilogram	orchestra	scrap	slot	soccer
group of people who play music						
long, thin opening						
small unwanted piece						

	crust	incidence	ram	senator	venue	verdict
hard outside part						
judgment						
place						

	alley	embassy	hardware	nutrition	threshold	tobacco
government building						
plant that is smoked in cigarettes						
small street between buildings						

	fling	forbid	harvest	shrink	simulate	vibrate
do not allow						
make smaller						
throw						

	activate	disclose	hug	intimidate	plunge	weep
cry						
tell						
turn on						

	diminish	exaggerate	explode	penetrate	transplant	verify
break into pieces violently						
get smaller						
move something to another place						

	adjacent	crude	fond	sane	spherical	swift
beside						
not crazy						
quick						

	abnormal	bulky	credible	greasy	magnificent	optical
believable						
oily						
unusual						

5,000 word level

	gown	maid	mustache	paradise	pastry	vinegar
hair on your upper lip						
perfect place						
small baked food						

	asthma	chord	jockey	monk	rectangle	vase
container for cut flowers						
group of musical notes that are played at the same time						
shape with two long and two short sides						

	batch	dentist	hum	lime	pork	scripture
green fruit						
low, constant sound						
meat from pigs						

	amnesty	claw	earthquake	perfume	sanctuary	wizard
liquid that is made to smell nice						
man who has magical powers						
safe place						

	altitude	diversion	hemisphere	pirate	robe	socket
height						
kind of clothing						
person who attacks ships						

	applaud	erase	jog	intrude	notify	wrestle
announce						
enter without permission						
remove						

	bribe	expire	immerse	meditate	persecute	shred
cut or tear into small pieces						
end						
think deeply						

	commemorate	growl	ignite	pierce	renovate	swap
catch fire						
exchange						
go into or through something						

	bald	eternal	imperative	lavish	moist	tranquil
calm and quiet						
having no hair						
slightly wet						

	diesel	incidental	mandatory	prudent	superficial	tame
not dangerous						
required						
using good judgment						

APPENDIX 3   25 useful word stems

This list gives 25 useful word stems, their meanings, and examples of words containing them (Wei & Nation, 2013).

The word stem, its meaning, a high-frequency word containing it, and an example of its connection to an unfamiliar word	Mid-frequency words containing the word stem
-spec (t)-, -spic-, -scope- = 'look' as in 'respect', 'to **look** upon sb with admiration' A **perspective** is a particular way of **looking** at things.	aspect, inspect, prospect, suspect, spectacle, speculate, perspective, spectrum, respective, spectacular, retrospect, spectator, inspectorate, specter, specify, specimen, despicable, conspicuous, microscope, kaleidoscope, telescope, stethoscope, sceptic*, spy*
-posit-, -pos- = 'put' as in 'position', 'a place where sb or sth is **put** To **pose** is to **put** sb or oneself into a particular position to be photographed.	impose, opposite, pose, dispose, compose, deposit, expose, proposition, compost, posture, disposition, provost*, superimpose, depose, repository, predispose, decompose, transpose, compound*
-vers-, -vert- = 'turn' as in' reverse', 'to **turn** sth the other way around' **Perverse** means thoroughly **turned** to the wrong way.	versus, adverse, diverse, diversify, diversion, perverse, traverse, convert, divert, inverse, revert, inadvertent, pervert, extrovert, vertebra, vertebrate, subvert, subversive
-vent-, -ven- = 'come' as in 'event', 'the **coming** of sth' A **convention** is a large meeting where people come together to discuss some issues.	invent, convention, advent, convent, circumvent, avenue, convenient, intervene, revenue, venue, convene, reconvene, convenor, contravene, souvenir, covenant
-ceive-, -cept- = 'take' as in 'receive', 'accept', 'to **take** what is offered' To **intercept** is to **take** sth when it is on its way from one place to another.	concept, intercept, deceive, deceptive, perception, perceive, reception, receipt*, receiver, receptive, misconception, perceptive, receptor, misconceive, susceptible

Note: Words marked with an asterisk (*) show variations in form.

-super- = 'above' as in 'super', 'being **above** sb or sth' To be **supervised** is to be directed by sb **above** you.	superb, supermarket, supervise, superior, superintendent, superficial, superman, supersede, superfluous, superstore, supernatural, superstar, superstructure, superpower, supersonic
-nam-, -nom-, -nym- = 'name' as in 'name' To **nominate** sb is to put sb's **name** forward for election.	surname, nickname, rename, nominate, nominal, misnomer, renown*, nominee, denomination, anonymous, synonym, acronym, anonymity, pseudonym, noun*
-sens-, -sent- = 'feel, sense' as in 'sense' **Consent** means having the same **feelings** and opinions about sth and therefore to be in agreement. **Sensual** means of the pleasures of the **senses**.	sentence, sensible, nonsense, sensitive, sensual, sensor, scent*, sensation, consensus, resent, sentiment, consent, assent, dissent
-sta-, -stan-, -stat- = 'stand' as in 'stand' **Instant** means happening quickly without anything **standing** in between two events.	stable, stall, status, distant, circumstance, instant, stance, static, obstacle, stool*, statue, pedestal, stature
-mit-, -mis- = 'send' as in 'committee', 'a group of people who are sent to be together to conduct some particular business' To **transmit** is to **send** out electric signals.	permit, transmit, submit, emit, remit, omit, message*, mission, premise, dismiss, missile, submission, demise, omission
-mid-, -med(i)- = 'middle' as in 'middle' **Mediocre** means being in the **middle** position ranging from good to bad.	immediate, medium, media, medieval, intermediate, Mediterranean, mediocre, mediate, meridian, meddle, median, intermediary, amid
-pris-, -pre- = 'take' as in 'surprise', 'sth which **takes** your attention unexpectedly' If sth **comprises** a number of things, it **takes** them in as its parts.	prison, enterprise, comprise, apprentice, prey, apprehend, comprehend, predatory, entrepreneur, incomprehensible, apprehension, comprehensive, entrepreneurial

-dict-, -dicate = 'say' as in 'indicate', 'to **say** sth indirectly' To **dedicate** a book or an artistic work to sb is to **say** that a book or an artistic work is produced or performed in sb's honor.	dictate, dedicate, abdicate, predicate, vindicate, predict, contradict, verdict, indict, diction, ditto*, index*
-cess- = 'go' as in 'process', 'actions **gone** through' Making a **concession** involves **going** along with sb's opinions.	access, excess, recession, concession, recess, ancestor*, predecessor, procession, succession, abscess, microprocessor, cease*
-form- = 'form' as in 'form' The **format** of a book is its **form**, such as its shape, size, and design.	formal, perform, transform, uniform, format, conform, formula, reform, deform, formative, morphology*
-tract- = 'draw' as in 'attract', 'to **draw** attention' To **extract** is to **draw** sth out.	extract, distract, abstract, subtract, detract, retract, contraction, protracted, traction, tractor, intractable
-graph- = 'write' as in 'paragraph', 'a **written** passage' A **telegraph** is a **written** message sent using radio signals.	telegraph, autobiography, biography, pornography, autograph, biographer, typographical, graph, graphic, topography, demography, geography
-gen- = 'produce' as in 'generate', 'produce' **Genes** are part of a cell that **produces** similar features in children.	genuine, gene, genesis, genetic, genius, indigenous, ingenuity, engender, congenital, genital, ingenious
-duce-, -duct- = 'lead' as in 'introduce', 'introduction', '**leading** sth/sb into a place, condition, or circle of people' To **induce** is to **lead** sb to do sth unwise.	induce, deduce, seduce, conducive*, conduct, abduct, viaduct, aqueduct, superconductor, subdue*
-voca-, -vok- is a variation of *-voic-* = 'voice' as in 'voice' To **advocate** is to **voice** one's opinions publicly to support sth.	advocate, vocabulary, vocal, invoke/invocation, equivocal, evoke/evocation, vowel*, advocacy

-cis-, -cid- = 'cut' as in 'decide', 'decision', 'a judgment about where to **cut** off (what to do or not to do)' To **excise** is to remove by **cutting** sth out.	precise, excise, circumcise, concise, incise, scissors, suicide, pesticide
-pla- is a variant of *-fla-* = 'flat' as in 'flat' A **plaice** is a **flat** sea fish.	plain, plane, plate, plaice, plateau, plot*, flounder*
-sec-, -sequ- = 'follow' as in 'second', '**following** the first' A **consequence** is what **follows** as an effect.	consequence, sequence, subsequent, consecutive, sequel, prosecute, consequential
-for(t)- = 'strong' as in 'force' A **fortress** is a very **strong** building for protecting people.	fortress, fortified, fortitude, comfort, effort, fort, enforce, reinforce, forte
-vis- = 'see' as in 'visit', 'go to **see** someone' Something **visible** can be **seen**.	visible, envisage, revise, supervise, visual, vision, television

APPENDIX 4 Word Part Levels Test: Intermediate

The Word Part Levels Test was created by Yosuke Sasao and Stuart Webb (2017). (For a version with answers, see www.oup.com/elt/teacher/hvil.)

Instructions

- This test has three sections: Form, Meaning, and Use.
- There is a total of 79 questions in the intermediate level.
- You cannot go back and change your answers.
- You must choose an answer that is most likely to be correct if you do not know it.
- There are no penalties for wrong answers.

1 Form section

- In order to use word part knowledge, you need to be able to recognize word parts.
- In this section, you are asked to choose a word part, a group of letters that change the meaning or the part of speech of a word.
- Wrong answers are strings of letters that occur in English words but do not change the meaning or the part of speech of a word.
- Here is an example:

(①) -ing (2) -nge (3) -eld (4) -kle

In this example, (1) *-ing* is correct, because it changes the part of speech of a word such as 'walk' (verb > noun). (2) *-nge* is wrong, because it appears in words like 'change' and 'orange', but does not change the meaning or the part of speech of *cha-* and *or-*.

The first part of this section is about prefixes (word parts that attach to the beginning of a word).

1	(1) ka-	(2) ze-	(3) de-	(4) ti-
2	(1) ba-	(2) oa-	(3) lu-	(4) ab-
3	(1) po-	(2) bu-	(3) wa-	(4) en-
4	(1) na-	(2) gi-	(3) em-	(4) ya-
5	(1) fe-	(2) qu-	(3) ra-	(4) bi-
6	(1) uni-	(2) dwe-	(3) haz-	(4) bal-
7	(1) vacat-	(2) super-	(3) stipu-	(4) schoo-

8	(1)	pro-	(2)	civ-	(3)	roc-	(4)	cha-
9	(1)	il-	(2)	ha-	(3)	fa-	(4)	ug-
10	(1)	daught-	(2)	circum-	(3)	carica-	(4)	manoeu-
11	(1)	sa-	(2)	za-	(3)	ex-	(4)	ut-

The second part of this section is about suffixes (word parts that attach to the end of a word).

12	(1)	-ous	(2)	-ney	(3)	-ope	(4)	-ime
13	(1)	-ism	(2)	-ike	(3)	-nda	(4)	-arf
14	(1)	-ible	(2)	-ight	(3)	-oach	(4)	-inue
15	(1)	-ent	(2)	-ead	(3)	-rol	(4)	-gue
16	(1)	-rse	(2)	-ack	(3)	-ful	(4)	-uin
17	(1)	-oud	(2)	-eep	(3)	-ant	(4)	-pse
18	(1)	-kout	(2)	-atic	(3)	-bour	(4)	-olve
19	(1)	-alia	(2)	-wise	(3)	-nana	(4)	-amel
20	(1)	-f	(2)	-y	(3)	-h	(4)	-g
21	(1)	-lf	(2)	-ss	(3)	-en	(4)	-mp
22	(1)	-lt	(2)	-ut	(3)	-al	(4)	-mb
23	(1)	-mme	(2)	-oom	(3)	-oad	(4)	-ive
24	(1)	-rove	(2)	-ulse	(3)	-some	(4)	-ribe
25	(1)	-eche	(2)	-eech	(3)	-ungr	(4)	-ence
26	(1)	-ition	(2)	-lause	(3)	-chool	(4)	-oards
27	(1)	-ward	(2)	-vern	(3)	-zzle	(4)	-vere
28	(1)	-hy	(2)	-ne	(3)	-ty	(4)	-rb
29	(1)	-ol	(2)	-th	(3)	-wn	(4)	-ak
30	(1)	-uit	(2)	-und	(3)	-eak	(4)	-eer
31	(1)	-ate	(2)	-rph	(3)	-yme	(4)	-uff
32	(1)	-aedia	(2)	-olors	(3)	-ation	(4)	-aight
33	(1)	-ways	(2)	-ause	(3)	-oice	(4)	-ript
34	(1)	-oard	(2)	-ogue	(3)	-laim	(4)	-most
35	(1)	-ly	(2)	-ma	(3)	-ra	(4)	-na
36	(1)	-hood	(2)	-ough	(3)	-erve	(4)	-inct
37	(1)	-ique	(2)	-less	(3)	-eeve	(4)	-itle

2 Meaning section

- This section is about word part meanings.
- For each item, a word part is presented with two example words. (The word part may also appear in other words.)
- You must choose the meaning of the word part from four choices.
- Here is an example:

-ed (walk<u>ed</u>; play<u>ed</u>)

((1))   past

(2)   not

(3)   many

(4)   person

The first part of this section is about prefixes (word parts that attach to the beginning of a word).

1 ex- (<u>ex</u>-wife; <u>ex</u>-member)
   (1)   earlier
   (2)   person
   (3)   bad
   (4)   can be

2 ab- (<u>ab</u>use; <u>ab</u>normal)
   (1)   person/thing
   (2)   times
   (3)   small
   (4)   away from

3 il- (<u>il</u>legal; <u>il</u>logical)
   (1)   between
   (2)   around
   (3)   person/thing
   (4)   not

4 circum- (<u>circum</u>polar; <u>circum</u>navigate)
   (1)   person/relating to
   (2)   small
   (3)   around
   (4)   beyond

5 uni- (<u>uni</u>sex; <u>uni</u>cycle)
   (1)   one
   (2)   person/thing
   (3)   not
   (4)   under

6 bi- (<u>bi</u>plane; <u>bi</u>sexual)
    (1)   person/thing
    (2)   two
    (3)   away from
    (4)   in advance

7 de- (<u>de</u>compose; <u>de</u>code)
    (1)   opposite
    (2)   person/thing
    (3)   together
    (4)   small

8 pro- (<u>pro</u>-democracy; <u>pro</u>-life)
    (1)   supporting
    (2)   against
    (3)   one
    (4)   too much

9 super- (<u>super</u>natural; <u>super</u>human)
    (1)   person
    (2)   half
    (3)   can be
    (4)   beyond

The second part of this section is about suffixes (word parts that attach to the end of a word).

10 -ism (socia<u>lism</u>; nationa<u>lism</u>)
    (1)   into another state/place
    (2)   theory of
    (3)   one
    (4)   small

11 -hood (child<u>hood</u>; mother<u>hood</u>)
    (1)   one
    (2)   halfway
    (3)   bad
    (4)   a state of

12 -th (four<u>th</u>; six<u>th</u>)
    (1)   person
    (2)   number
    (3)   not
    (4)   small

13 -ways (side<u>ways</u>; length<u>ways</u>)
    (1)   not
    (2)   person/thing
    (3)   wrongly
    (4)   direction

14 -ful (hand<u>ful</u>; mouth<u>ful</u>)
  (1)   not
  (2)   person
  (3)   small
  (4)   amount

15 -wise (clock<u>wise</u>; step<u>wise</u>)
  (1)   person
  (2)   direction
  (3)   new
  (4)   one

16 -en (wood<u>en</u>; gold<u>en</u>)
  (1)   one
  (2)   beyond
  (3)   opposite
  (4)   made of

17 -ible (access<u>ible</u>; convert<u>ible</u>)
  (1)   can be
  (2)   person/relating to
  (3)   after
  (4)   times

18 -less (end<u>less</u>; use<u>less</u>)
  (1)   before
  (2)   without
  (3)   the furthest
  (4)   person

19 -ward (up<u>ward</u>; back<u>ward</u>)
  (1)   direction
  (2)   person
  (3)   self
  (4)   without

20 -eer (mountain<u>eer</u>; engin<u>eer</u>)
  (1)   not
  (2)   after
  (3)   amount
  (4)   person

21 -most (top<u>most</u>; upper<u>most</u>)
  (1)   the furthest
  (2)   half
  (3)   person
  (4)   opposite

3 Use section

- Some affixes have the function of changing the part of speech of a word. For example, some word parts change a noun to a verb.
- For each item, a word part is presented with two example words. (The word part may also appear in other words.)
- You must choose the part of speech of the two example words, from noun, verb, adjective, and adverb.
- Here are examples of the four parts of speech.

    (1) Noun: 'house' ('My <u>house</u> is old.'); 'water' ('They drink <u>water</u>.')

    (2) Verb: 'know' ('I <u>know</u> her.'); 'talk' ('They <u>talk</u> a lot.')

    (3) Adjective: 'young' ('He is <u>young</u>.'); 'new' ('This is a <u>new</u> book.')

    (4) Adverb: 'too' ('She likes it <u>too</u>.'); 'often' ('He <u>often</u> plays football.')

- Here is an example.

-ed (walk<u>ed</u>; play<u>ed</u>)

(1)   Noun
(2)   Verb
(3)   Adjective
(4)   Adverb

The example words 'walked' and 'played' are verbs, because these words are used in sentences such as 'She walked home.' and 'He played soccer yesterday.'

  1 en- (<u>en</u>sure; <u>en</u>able)
    (1)   Noun
    (2)   Verb
    (3)   Adjective
    (4)   Adverb

  2 em- (<u>em</u>power; <u>em</u>body)
    (1)   Noun
    (2)   Verb
    (3)   Adjective
    (4)   Adverb

  3 -y (difficult<u>y</u>; honest<u>y</u>)
    (1)   Noun
    (2)   Verb
    (3)   Adjective
    (4)   Adverb

4 -ent (differ<u>ent</u>; excell<u>ent</u>)
   (1)   Noun
   (2)   Verb
   (3)   Adjective
   (4)   Adverb

5 -atic (system<u>atic</u>; problem<u>atic</u>)
   (1)   Noun
   (2)   Verb
   (3)   Adjective
   (4)   Adverb

6 -ation (consider<u>ation</u>; present<u>ation</u>)
   (1)   Noun
   (2)   Verb
   (3)   Adjective
   (4)   Adverb

7 -ate (formul<u>ate</u>; activ<u>ate</u>)
   (1)   Noun
   (2)   Verb
   (3)   Adjective
   (4)   Adverb

8 -en (wood<u>en</u>; gold<u>en</u>)
   (1)   Noun
   (2)   Verb
   (3)   Adjective
   (4)   Adverb

9 -ition (add<u>ition</u>; oppos<u>ition</u>)
   (1)   Noun
   (2)   Verb
   (3)   Adjective
   (4)   Adverb

10 -al (propos<u>al</u>; approv<u>al</u>)
   (1)   Noun
   (2)   Verb
   (3)   Adjective
   (4)   Adverb

11 -ence (differ<u>ence</u>; exist<u>ence</u>)
   (1)   Noun
   (2)   Verb
   (3)   Adjective
   (4)   Adverb

12 -ly (live<u>ly</u>; friend<u>ly</u>)
   (1)   Noun
   (2)   Verb
   (3)   Adjective
   (4)   Adverb

13 -less (end<u>less</u>; use<u>less</u>)
   (1)   Noun
   (2)   Verb
   (3)   Adjective
   (4)   Adverb

14 -some (trouble<u>some</u>; fear<u>some</u>)
   (1)   Noun
   (2)   Verb
   (3)   Adjective
   (4)   Adverb

15 -al (person<u>al</u>; tradition<u>al</u>)
   (1)   Noun
   (2)   Verb
   (3)   Adjective
   (4)   Adverb

16 -ive (act<u>ive</u>; effect<u>ive</u>)
   (1)   Noun
   (2)   Verb
   (3)   Adjective
   (4)   Adverb

17 -ant (result<u>ant</u>; pleas<u>ant</u>)
   (1)   Noun
   (2)   Verb
   (3)   Adjective
   (4)   Adverb

18 -ible (access<u>ible</u>; convert<u>ible</u>)
   (1)   Noun
   (2)   Verb
   (3)   Adjective
   (4)   Adverb

19 -ous (danger<u>ous</u>; continu<u>ous</u>)
   (1)   Noun
   (2)   Verb
   (3)   Adjective
   (4)   Adverb

20 -ate (passion<u>ate</u>; fortun<u>ate</u>)
   (1)   Noun
   (2)   Verb
   (3)   Adjective
   (4)   Adverb

21 -ty (safe<u>ty</u>; uncertain<u>ty</u>)
   (1)   Noun
   (2)   Verb
   (3)   Adjective
   (4)   Adverb

GLOSSARY

Academic Collocations List (ACL): A list of 2,468 adjective/noun, noun/noun, verb/noun, verb/adjective, verb/adverb, and adverb/verb collocations that are high frequency across a range of academic disciplines (Ackermann & Chen, 2013).

academic vocabulary: Words that are high frequency across a range of academic disciplines and less frequent outside academic discourse.

Academic Vocabulary List (AVL): A list of the 3,000 most frequent academic word families ordered according to their frequency (Gardner & Davies, 2014).

Academic Word List (AWL): A list of the 570 most frequent academic word families broken down into ten sub-lists (Coxhead, 2000).

alliteration: The use of the same letter or sounds at the beginning of words in a phrase (for example, 'sing a song of sixpence').

apposition: The use of a noun phrase immediately after another noun phrase that refers to the same thing (for example, 'Canberra, the capital of Australia').

association: A mental connection between ideas.

assonance: The use of two syllables close together with the same vowel sound but different consonants, or the same consonants but different vowels (for example, 'no one knows').

autonomous learning: Learning independently, without the support of teachers.

bilingual dictionary: A dictionary that provides information about L2 words in the L1.

bilingualized dictionary: A dictionary that provides information about the L2 words in both the L1 and L2.

British National Corpus (BNC): A 100 million-word collection of samples of written and spoken language that was designed to be representative of British English.

cognate: A word with the same origin as another word.

collocation: Words that commonly occur together (for example, 'point out', 'long term', 'make sure'). See also *multi-word combination.*

comprehensible input: A term introduced by Stephen Krashen and commonly used within applied linguistics to refer to language that can be understood by learners. See also *meaning-focused input.*

concordance: A list showing all the examples of an individual word in a text, corpus, etc.

consonance: Recurring consonant sounds within a phrase. See also *alliteration.*

content and language integrated learning (CLIL): Learning a language through the study of both language and academic content. See also *content-based language teaching (CBLT).*

content-based language teaching (CBLT): Teaching a second language through the study of subjects such as mathematics, science, and history. See also *content and language integrated learning (CLIL).*

content word: A word that conveys meaning, such as a noun, a verb, an adjective, or an adverb.

contextual clue: Information within a sentence, paragraph, or text that can be used to help infer the meaning of an unknown word.

contrastive analysis: The systematic study of two languages in order to identify similarities and differences in structure.

core meaning: The central or common meaning across several definitions of a word.

corpus (plural: **corpora**): A collection of texts that is designed to be representative of some aspect of language. For example, learner corpora are representative of the language used by learners of a second or foreign language.

Corpus of Contemporary American English (COCA): A 520 million-word collection of samples of language from spoken sources and written sources including fiction, magazines, newspapers, and academic texts that was designed to be representative of American English.

decontextualized: In isolation rather than in a phrase, sentence, or paragraph. Decontextualization limits the amount of information that can be learned about an unknown word.

deliberate learning: Learning, for example, vocabulary through the completion of exercises and tasks where the primary aim of the activity is to learn target words. Also known as intentional or explicit learning.

derivation: A change to the form of a headword through the addition of an affix (*un-*, *non-*, *hyper-*, *-ment*, *-tion*, *-able*, etc.). For example, 'add' (headword), 'addition', 'additions', 'additional', 'additionally', etc. (derivations). Derivations change the meaning of the headword (for example, 'happy' – 'unhappy') or the part of speech ('inform' – 'information').

dictogloss: A supported dictation activity where learners reconstruct a text by listening and noting down key words.

dual coding: The theory that both verbal information (relating to form) and non-verbal information (relating to the image that a word can convey) can contribute to learning. Words that are encoded both verbally and non-verbally (for example, 'tree', 'bird') are easier to learn than those that can only be encoded verbally (for example, 'adapt', 'appointment').

elaboration: Helping a word stick in memory by, for example, associating it with images, finding extra information about the word, doing word part analysis, or applying mnemonic tricks.

English as a Foreign Language (EFL)**:** English taught in contexts where English is not commonly used for communication (for example, Brazil, China, France, Japan).

English as a Second Language (ESL)**:** English taught in contexts where English is commonly used for communication (for example, the United States, Canada, the United Kingdom, Australia, and New Zealand).

English for Academic Purposes (EAP)**:** Programmes which prepare learners for study at English-medium universities.

Essential Word List (EWL)**:** A list made up of the 800 lemmas that are most frequent in spoken and written English, providing a useful lexical foundation for beginners.

etymology: The study of the origin of words. Knowing how the meaning of a word (or word sequence) was derived may help learners to remember it.

extensive listening: Listening to large amounts of L2 spoken text for interest or pleasure from, for example, the radio, podcasts, online sites, music, audio versions of graded readers and e-books. Materials should be at the appropriate level with a maximum of 5% of unknown words.

extensive reading: Reading large amounts of L2 text for interest or pleasure. Texts should be at the appropriate level with a maximum of 2% of unknown words so that learners process the language in a similar way to native speakers.

extensive viewing: Watching large amounts of L2 video for interest or pleasure. Sources of input include television, films, TED Talks, and YouTube. The language should be at the appropriate level, with a maximum of 5% of unknown words.

flashcard: A card with an L2 word or phrase on one side and the L1 meaning on the other. The primary aim of using flashcards is to link the form of an L2 word to its meaning and vice versa.

fluency development: One of Nation's four strands (see *principle of the four strands*). The focus is on learning to process language in a faster, more native-like way, using activities such as speed-reading, 4/3/2, and ten-minute writing. This should represent about one quarter of a vocabulary learning programme, split across the four skills of listening, speaking, reading, and writing.

form–meaning connection: Linking an L2 form to the L1 meaning. This is the most important aspect of vocabulary knowledge, because it is central to comprehension.

formulaic language: Combinations of words such as collocations, idioms, and phrasal verbs. Wray (2002) defines it as 'sequences of words that are stored and retrieved as wholes'. See also *multi-word combination*.

frequency list: A list of words derived from their frequency and range of occurrence in language, for example the General Service List (West, 1953) and the BNC/COCA word lists (Nation, 2012).

General Service List (GSL)**:** A frequency list developed in 1953 by Michael West, of about 2,000 word families viewed as being most useful for beginners. There are now several lists that better reflect the high-frequency words that are used today.

glossing: The explanation of difficult words in a text via L1 translation, L2 definition, or pictures to aid comprehension and vocabulary learning.

graphic organizer: A visual communication tool for expressing facts or ideas and the relationships between them.

guessing from context: A principled strategy which involves inferring the meanings of unknown words that are encountered by examining the surrounding context.

headword: The word that begins each entry in a word list or dictionary. (See also *derivation* and *inflection*.)

high-frequency: Vocabulary that is frequent across a range of spoken and written text types. The 2,000 highest-frequency word families typically account for about 70–90% of the words in a text and represent an important learning target.

homograph: A word with the same written form as another, but a different pronunciation and meaning; for example, 'attribute' (noun, verb), 'bow' (noun, verb), 'content' (noun, adj), 'lead' (noun, verb), 'row' (noun, verb).

homonym: A word with the same spoken and written form as another, but an unrelated meaning; for example, 'bank' (noun, noun), 'bat'(noun, noun, verb), 'fine' (noun, verb, adverb), 'light' (noun, verb, adj), 'novel' (noun, adj).

homophone: A word with the same spoken form as another, but a different written form and an unrelated meaning (for example, 'eye' and 'I', 'buy' and 'by', 'cereal' and 'serial', 'flour' and 'flower').

imaging: The process of deliberately creating a visual image related to the meaning of the word. The keyword technique is an example of an activity that uses imaging to learn words.

implicit knowledge: The information that learners have that they are unable to express (unconscious knowledge). The opposite, explicit knowledge, refers to information that can be stated verbally, such as the spelling of a word or its meaning.

incidental learning: Learning as a by-product of another task.

Incidental Learning Hypothesis: The theory that the impressive lexical growth of children is primarily the result of learning words incidentally through doing large amounts of reading. (Also known as the Default Learning Hypothesis.)

inflection: A change to the form of a headword through the addition of an affix (for example, *-ing, -ed, -s*) to reflect a grammatical function. For example, 'add' (headword), 'adds', 'adding', 'added' (inflections). The most common inflections entail changes in verb tense.

instantiation: The association of a word with a particular real-life occurrence of that word. Instantiation can help learners to remember words. For example, they might learn and remember the word 'fireworks' more effectively when it is learned while viewing fireworks.

intensive reading: A reading activity that involves a deliberate focus on language learning. Texts used for intensive reading typically include a proportion of unknown words greater than 2%.

interference: The problem created when factors within the learning condition reduce the potential to learn. This most often occurs when learning words that have similar meanings, such as synonyms, antonyms, lexical sets (for example, 'carrot', 'cabbage', 'onion', etc.) or similar forms (for example, 'affect' and 'effect', 'different' and 'difficult', 'Tuesday' and 'Thursday').

Involvement Load Hypothesis: A theory which Batia Laufer and Jan Hulstijn (2001) developed as a means to allow teachers to evaluate the effectiveness of activities. Activities can be analysed and scored for the inclusion of three learning conditions (need, search, evaluation) that indicate the extent to which they are likely to be effective (see also *Technique Feature Analysis*). It was a huge improvement on earlier systems of evaluation because it provided a quantifiable approach to determining the value of vocabulary learning activities.

keyword technique: An activity that involves creating an image linking the meaning of an L2 word with an L1 word that has a similar spoken form. It has been found to contribute to durable long-term vocabulary learning.

language-focused learning: One of Nation's four strands (see *principle of the four strands*). The focus is on deliberately learning words and developing strategies to learn more effectively. This should represent no more than one quarter of a vocabulary learning programme.

learning burden: The difficulty of learning a word, or the effort required to learn it. Words that follow established patterns in spelling, pronunciation, and grammar and have a high degree of overlap with L1 meanings have a lower learning burden than those that do not.

lemma: A unit of counting words. Lemmas are made up of a headword (for example, 'add') and its inflections ('add', 'adding', 'added'). Lemmas are useful as a unit of counting for beginners, who have yet to learn derivations.

lexical coverage: The percentage of known words. Usually referred to in relation to learners with varying vocabulary sizes (learners who know the 1,000/2,000 most frequent words, etc.). For example, research indicates that a lexical coverage of 95% may allow students to understand spoken discourse (van Zeeland & Schmitt, 2013), and a lexical coverage of 98% may allow students to understand written discourse (Hu & Nation, 2000).

lexical profiler: A tool that reveals frequency information about a text, such as the frequency level of each word, the lexical coverage of a text for learners with different vocabulary sizes, and which words are most likely to be unknown.

lexical set: A set of words with related meanings, such as colours, vehicles, and weather adjectives.

linked skills: An activity in which learners deal with the same content across the four skills of listening, speaking, reading, and writing.

loanword: A word adopted from a foreign language with little or no modification.

longitudinal study: A research method in which data is gathered on the same subject repeatedly over a period of time.

low-frequency: Vocabulary that is not common across a range of spoken and written text types. Low-frequency vocabulary is typically less frequent than the 2,000 most frequent word families. However, Schmitt and Schmitt (2012) suggest that it would be better to define low-frequency words as those that are less frequent than the 9,000 most frequent word families.

Matthew effect: A phenomenon where greater initial knowledge contributes to greater learning. Learners with less knowledge are likely to fall further and further behind, because the learners who are more advanced keep making greater gains than they do.

meaning-focused input: One of Nation's four strands (see *principle of the four strands*). The focus is on learning from comprehensible spoken and written text through extensive reading, listening, and viewing so that learners develop knowledge about how words are used, as well as about form and meaning. This should represent about one quarter of a vocabulary learning programme.

meaning-focused output: One of Nation's four strands (see *principle of the four strands*). The focus is on learning through producing language for the purpose of communication, namely speaking and writing. This should represent about one quarter of a vocabulary learning programme.

metalanguage: The words that are used to convey the rules of English (for example, 'noun', 'tense', 'metaphor'). They are low-frequency, with little value for communication, but important for teaching and learning purposes.

mid-frequency: Vocabulary from the 3–9,000 most frequent word families. These items are needed for comprehension of written text types such as newspapers and novels, and represent an important learning target for advanced students.

mnemonic: A strategy or device to help remember information. The keyword technique is an example of a mnemonic device that uses imagery.

monolingual dictionary: A dictionary typically used by native speakers. An English monolingual dictionary provides information about the words in English.

monosemic bias: The idea that if two words have the same or similar forms, they should be assumed to have the same meaning.

morpheme: The smallest grammatical unit (word part) in a language (for example, 'go', 'bed', *-less*, *-ing*).

morphology: The study of different forms of words and word parts.

multi-word combination: An umbrella term for a sequence of words that tends to function as a single unit (for example, 'How are you?', 'of course', 'lose weight', 'have to', 'the effects of'). The use of unusual combinations of words can differentiate advanced language learners from native-speakers.

narrow reading: Reading different texts about the same topic. This activity supports comprehension by developing background knowledge of a topic area and is less lexically demanding, because the same words tend to be repeated in related texts.

narrow viewing: Watching different episodes of the same television series in sequence. This activity is less lexically demanding than watching different programmes because more words tend to be repeated. Also, words that may be unknown are more likely to be repeated, which increases the potential for incidental vocabulary learning.

needs analysis: A careful consideration of the language needs of the learner in order to drive the objectives of a language course.

negotiation: A language-focused interaction between learners around the forms or meanings of unknown words.

new-General Service List (new-GSL)**:** A high-frequency word list developed in 2015 by Brezina and Gablasova.

noticing: The process of becoming aware that something is unknown in encountered input, for example a word's spelling, pronunciation, word parts, meaning, associations, collocations, grammatical functions, when and how often it is used.

parallelism: The use of repeated forms, sounds, rhythms, etc. in a text.

paraphrase: A restatement of the meaning of a text using other words

phonological awareness: Awareness of the sound structure of language.

phonology: The study of the system of sounds in a language.

phrasal expression: See *multi-word combination.*

Phrasal Expressions List: A list of the most frequent multi-word combinations (Martinez & Schmitt, 2012).

polysemous: With more than one meaning (for example, 'bank' – place to keep money / side of a river; 'head' – part of the body / leading person in a group).

post-test: A test administered after learning. Some are completed immediately after learning (immediate ~) and some are completed several days or weeks after learning (delayed ~).

pragmatics: The branch of linguistics dealing with language use in context.

pre-test: A test administered after learning.

principle of the four strands: Nation (2007) suggests that a well-balanced vocabulary learning programme should include the four strands of *meaning-focused input*, *meaning-focused output*, *language-focused learning*, and *fluency development*. The central principle behind the four strands is that no one form of learning is likely to be effective on its own and that each of the strands helps to develop a different aspect of language knowledge.

productive knowledge: The knowledge required to use a word, for example, its spoken or written form, its derivations and inflections, associations, and collocations. Gaining productive knowledge tends to take longer and occur after gaining receptive knowledge. Productive knowledge is also known as active knowledge.

productive learning: Producing language through speaking or writing, for example in communicative tasks, cloze activities, and crosswords.

receptive knowledge: The knowledge required to understand words through listening or reading. Gaining receptive knowledge allows us to recognize a word's spoken form, written form, derivations and inflections, meanings, associations, collocations, grammatical functions, and when and how often it is used. Because the majority of language learning is receptive and it is easier to gain receptive knowledge than productive knowledge, people tend to have greater receptive knowledge than productive knowledge. Receptive knowledge is also known as passive knowledge.

receptive learning: Encountering language and trying to understand it, for example, during reading, listening, and matching L2 words with their meanings.

referent: The person, thing, or idea that a word or phrase stands for or is a symbol for.

retention: The extent to which information about a word can be remembered.

retrieval: The process of searching for the form or meaning of a word. There are two types of retrieval: recall and recognition. Recall involves retrieving information from memory (for example, in a translation test). Recognition involves recognizing the correct information from different choices (for example, in a multiple-choice test). Spaced retrieval involves searching for the form or meaning of a word after some time has passed since the previous encounter or use. Spacing increases the effort required to retrieve the form or meaning of a word, which in turn increases the benefits of retrieval to lexical development.

rich instruction: A time-intensive series of activities designed to develop comprehensive knowledge of a target word, such as written form, spoken form, word parts, meaning, collocations, and grammatical functions. It is only worth using for the most important words.

rote-learning: A memorization technique based on repetition (for example, using flashcards).

running word: A word that is encountered in spoken or written text (for example, 'In this sentence there are eight running words.').

semantic mapping: Building a map of words and phrases associated with a topic. See also *graphic organizer*.

semantically related: Similar in meaning (for example, 'car', 'vehicle', 'truck', 'van'; 'blue', 'red', 'yellow', 'green').

slant rhyme: A rhyme formed by words with similar but not identical sounds (for example, 'years' and 'yours', 'fall' and 'bell').

speed-reading: A fluency development technique designed to increase the rate of reading speed.

sub-technical: Synonymous with *academic vocabulary*, occurring across a range of academic subjects rather than in a single subject.

synform: A word that looks or sounds like the wanted word but is not the wanted word, for example 'prize' and 'price', 'industrial' and 'industrious' (Laufer, 1988). Synforms are more difficult to learn than words that have unrelated forms.

synonym: A word or phrase that has the same meaning as another word or phrase.

syntax: The way in which words and phrases are organized in a language to create sentences.

technical vocabulary: Words that are high in frequency in a specific subject area and less frequent outside that area (for example, in medicine: 'pulmonary', 'anaemia', 'biopsy', 'renal').

Technique Feature Analysis: A method of evaluating the effectiveness of activities (Nation & Webb, 2011) that involves answering a series of 18 questions about the psychological conditions generated by an activity. Research indicates that it is more accurate in determining the value of activities than the Involvement Load Hypothesis (Hu & Nassaji, 2016).

testing effect: The likely improvement in score on the second administration of a test.

textual enhancement: A technique for drawing attention to important words in a text to increase the chances that they are learned (for example, bold, underlining, italics, highlighting). This term is sometimes used to refer to highlighting of a particular sort, but it is also used more broadly to refer to any kind of assistance which is used to help with the reading of a text, such as guiding questions, or glossing.

varied encounter: Encountering a word in a context which is different from a previous encounter. Note that it differs from the term 'generative use' (Joe, 1995, 1998), which was previously used for this concept. This is the result of a continuing attempt to find more transparent terminology and does not reflect a change in meaning.

varied use: Using a word in a way which is different from a previous use. Note that it differs from the term 'creative use' (Nation, 2013a), which was previously used for this concept. This is the result of a continuing attempt to find more transparent terminology and does not reflect a change in meaning.

Vocabulary Levels Test (VLT)**:** A test designed to measure knowledge of the most frequent English words. It is the most useful test for determining which words are known and which words should be learned. There are several versions; see Appendix 2 for Webb, Sasao, and Ballance's (2017) updated version of the test.

vocabulary load: The lexical difficulty involved in understanding the words in spoken or written text. A text with a lot of unknown words has a higher vocabulary load than a text with few unknown words.

word consciousness: A general awareness of words and various aspects of what it means to know a word.

word family: A unit of counting words. Word families are made up of a headword (for example, 'add'), its inflections ('adds', 'adding', 'added'), and its derivations ('addition', 'additions', 'additional', 'additionally', etc.). Word families are most useful as a unit of counting for receptive knowledge.

word list: A list of words that are deemed to be particularly important for learning a language or an aspect of a language.

word part: See *morpheme*.

word part analysis: Breaking a word down into parts to see how the parts contribute to the meaning of the word.

word type: A unit of counting words. Word types are every different word in a text (a second occurrence of a word is not different and is not counted). Word types are useful as a unit of counting for beginners, who have yet to learn inflections and derivations.

Zipf's law: The discovery that if we rank words according to their use, there is a patterned decrease in the frequency of items (Zipf, 1949). By examining the frequency of words in English, Zipf found that the number of occurrences of each word followed a logical progression; the most frequent word was about twice as frequent as the next most frequent word, approximately three times as frequent as the next most frequent word, and so on. Zipf's law highlights the fact that there are relatively few high-frequency words and many more low-frequency words.

WEBSITE REFERENCES

People and organizations

Mark Davies/Brigham Young University corpus

http://corpus.byu.edu

Center for English Corpus Linguistics, Université Catholique de Louvain

https://uclouvain.be/en/research-institutes/ilc/cecl

Compass Publishing

www.compasspub.com/eng/compass/book_level.asp

Compleat Lexical Tutor

www.lextutor.ca

Averil Coxhead

www.victoria.ac.nz/lals/about/staff/averil-coxhead

Nick Ellis

www-personal.umich.edu/~ncellis/NickEllis/Home.html

Extensive Reading Foundation

http://erfoundation.org

Paul Nation

www.victoria.ac.nz/lals/about/staff/paul-nation

Norbert Schmitt

www.norbertschmitt.co.uk

Stuart Webb

www.edu.uwo.ca/faculty-profiles/stuart-webb.html

Voice of America Learning English

http://learningenglish.voanews.com

Resources

Anki

https://apps.ankiweb.net

AntWordProfiler

www.laurenceanthony.net/software/antwordprofiler

Academic Vocabulary List

www.academicwords.info

BBC Learning English

www.bbc.co.uk/learningenglish

Flashcards+

www.chegg.com/mobile

List of graded readers

http://erfoundation.org/wordpress/graded-readers/graded-reader-list

www.lextutor.ca/ra_read

Guessing from Context Test

http://ysasaojp.info/testen.html

Guide to extensive reading

http://erfoundation.org/wordpress/useful-resources

Picture Vocabulary Size Test

www.laurenceanthony.net/software/pvst

Poll Everywhere

www.polleverywhere.com

Speed-reading courses

www.victoria.ac.nz/lals/about/staff/paul-nation#readers

www.victoria.ac.nz/lals/about/staff/sonia-millett

TED Talks

www.TED.com/talks

Vocabulary Levels Test

www.edu.uwo.ca/faculty-profiles/stuart-webb.html

Early versions of the Vocabulary Levels Test

www.norbertschmitt.co.uk/resources.html

VocabProfile

www.lextutor.ca/vp

Vocabulary Size Test

www.victoria.ac.nz/lals/about/staff/paul-nation

www.lextutor.ca

www.my.vocabularysize.com

Word Neighbors concordancer

http://wordneighbors.ust.hk

Word Part Levels Test

http://ysasaojp.info/testen.html

YouTube

www.youtube.com

BIBLIOGRAPHY

Ackermann, K., & **Chen, Y.** (2013). Developing the academic collocation list (ACL) – a corpus-driven and expert-judged approach. *Journal of English for Academic Purpos*es, *12(4)*, 235–247.

Alderson, J. C. (2007). Judging the frequency of English words. *Applied Linguistics*, *28(3)*, 383–409.

Anderson, R. C., **Stevens, K. C.**, **Shifrin, Z.**, & **Osborn, J.** (1978). Instantiation of word meanings in children. *Journal of Reading Behaviour*, *10(2)*, 149–157.

Anglin, J. M. (1993). Vocabulary development: a morphological analysis. *Monographs of the Society for Research in Child Development*, *58(10)*, 1–166.

Arevart, S., & **Nation, I. S. P.** (1991). Fluency improvement in a second language. *RELC Journal, 22(1)*, 84–94.

Astika, G. G. (1993). Analytical assessment of foreign students' writing. *RELC Journal, 24(1)*, 61–72.

Atkins, B. T. S., & **Knowles, F. E.** (1990). Interim report on the EURALEX/AILA research project into dictionary use. *BudaLex 88 proceedings*, 391–392.

Baddeley, A. D. (1990). *Human memory*. London: Lawrence Erlbaum Associates.

Bahrick, H. P., **Bahrick, L. E.**, **Bahrick, A. S.**, & **Bahrick, P. E.** (1993). Maintenance of foreign language vocabulary and the spacing effect. *Psychological Science, 4(5)*, 316–321.

Barcroft, J. (2006). Can writing a new word detract from learning it? More negative effects of forced output during vocabulary learning. *Second Language Research, 22(4)*, 487–497.

Barcroft, J. (2007). Effects of opportunities for word retrieval during second language vocabulary learning. *Language Learning, 57(1)*, 35–56.

Barcroft, J. (2009). Effects of synonym generation on incidental and intentional L2 vocabulary learning during reading. *TESOL Quarterly, 43(1)*, 79–103.

Barcroft, J. (2015). Can retrieval opportunities increase vocabulary learning during reading? *Foreign Language Annals, 48(2)*, 236–249.

Barnard, H. (1961). A test of P.U.C. students' vocabulary in Chotanagpur. *Bulletin of the Central Institute of English, 1*, 90–100.

Bauer, L., & **Nation, I. S. P.** (1993). Word families. *International Journal of Lexicography, 6(4)*, 253–279.

Beglar, D. (2010). A Rasch-based validation of the Vocabulary Size Test. *Language Testing, 27(1)*, 101–118.

Biber, D., & **Conrad, S.** (2001). Quantitative corpus-based research: Much more than bean counting. *TESOL Quarterly, 35*, 331–336.

Biemiller, A., & **Slonim, N.** (2001). Estimating root word vocabulary growth in normative and advantaged populations: evidence for a common sequence of vocabulary acquisition. *Journal of Educational Psychology, 93(3)*, 498–520.

Biemiller, A., & **Boote, C.** (2006). An effective method for building meaning vocabulary in primary grades. *Journal of Educational Psychology, 98(1)*, 44–62.

Bishop, H. (2004). The effect of typographic salience on the look up and comprehension of unknown formulaic sequences. In N. Schmitt (Ed.), *Formulaic sequences: acquisition, processing, and use* (pp. 227–248). Amsterdam: John Benjamins.

Boers, F., **Demecheleer, M.**, & **Eyckmans, J.** (2004). Etymological elaboration as a strategy for learning figurative idioms. In P. Bogaards & B. Laufer (Eds.), *Vocabulary in a second language: selection, acquisition and testing* (pp. 53–78). Amsterdam: John Benjamins.

Boers, F., **Eyckmans, J.**, & **Stengers, H.** (2007). Presenting figurative idioms with a touch of etymology: more than mere mnemonics? *Language Teaching Research, 11(1)*, 43–62.

Boers, F., & **Lindstromberg, S.** (2009). *Optimizing a lexical approach to instructed second language acquisition*. Basingstoke: Palgrave Macmillan.

Boers, F., **Siyanova-Chanturia, A.**, & **Warren, P.** (2013). Does adding pictures to glosses promote uptake of new words? Paper presented at Vocab@Vic conference, University of Wellington, New Zealand.

Boers, F. (2014). A reappraisal of the 4/3/2 activity. *RELC Journal, 45(3)*, 221–235.

Boers, F., **Lindstromberg, S.**, & **Webb, S.** (2014). Further evidence of the comparative memorability of alliterative expressions in second language learning. *RELC Journal, 45(1)*, 85–99.

Boers, F., **Demecheleer, M.**, **Coxhead, A.**, & **Webb, S.** (2014). Gauging the effects of exercises on verb-noun collocations. *Language Teaching Research, 18(1)*, 54–74.

Bowles, M. A. (2004). L2 glossing: to CALL or not to CALL. *Hispania, 87(3)*, 541–52.

Brezina, V., & **Gablasova, D.** (2015). Is there a core general vocabulary? Introducing the New General Service List. *Applied Linguistics, 36(1)*,1–22.

Brown, R., **Waring, R.**, & **Donkaewbua, S.** (2008). Incidental vocabulary acquisition from reading, reading-while-listening, and listening to stories. *Reading in a Foreign Language, 20(2)*, 136–163.

Bruton, A. (2007). Vocabulary learning from dictionary reference in collaborative EFL translational writing. *System, 35(3)*, 353–367.

Campion, M. E., & **Elley, W. B.** (1971). *An academic vocabulary list.* Wellington: New Zealand Council for Educational Research.

Carlo, M. S., **August, D.**, **Mclaughlin, B.**, **Snow, C. E.**, **Dressler, C.**, **Lippman, D. N.**, **Lively, T. J.**, & **White, C. E.** (2004). Closing the gap: addressing the vocabulary needs of English-language learners in bilingual and mainstream classrooms. *Reading Research Quarterly, 39(2)*,188–215.

Carroll, J. B., **Davies, P.**, & **Richman, B.** (1971). *The American heritage word frequency book.* New York: Houghton Mifflin, Boston American Heritage.

Carver, R. P. (1992). Reading rate: theory, research, and practical implications. *Journal of Reading, 36(2)*, 84–95.

Chang, A. C.-S. (2007). The impact of vocabulary preparation on L2 listening comprehension, confidence and strategy use. *System, 35(4)*, 534–550.

Chapple, L., & **Curtis, A.** (2000). Content-based instruction in Hong Kong: student responses to film. *System, 28(3)*, 419–433.

Chaudron, C. (1982). Vocabulary elaboration in teachers' speech to L2 learners. *Studies in Second Language Acquisition, 4(2)*,170–180.

Chung, T. M., & **Nation, I. S. P.** (2003). Technical vocabulary in specialised texts. *Reading in a Foreign Language, 15(2)*, 103–116.

Chung, M., & **Nation, I. S. P.** (2006). The effect of a speed reading course. *English Teaching, 61(4)*,181–204.

Clarke, D. F., & **Nation, I. S. P.** (1980). Guessing the meanings of words from context: strategy and techniques. *System, 8(3)*, 211–220.

Cobb, T. (2007). Computing the vocabulary demands of L2 reading. *Language Learning & Technology, 11(3)*, 38–63.

Cobb, T. (2010). Learning about language and learners from computer programs. *Reading in a Foreign Language, 22(1)*,181–200.

Cohen, A. D. (1989). Reformulation: a technique for providing advanced feedback in writing. *Guidelines, 11(2)*, 1–9.

Coxhead, A. (2000). A new academic word list. *TESOL Quarterly, 34(2)*, 213–238.

Coxhead, A. (2007). Factors and aspects of knowledge affecting L2 word use in writing. In P. Davidson, C. Coombe, D. Lloyd, & D. Palfreyman (Eds.), *Teaching and learning vocabulary in another language* (pp. 331–342). Dubai: TESOL Arabia.

Coxhead, A., & **Hirsh, D.** (2007). A pilot science word list for EAP. *Revue Française de Linguistique Appliqueé, XII(2)*, 65–78.

Coxhead, A., & **Walls, R.** (2012). TED Talks, vocabulary, and listening for EAP. *TESOLANZ Journal, 20(1)*, 55–67.

Coxhead, A., **Nation, I. S. P.**, & **Sim, D.** (2015). Measuring the vocabulary size of native speakers of English in New Zealand secondary schools. *New Zealand Journal of Educational Studies, 50(1)*, 121–135.

Craik, F. I. M., & **Lockhart, R. S.** (1972). Levels of processing: a framework for memory research. *Journal of Verbal Learning and Verbal Behavior, 11*, 671–684.

Craik, F. I. M., & **Tulving, E.** (1975). Depth of processing and the retention of words in episodic memory. *Journal of Experimental Psychology,104(3)*, 268–294.

Crothers, E., & **Suppes, P.** (1967). *Experiments in Second-Language Learning.* New York: Academic Press.

d'Agostino, P. R., **O'Neill, B. J.**, & **Paivio, A.** (1977). Memory for pictures and words as a function of level of processing: depth or dual coding? *Memory & Cognition, 5(2)*, 252–256.

d'Anna, C. A., **Zechmeister, E. B.**, & **Hall, J. W.** (1991). Toward a meaningful definition of vocabulary size. *Journal of Literacy Research, 23(1)*, 109–122.

Daneman, M., & **Green, I.** (1986). Individual differences in comprehending and producing words in context. *Journal of Memory and Language, 25(1)*, 1–18.

Dang, T. N. Y., & **Webb, S.** (2014). The lexical profile of academic spoken English. *English for Specific Purposes*, *33*, 66–76.

Dang, T. N. Y., & **Webb, S.** (2016a). Evaluating lists of high-frequency words. *International Journal of Applied Linguistics*, *167(2)*, 132–158.

Dang, T. N. Y., & **Webb, S.** (2016b). Making an essential word list for beginners. In I. S. P. Nation, *Making and using word lists for language learning and testing* (pp. 153–167, 188–195). Amsterdam: John Benjamins.

Danelund, L. (2013). Exploring the level and development of Danish high school EFL learners' receptive and productive vocabulary knowledge. Unpublished MA thesis, University of Copenhagen, Denmark.

Daulton, F. E. (2008). *Japan's built-in lexicon of English-based loanwords.* Clevedon: Multilingual Matters.

Day, R. R., **Omura, C.**, & **Hiramatsu, M.** (1991). Incidental EFL vocabulary learning and reading. *Reading in a Foreign Language*, *7(2)*, 541–551.

Day, R., & **Bamford, J.** (2002). Top ten principles for teaching extensive reading. *Reading in a Foreign Language*, *14(2),* 136–141.

de Bot, K., **Paribakht, T. S.**, & **Wesche, M. B.** (1997). Toward a lexical processing model for the study of second language vocabulary acquisition. *Studies in Second Language Acquisition*, *19(3)*, 309–329.

de Groot, A. M. B. (2006). Effects of stimulus characteristics and background music on foreign language vocabulary learning and forgetting. *Language Learning*, *56(3)*, 463–506.

deHaan, J., **Reed, W. M.**, & **Kuwada, K.** (2010). The effect of interactivity with a music video game on second language vocabulary recall. *Language Learning & Technology*, *14(2)*, 79–94.

de la Fuente, M. J. (2002). Negotiation and oral acquisition of L2 vocabulary. *Studies in Second Language Acquisition*, *24(1)*, 81–112.

de la Fuente, M. J. (2003). Is SLA interactionist theory relevant to CALL? A study on the effects of computer-mediated interaction in L2 vocabulary acquisition. *Computer Assisted Language Learning*, *16(1)*, 47–81.

de Ridder, I. (2002). Visible or invisible links: does the highlighting of hyperlinks affect incidental vocabulary learning, text comprehension, and the reading process? *Language Learning and Technology*, *6(1)*, 123–146.

Dobao, A. F. (2014a). Attention to form in collaborative writing tasks: comparing pair and small group interaction. *The Canadian Modern Language Review / La Revue Canadienne Des Langues Vivantes*, *70(2)*, 158–187.

Dobao, A. F. (2014b). Vocabulary learning in collaborative tasks: a comparison of pair and small group work. *Language Teaching Research*, *18(4)*, 497–520.

Durrant, P., & **Schmitt, N.** (2010). Adult learners' retention of collocations from exposure. *Second Language Research*, *26(2)*, 163–188.

Elgort, I. (2011). Deliberate learning and vocabulary acquisition in a second language. *Language Learning*, *61(2)*, 367–413.

Elley, W. B., & **Mangubhai, F.** (1981a). *The impact of a book flood in Fiji primary schools.* Wellington: New Zealand Council for Educational Research.

Elley, W. B., & **Mangubhai, F.** (1981b). The long-term effects of a book flood on children's language growth. *Directions*, *7*, 15–24.

Elley, W. B. (1989). Vocabulary acquisition from listening to stories. Reading *Research Quarterly*, *24(2)*, 174–187.

Ellis, N. C., & **Beaton, A.** (1993). Psycholinguistic determinants of foreign language vocabulary learning. *Language Learning*, *43(4)*, 559–617.

Ellis, R. (1991). The interaction hypothesis: a critical evaluation. In E. Sadtono (Ed.), *Language acquisition and the second/foreign language classroom* (pp. 179–211). RELC Anthology: Series 28. Singapore: SEAMEO-RELC.

Ellis, R., **Tanaka, Y.**, & **Yamazaki, A.** (1994). Classroom interaction, comprehension, and the acquisition of L2 word meanings. *Language Learning*, *44(3)*, 449–491.

Ellis, R. (1997). *SLA research and language teaching.* Oxford: Oxford University Press.

Ellis, R., & **Heimbach, R.** (1997). Bugs and birds: children's acquisition of second language vocabulary through interaction. *System*, *25(2)*, 247–259.

Ellis, R. (1999). *Learning a second language through interaction.* Amsterdam: John Benjamins.

Ellis, R., & **He, X.** (1999). The roles of modified input and output in the incidental acquisition of word meanings. *Studies in Second Language Acquisition*, *21(2)*, 285–301.

Engber, C. A. (1995). The relationship of lexical proficiency to the quality of ESL compositions. *Journal of Second Language Writing*, *4(2)*, 139–155.

Engels, L. K. (1968). The fallacy of word-counts. *International Review of Applied Linguistics in Language Teaching*, *6(1/4)*, 213–231.

Erman, B., & **Warren, B.** (2000). The idiom principle and the open choice principle. *Text, 20(1)*, 29–62.

Erten, I. H., & **Tekin, M.** (2008). Effects on vocabulary acquisition of presenting new words in semantic sets versus semantically unrelated sets. *System, 36(3)*, 407–422.

Flowerdew, J. (1992). Definitions in science lectures. *Applied Linguistics, 13(2),* 202–221.

Francis, W. N., & **Kučera, H.** (1982). *Frequency analysis of English usage*. Boston, MA: Houghton Mifflin.

Fraser, C. A. (1999). Lexical processing strategy use and vocabulary learning through reading. *Studies in Second Language Acquisition, 21(2)*, 225–241.

Fraser, S. (2007). Providing ESP learners with the vocabulary they need: corpora and the creation of specialized word lists. *Hiroshima Studies in Language and Language Education, 10*, 127–143.

Fukkink, R. G., & **de Glopper, K.** (1998). Effects of instruction in deriving word meaning from context: a meta-analysis. *Review of Educational Research, 68(4)*, 450–469.

Gardner, D., & **Davies, M.** (2014). A new Academic Vocabulary List. *Applied Linguistics, 35(3)*, 305–327.

Gass, S. (1999). Discussion: Incidental vocabulary learning. *Studies in Second Language Acquisition, 21(2)*, 319–333.

Gathercole, S. E., & **Baddeley, A. D.** (1989). Evaluation of the role of phonological STM in the development of vocabulary in children: a longitudinal study. *Journal of Memory and Language, 28(2)*, 200–213.

Gettys, S., **Imhof, L. A.**, & **Kautz, J. O.** (2001). Computer-assisted reading: the effect of glossing format on comprehension and vocabulary retention. *Foreign Language Annals, 34(2)*, 91–106.

Gieve, S., & **Clark, R.** (2005). The Chinese approach to learning: cultural trait or situated response? The case of a self-directed learning programme. *System, 33(2)*, 261–276.

Goulden, R., **Nation, I. S. P.**, & **Read, J.** (1990). How large can a receptive vocabulary be? *Applied Linguistics, 11(4)*, 341–363.

Grant, L., & **Nation, I. S. P.** (2006). How many idioms are there in English? *International Journal of Applied Linguistics (ITL), 151*, 1–14.

Graves, M. F. (2006). *The vocabulary book: learning and instruction*. Newark: International Reading Association.

Griffin, G. F., & **Harley, T. A.** (1996). List learning of second language vocabulary. *Applied Psycholinguistics, 17(4)*, 443–460.

Gu, P. Y. (2003). Fine brush and freehand: the vocabulary-learning art of two successful Chinese EFL learners. *TESOL Quarterly, 37(1)*, 73–104.

Haastrup, K. (1989). *Lexical inferencing procedures Vols 1 and 2.* Copenhagen: Handelshojskolen i Kobenhavn.

Hall, S. J. (1991). Using split information tasks to learn mathematics vocabulary. *Guidelines, 14(1)*, 72–77.

Hayes, D. P. (1988). Speaking and writing: Distinct patterns of word choice. *Journal of Memory and Language, 27(5)*, 572–585.

Higa, M. (1963). Interference effects of intralist word relationships in verbal learning. *Journal of Verbal Learning and Verbal Behavior, 2(2)*, 170–175.

Higa, M. (1965). The psycholinguistic concept of 'difficulty' and the teaching of foreign language vocabulary. *Language Learning, 15(3–4)*, 167–179.

Hill, J. (2001). Revising priorities: from grammatical failure to collocational success. In M. Lewis (Ed.), *Teaching collocation: further development in the lexical approach* (pp. 47–69). Hove: LTP.

Holdaway, D. (1979). *The foundations of literacy.* Sydney: Ashton Scholastic.

Horst, M., **Cobb, T.**, & **Meara, P. M.** (1998). Beyond a clockwork orange: acquiring second language vocabulary through reading. *Reading in a Foreign Language, 11(2)*, 207–223.

Horst, M., & **Collins, L.** (2006). From 'faible' to strong: how does their vocabulary grow? *Canadian Modern Language Review, 63(1)*, 83–108.

Hsu, W. (2013). Bridging the vocabulary gap for EFL medical undergraduates: the establishment of a medical word list. *Language Teaching Research, 17(4)*, 454–484.

Hsu, W. (2014). Measuring the vocabulary load of engineering textbooks for EFL undergraduates. *English for Specific Purposes, 33(1)*, 54–65.

Hu, C.-F. (2008). Rate of acquiring and processing L2 color words in relation to L1 phonological awareness. *Modern Language Journal, 92(1)*, 39–52.

Hu, H. M., & **Nation, I. S. P.** (2000). Unknown vocabulary density and reading comprehension. *Reading in a Foreign Language, 13(1)*, 403–430.

Hu, H. M., & **Nassaji, H.** (2016). Effective vocabulary learning tasks: Involvement Load Hypothesis versus Technique Feature Analysis. *System*, *56*, 28–39.

Hughes, P. (2001). Animals, values and tourism – structural shifts in UK dolphin tourism provision. *Tourism Management*, *22(4)*, 321–329.

Hulstijn, J. H. (1992). Retention of inferred and given word meanings: experiments in incidental vocabulary learning. In P. J. L. Arnaud & H. Bejoint (Eds.), *Vocabulary and applied linguistics* (pp. 113–125). London: Macmillan.

Hulstijn, J., **Hollander, M.**, & **Greidanus, T.** (1996). Incidental vocabulary learning by advanced foreign language students: the influence of marginal glosses, dictionary use, and reoccurrence of unknown words. *Modern Language Journal*, *80(3)*, 327–339.

Hulstijn, J. H., & **Laufer, B.** (2001). Some empirical evidence for the involvement load hypothesis in vocabulary acquisition. *Language Learning*, *51(3)*, 539–558.

Hwang, K., & **Nation, I. S. P.** (1989). Reducing the vocabulary load and encouraging vocabulary learning through reading newspapers. *Reading in a Foreign Language*, *6(1)*, 323–335.

Hyland, K., & **Tse, P.** (2007). Is there an 'academic vocabulary'? *TESOL Quarterly*, *41(2)*, 235–253.

Ishii, T. (2013). Reexamining semantic clustering: insight from memory models. *Vocabulary Learning and Instruction, 2(1)*, 1–7.

Jacobs, G. M., **Dufon, P.**, & **Hong, F. C.** (1994). L1 and L2 vocabulary glosses in L2 reading passages: their effectiveness for increasing comprehension and vocabulary knowledge. *Journal of Research in Reading*, *17(1)*, 19–28.

Jenkins, J. R., & **Dixon, R.** (1983). Vocabulary learning. *Contemporary Educational Psychology, 8(3)*, 237–260.

Jenkins, J. R., **Stein, M. L.**, & **Wysocki, K.** (1984). Learning vocabulary through reading. *American Educational Research Journal*, *21*, 767–787.

Joe, A. (1995). Text-based tasks and incidental vocabulary learning. *Second Language Research*, *11(2)*,149–158.

Joe, A. (1998). What effects do text-based tasks promoting generation have on incidental vocabulary acquisition? *Applied Linguistics*, *19(3)*, 357–377.

Johannsen, K. L., & **Tarver Chase, R.** (2010). *Word English 3*. Boston, M.A.: Heinle Cengage Learning.

Jordan, R. R. (1990). Pyramid discussions. *ELT Journal*, *44(1)*, 46–54.

Joseph, S. R. H., **Watanabe, Y.**, **Shiung, Y. J.**, **Choi, B.**, & **Robbins, C.** (2009). Key aspects of computer assisted vocabulary learning (CAVL): combined effects of media, sequencing and task type. *Research and Practice in Technology Enhanced Learning, 4(2)*, 133–168.

Karpicke, J. D., & **Blunt, J. R.** (2011). Response to comment on 'Retrieval practice produces more learning than elaborative studying with concept mapping.'. *Science, 334(6055)*, 453–453.

Kim, Y. J. (2008a). The role of task-induced involvement and learner proficiency in L2 vocabulary acquisition. *Language Learning, 58(2)*, 285–325.

Kim, Y. (2008b). The contribution of collaborative and individual tasks to the acquisition of L2 vocabulary. *Modern Language Journal, 92(1)*, 114–130.

King, J. (2002). Using DVD feature films in the EFL classroom. *Computer Assisted Language Learning, 15(5)*, 509–523.

Knight, S. M. (1994). Dictionary use while reading: the effects on comprehension and vocabulary acquisition for students of different verbal abilities. *Modern Language Journal, 78(3)*, 285–299.

Ko, M. H. (2005). Glosses, comprehension, and strategy use. *Reading in a Foreign Language, 17(2)*, 125–143.

Konstantakis, N. (2007). Creating a business word list for teaching Business English. *Estudios de Lingüística Inglesa Aplicada, 7*, 79–102.

Koolstra, C. M., & **Beentjes, J. W.** (1999). Children's vocabulary acquisition in a foreign language through watching subtitled television programs at home. *Educational Technology Research and Development, 47(1)*, 51–60.

Kötter, M. (2003). Negotiation of meaning and codeswitching in online tandems. *Language Learning & Technology, 7(2)*, 145–72.

Krashen, S. D. (1981). The 'fundamental pedagogical principle' in second language teaching. *Studia Linguistica, 35(1–2)*, 50–70.

Krashen, S. (1985). *The input hypothesis: issues and implications*. London: Longman.

Krashen, S. (1989). We acquire vocabulary and spelling by reading: additional evidence for the input hypothesis. *The Modern Language Journal, 73(4)*, 440–464.

Krashen, S. D. (2004). *The power of reading: insights from the research, second edition*. Portsmouth, NH: Heinemann.

Kraus-Srebrič, E., **Brakus, L.**, & **Kentrič, D.** (1981). A six-tier cake: an experiment with self-selected learning tasks. *ELT Journal, 36(1)*, 19–23.

Kuhn, M. R., & **Stahl, S. A.** (1998). Teaching children to learn word meanings from context. *Journal of Literacy Research, 30(1)*, 119–138.

Kweon, S.-O., & **Kim, H. R.** (2008). Beyond raw frequency: incidental vocabulary acquisition in extensive reading. *Reading in a Foreign Language, 20(2)*, 191–215.

Lado, R., **Baldwin, B.**, & **Lobo, F.** (1967). *Massive vocabulary in a foreign language beyond the basic course: the effects of stimuli, timing and order of presentation*. Washington, D.C.: U.S. Department of Health, Education, and Welfare.

Landauer, T. K., & **Bjork, R. A.** (1978). Optimum rehearsal patterns and name learning. *Practical Aspects of Memory, 1*, 625–632.

Laufer, B., & **Sim, D. D.** (1985). Measuring and explaining the reading threshold needed for English for academic purposes texts. *Foreign Language Annals, 18(5)*, 405–411.

Laufer, B. (1988). The concept of 'synforms' (similar lexical forms) in vocabulary acquisition. *Language and Education, 2(2)*, 113–132.

Laufer, B. (1997). What's in a word that makes it hard or easy? Intralexical factors affecting the difficulty of vocabulary acquisition. In N. Schmitt & M. McCarthy (Eds.), *Vocabulary: description, acquisition and pedagogy* (pp. 140–155). Cambridge: Cambridge University Press.

Laufer, B., & **Hadar, L.** (1997). Assessing the effectiveness of monolingual, bilingual, and 'bilingualised' dictionaries in the comprehension and production of new words. *Modern Language Journal, 81(2)*, 189–196.

Laufer, B., & **Shmueli, K.** (1997). Memorizing new words: does teaching have anything to do with it? *RELC Journal, 28(1)*, 89–108.

Laufer, B., & **Hill, M.** (2000). What lexical information do L2 learners select in a CALL dictionary and how does it affect word retention? *Language Learning & Technology, 3(2)*, 58–76.

Laufer, B. (2001). Reading, word-focused activities and incidental vocabulary acquisition in a second language. *Prospect, 16(3)*, 44–54.

Laufer, B., & **Hulstijn, J.** (2001). Incidental vocabulary acquisition in a second language: the construct of task-induced involvement. *Applied Linguistics, 22(1)*, 1–26.

Laufer, B. (2003). Vocabulary acquisition in a second language: do learners really acquire most vocabulary by reading? *Canadian Modern Language Review, 59(4)*, 565–585.

Laufer, B., & **Goldstein, Z.** (2004). Testing vocabulary knowledge: size, strength, and computer adaptiveness. *Language Learning, 54(3)*, 399–436.

Laufer, B., **Elder, C.**, **Hill, K.**, & **Congdon, P.** (2004). Size and strength: do we need both to measure vocabulary knowledge? *Language Testing, 21(2)*, 202–226.

Laufer, B. (2005). Lexical frequency profiles: from Monte Carlo to the real world. A response to Meara (2005). *Applied Linguistics, 26(4)*, 582–588.

Laufer, B., & **Rozovski-Roitblat, B.** (2011). Incidental vocabulary acquisition: the effects of task type, word occurrence and their combination. *Language Teaching Research, 15(4)*, 391–411.

Laufer, B., & **Rozovski-Roitblat, B.** (2015). Retention of new words: quantity of encounters, quality of task, and degree of knowledge. *Language Teaching Research, 19(6)*, 687–711.

Lee, S. H. (2003). ESL learners' vocabulary use in writing and the effects of explicit vocabulary instruction. *System, 31(4)*, 537–561.

Lee, S. H., & **Muncie, J.** (2006). From receptive to productive: improving ESL learners' use of vocabulary in a post-reading composition task. *TESOL Quarterly, 40(2)*, 295–320.

Leech, G., **Rayson, P.**, & **Wilson, A.** (2001). *Word frequencies in written and spoken English.* Harlow: Longman.

Lindstromberg, S., & **Boers, F.** (2008). Phonemic repetition and the learning of lexical chunks: The power of assonance. *System, 36(3)*, 423–436.

Liu, D. (2010). Going beyond patterns: involving cognitive analysis in the learning of collocations. *TESOL Quarterly, 44(1)*, 4–30.

Liu, D. (2012). The most frequently-used multi-word constructions in academic written English: a multi-corpus study. *English for Specific Purposes, 31(1)*, 25–35.

Liu, N., & **Nation, I. S. P.** (1985). Factors affecting guessing vocabulary in context. *RELC Journal, 16(1)*, 33–42.

Luppescu, S., & **Day, R. R.** (1993). Reading, dictionaries and vocabulary learning. *Language Learning, 43(2)*, 263–287.

Martínez, I. A., **Beck, S. C.**, & **Panza, C. B.** (2009). Academic vocabulary in agriculture research articles: a corpus-based study. *English for Specific Purposes, 28(3)*, 183–198.

Martinez, R., & **Schmitt, N.** (2012). A phrasal expressions list. *Applied Linguistics, 33(3)*, 299–320.

Maurice, K. (1983). The fluency workshop. *TESOL Newsletter*, *17(4)*, 29.

McDonough, K., & **Sunitham, W.** (2009). Collaborative dialogue between Thai EFL learners during self-access computer activities. *TESOL Quarterly*, *43(2)*, 231–254.

McLaughlin, B. (1990). Restructuring. *Applied Linguistics*, *11(2)*, 113–128.

Merton, R. K. (1968). The Matthew effect in science. *Science*, *159(3810)*, 56–63.

Milton, J., & **Meara, P.** (1998). Are the British really bad at learning foreign languages? *Language Learning Journal*, *18(1)*, 68–76.

Milton, J. (2006a). X-Lex: the Swansea Vocabulary Levels Test. In C. Coombe, P. Davidson, & D. Lloyd (Eds.), *Proceedings of the 7th and 8th Current Trends in English Language Testing (CTELT) Conference, Vol. 4* (pp. 29–39). UAE: TESOL Arabia.

Milton, J. (2006b). Language lite: learning French vocabulary in school. *Journal of French Language Studies*, *16(2)*, 187–205.

Min, H. (2008). EFL vocabulary acquisition and retention: reading plus vocabulary enhancement activities and narrow reading. *Language Learning*, *58(1)*, 73–115.

Mol, S., **Bus, A.**, & **de Jong, M.** (2009). Interactive book reading in early education: a tool to stimulate print knowledge as well as oral language. *Review of Educational Research*, *79(2)*, 979–1007.

Mondria, J. A. (2003). The effects of inferring, verifying and memorizing on the retention of L2 word meanings. *Studies in Second Language Acquisition*, *25(4)*, 473–499.

Mondria, J. A., & **Wiersma, B.** (2004). Receptive, productive, and receptive + productive L2 vocabulary learning: what difference does it make? In P. Bogaards & B. Laufer (Eds.), *Vocabulary in a second language: selection, acquisition, and testing* (pp. 79–100). Amsterdam: John Benjamins.

Morgan, B. Q., & **Oberdeck, L. M.** (1930). Active and passive vocabulary. In E. W. Bagster-Collins (Ed.), *Studies in modern language teaching* (pp. 213–221). London: Macmillan.

Moseley, D. (1994). From theory to practice: errors and trials. In G. D. A. Brown & N. C. Ellis (Eds.), *Handbook of spelling* (pp. 459–479). Chichester: John Wiley & Sons.

Nagy, W. E., **Herman, P. A.**, & **Anderson, R. C.** (1985). Learning words from context. *Reading Research Quarterly*, *20(2)*, 233–253.

Nagy, W. E., & **Herman, P. A.** (1987). Breadth and depth of vocabulary knowledge: implications for acquisition and instruction. In M. G. McKeown & M. E. Curtis (Eds.), *The nature of vocabulary acquisition* (pp. 19–36). Hillsdale, NJ: Erlbaum.

Nakata, T. (2011). Computer-assisted second language vocabulary learning in a paired-associate paradigm: a critical investigation of flashcard software. *Computer Assisted Language Learning, 24(1)*, 17–38.

Nakata, T. (2015). Effects of expanding and equal spacing on second language vocabulary learning. *Studies in Second Language Acquisition, 37(4)*, 677–711.

Nakata, T., & **Webb, S.** (2016). Does studying vocabulary in smaller sets increase learning?: the effects of part and whole learning on second language vocabulary acquisition. *Studies in Second Language Acquisition, 38*, 523–552.

Nesselhauf, N. (2003). The use of collocations by advanced learners of English and some implications for teaching. *Applied Linguistics, 24(2)*, 223–242.

Nation, I. S. P. (1983). Testing and teaching vocabulary. *Guidelines, 5(1)*, 12–25.

Nation, I. S. P. (1988). Using techniques well: information transfer. *Guidelines, 10(1)*, 17–23.

Nation, I. S. P. (1989). Improving speaking fluency. *System, 17(3)*, 377–384.

Nation, I. S. P. (1990). *Teaching and learning vocabulary*. Rowley, MA: Newbury House.

Nation, I. S. P. (1991a). Managing group discussion: problem-solving tasks. *Guidelines, 13(1)*, 1–10.

Nation, I. S. P. (1991b). Dictation, dicto-comp and related techniques. *English Teaching Forum, 29(4)*, 12–14.

Nation, I. S. P., & **Hwang, K.** (1995). Where would general service vocabulary stop and special purposes vocabulary begin? *System, 23(1)*, 35–41.

Nation, I. S. P. (2000). Learning vocabulary in lexical sets: dangers and guidelines. *TESOL Journal, 9(2)*, 6–10.

Nation, I. S. P., & **Hamilton-Jenkins, A.** (2000). Using communicative tasks to teach vocabulary. *Guidelines, 22(2)*, 15–19.

Nation, I. S. P. (2001). *Learning vocabulary in another language*. Cambridge: Cambridge University Press.

Nation, I. S. P., & **Heatley, A.** (2002). RANGE: A program for the analysis of vocabulary in texts. http://www.victoria.ac.nz/lals/about/staff/paul-nation. Retrieved 4 April 2011.

Nation, I. S. P. (2004a). A study of the most frequent word families in the British National Corpus. In P. Bogaards & B. Laufer (Eds.), *Vocabulary in a second language: selection, acquisition and testing* (pp. 3–13). Amsterdam: John Benjamins.

Nation, I. S. P. (2004b). Vocabulary learning and intensive reading. *EA Journal, 21(2)*, 20–29.

Nation, I. S. P. (2005). Reading faster. *PASAA, 36*, 21–37.

Nation, I. S. P. (2006). How large a vocabulary is needed for reading and listening? *Canadian Modern Language Review, 63(1)*, 59–82.

Nation, I. S. P. (2007). The four strands. *Innovation in Language Learning and Teaching, 1(1)*, 1–12.

Nation, I. S. P., & **Beglar, D.** (2007). A vocabulary size test. *The Language Teacher, 31(7)*, 9–13.

Nation, I. S. P., & **Malarcher, C.** (2007). *Reading for speed and fluency*. Seoul: Compass Publishing.

Nation, I. S. P. (2008). Teaching vocabulary: strategies and techniques. Boston, M.A.: Heinle Cengage Learning.

Nation, I. S. P., & **Newton, J.** (2008). *Teaching ESL/EFL listening and speaking*. New York: Routledge.

Nation, I. S. P., & **Webb, S.** (2011). *Researching and analysing vocabulary*. Boston, M.A.: Heinle Cengage Learning.

Nation, I. S. P. (2012). The BNC/COCA word family lists. http://www.victoria.ac.nz/lals/about/staff/paul-nation. Retrieved 17 November 2015.

Nation, I. S. P., & **Yamamoto, A.** (2012). Applying the four strands to language learning. International *Journal of Innovation in English Language Teaching and Research, 1(2)*, 167–181.

Nation, I. S. P. (2013a). *Learning vocabulary in another language, second edition*. Cambridge: Cambridge University Press.

Nation, I. S. P. (2013b). *What should every ESL teacher know?* Seoul: Compass Publishing.

Nation, I. S. P. (2013c). *What should every EFL teacher know?* Seoul: Compass Publishing.

Nation, I. S. P., & **Anthony, L.** (2013). Mid-frequency readers. *Journal of Extensive Reading, 1(1)*, 5–16.

Nation, I. S. P., & **Waring, R.** (2013*). Extensive reading and graded readers.* Seoul: Compass Publishing.

Nation, I. S. P. (2014). How much input do you need to learn the most frequent 9,000 words? *Reading in a Foreign Language, 26(2)*, 1–16.

Nation, I. S. P. (2015). Principles guiding vocabulary learning through extensive reading. *Reading in a Foreign Language, 27(1)*, 136–145.

Nation, I. S. P., & **Anthony, L.** (2016). The picture vocabulary size test. Poster session presented at Vocab@Tokyo, Tokyo, Japan.

Neuman, S. B., & **Koskinen, P. S.** (1992). Captioned television as comprehensible input: effects of incidental word learning from context for language minority students. *Reading Research Quarterly, 27(1)*, 95–106.

Newton, J. (1995). Task-based interaction and incidental vocabulary learning: a case study. *Second Language Research, 11(2)*, 159–177.

Newton, J. (2013). Incidental vocabulary learning in classroom communication tasks. *Language Teaching Research, 17(2)*, 164–187.

Nguyen, L. T. C. (2015). Written fluency improvement in a foreign language. *TESOL Journal, 6(4)*, 707–730.

Nurmukhamedov, U., & **Sadler, R.** (2011). Podcasts in four categories: applications to language learning. In B. Facer & M. Abdous (Eds.), *Academic podcasting and mobile-assisted language learning: applications and outcomes* (pp.176–195). Hershey, P.A.: Information Science Reference.

Nurweni, A., & **Read, J.** (1999). The English vocabulary knowledge of Indonesian university students. *English for Specific Purposes, 18(2)*, 161–175.

Organization for Economic Co-operation and Development (2007). Communications outlook 2007. http://213.253.134.43/oecd/pdfs/ browseit/9307021E.PDF. Paris, France: OECD.

Oller, J. W., & **Streiff, V.** (1975). Dictation: a test of grammar based expectancies. *ELT Journal, 30(1)*, 25–36.

Orosz, A. (2009). The growth of young learners' English vocabulary size. In M. Nikolov (Ed.), *Early learning of modern foreign languages* (pp. 181–194). Bristol: Multilingual Matters.

Paivio, A., & **Desrochers, A.** (1981). Mnemonic techniques in second-language learning. *Journal of Educational Psychology, 73(6)*, 780–795.

Palmer, D. M. (1982). Information transfer for listening and reading. *English Teaching Forum, 20(1)*, 29–33

Parent, K. (2012). The most frequent English homonyms. *RELC Journal, 43(1),* 69–81.

Paribakht, T. S., & **Wesche, M. B.** (1996). Enhancing vocabulary acquisition through reading: A hierarchy of text-related exercise types. *Canadian Modern Language Review, 52(2),* 155–178.

Paribakht, T. S., & **Wesche, M. B.** (1999). Reading and 'incidental' L2 vocabulary acquisition. *Studies in Second Language Acquisition, 21(2),* 195–224.

Pawley, A., & **Syder, F. H.** (1983). Two puzzles for linguistic theory: nativelike selection and nativelike fluency. In J. C. Richards & R. W. Schmidt (Eds.), *Language and communication* (pp. 191–225). London: Longman.

Pellicer-Sanchez, A., & **Schmitt, N.** (2010). Incidental vocabulary acquisition from an authentic novel: Do Things Fall Apart? *Reading in a Foreign Language, 22(1),* 31–55.

Pellicer-Sánchez, A. (2016). Incidental L2 vocabulary acquisition from and while reading: an eye-tracking study. *Studies in Second Language Acquisition, 38(1),* 97–130.

Peters, E. (2007). Manipulating L2 learners' online dictionary use and its effect on L2 word retention. *Language Learning & Technology, 11(2),* 36–58.

Peters, E. (2012). Learning German formulaic sequences: the effect of two attention-drawing techniques. *The Language Learning Journal, 40(1),* 65–79.

Pigada, M., & **Schmitt, N.** (2006). Vocabulary acquisition from extensive reading: a case study. *Reading in a Foreign Language, 18(1),* 1–28.

Praninskas, J. (1972). *American university word list.* London: Longman.

Pressley, M. (1977). Children's use of the keyword method to learn simple Spanish vocabulary words. *Journal of Educational Psychology, 69(5),* 465–472.

Pulido, D. (2003). Modelling the role of second language proficiency and topic familiarity in second language incidental vocabulary acquisition through reading. *Language Learning, 53(2),* 233–84.

Pulido, D. (2007). The effects of topic familiarity and passage sight vocabulary on L2 lexical inferencing and retention through reading. *Applied Linguistics, 28(1),* 66–86.

Quero, B. (2015). Estimating the vocabulary size of L1 Spanish ESP learners and the vocabulary load of medical textbooks. Unpublished PhD thesis, Victoria University of Wellington, New Zealand.

Quinn, G. (1968). The English vocabulary of some Indonesian university entrants. *English Department Monograph IKIP Kristen Satya Watjana: Salatiga, 7(4)*.

Read, J. (2000). *Assessing Vocabulary*. Cambridge: Cambridge University Press.

Rice, M. L., & **Woodsmall, L.** (1988). Lessons from television: children's word learning when viewing. *Child Development, 59(2)*, 420–429.

Rodgers, M. P. H., & **Webb, S.** (2011). Narrow viewing: the vocabulary in related television programs. *TESOL Quarterly, 45(4)*, 689–717.

Rodgers, M. P. H. (2013). English language learning through viewing television: an investigation of comprehension, incidental vocabulary acquisition, lexical coverage, attitudes, and captions. Unpublished PhD thesis, Victoria University of Wellington, New Zealand.

Rodgers, T. S. (1969). On measuring vocabulary difficulty: an analysis of item variables in learning Russian-English vocabulary pairs. *IRAL, 7(4)*, 327–343.

Rogers, J., **Webb, S.**, & **Nakata, T.** (2015). Do the cognacy characteristics of loanwords make them more easily learned than noncognates?. *Language Teaching Research, 19(1)*, 9–27.

Rott, S. (1999). The effect of exposure frequency on intermediate language learners' incidental vocabulary acquisition through reading. *Studies in Second Language Acquisition, 21(1)*, 589–619.

Rott, S., **Williams, J.**, & **Cameron, R.** (2002). The effect of multiple-choice L1 glosses and input-output cycles on lexical acquisition and retention. *Language Teaching Research, 6(3)*, 183–222.

Rott, S. (2007). The effect of frequency of input-enhancements on word learning and text comprehension. *Language Learning, 57(2)*, 165–199.

Royer, J. M. (1973). Memory effects for test-like-events during acquisition of foreign language vocabulary. *Psychological Reports, 32*, 195–198.

Ruhl, C. (1989). *On monosemy: a study in linguistic semantics*. Albany: State University of New York Press.

Salisbury, D. F., & **Klein, J. D.** (1988). A comparison of a microcomputer progressive state drill and flashcards for learning paired associates. *Journal of Computer-Based Instruction, 15(4)*, 136–143.

Samuels, S. J. (1970). Effects of pictures on learning to read, comprehension and attitudes. *Review of Educational Research*, *40(3)*, 397–407.

Saragi, T., **Nation, I. S. P.**, & **Meister, G. F.** (1978). Vocabulary learning and reading. *System*, *6(2)*, 72–78.

Sasao, Y. (2013). Diagnostic tests of English vocabulary learning proficiency: guessing from context and knowledge of word parts. Unpublished PhD thesis, Victoria University of Wellington, New Zealand.

Sasao, Y., & **Webb, S.** (2017). The Word Part Levels Test. Language Teaching *Research*. *21(1)*. 12–30.

Sawada, K. (2009). Vocabulary acquisition through listening and its relation to learning channel Preferences. Unpublished PhD thesis, Temple University, Tokyo, Japan.

Sawyer, J., & **Silver, S.** (1961). Dictation in language learning. *Language Learning*, *11(1–2)*, 33–42.

Schmidt, R. W. (1990). The role of consciousness in second language learning. *Applied Linguistics*, *11(2)*, 129–158.

Schmitt, N. (1997). Vocabulary learning strategies. In N. Schmitt & M. McCarthy (Eds.), *Vocabulary: description, acquisition and pedagogy* (pp. 199–227). Cambridge: Cambridge University Press.

Schmitt, N. (2000). *Vocabulary in language teaching*. Cambridge: Cambridge University Press.

Schmitt, N., & **Carter, R.** (2000). The lexical advantages of narrow reading for second language learners. *TESOL Journal*, *9(1)*, 4–9.

Schmitt, N., **Schmitt, D.**, & **Clapham, C.** (2001). Developing and exploring the behaviour of two new versions of the Vocabulary Levels Test. *Language Testing*, *18(1)*, 55–88.

Schmitt, N., **Jiang, X.**, & **Grabe, W.** (2011). The percentage of words known in a text and reading comprehension. *Modern Language Journal*, *95(1)*, 26–43.

Schmitt, N., & **Schmitt, D.** (2014). A reassessment of frequency and vocabulary size in L2 vocabulary teaching. *Language Teaching*, *47(4)*, 484–503.

Schuetze, U. (2015). Spacing techniques in second language vocabulary acquisition: short-term gains vs. long-term memory. *Language Teaching Research*, *19(1)*, 28–42.

Scott, J. A., & **Nagy, W. E.** (2004). Developing word consciousness. In J. F. Baumann & E. J. Kame'enui (Eds.), *Vocabulary instruction: research to practice* (pp. 201–217). New York: Guilford Press.

Service, E. (1992). Phonology, working memory, and foreign language learning. *Quarterly Journal of Experimental Psychology*, *45(1)*, 21–50.

Shin, D., & **Nation, I. S. P.** (2008). Beyond single words: the most frequent collocations in spoken English. *ELT Journal*, *62(4)*, 339–348.

Simpson-Vlach, R., & **Ellis, N. C.** (2010). An academic formulas list: new methods in phraseology research. *Applied Linguistics*, *31(4)*, 487–512.

Smith, B. (2005). The relationship between negotiated interaction, learner uptake, and lexical acquisition in task-based computer-mediated communication. *TESOL Quarterly*, *39(1)*, 33–58.

Smith, J. W. A., & **Elley, W. B.** (1997). *How children learn to read.* Auckland: Addison Wesley Longman.

Smith, L. C., & **Mare, N. N.** (2011). *Reading for Today 3: Issues for Today, fourth edition,* Heinle Cengage Learning.

Smith, M. (1941). Measurement of the size of general English vocabulary through the elementary grades and high school. *Genetic Psychological Monographs*, *24*, 311–345.

Sokmen, A. J. (1992). Students as vocabulary generators. *TESOL Journal*, *1(4)*, 16–18.

Sonbul, S., & **Schmitt, N.** (2010). Direct teaching of vocabulary after reading: is it worth the effort? *ELT Journal*, *64(3)*, 253–60.

Sonbul, S., & **Schmitt, N.** (2013). Explicit and implicit lexical knowledge: acquisition of collocations under different input conditions. *Language Learning*, *63(1)*, 121–159.

Stahl, S. A., & **Vancil, S. J.** (1986). Discussion is what makes semantic maps work in vocabulary instruction. *The Reading Teacher, 40(1)*, 62–67.

Stahl, S. A., & **Clark, C. H.** (1987). The effects of participatory expectations in classroom discussion on the learning of science vocabulary. *American Educational Research Journal*, *24(4)*, 541–545.

Statistics Canada (1998). Average time spent on activities, by sex. Ottawa, Ontario: Author. http://www40.statcan.ca/l01/cst01/famil36a.htm, Retrieved October 21 2007.

Stauffer, R. G. (1942). A study of prefixes in the Thorndike list to establish a list of prefixes that should be taught in the elementary school. *Journal of Educational Research*, *35(6)*, 453–458.

Stoddard, G. D. (1929). An experiment in verbal learning. *Journal of Educational Psychology*, *20(6)*, 452–457.

Sueyoshi, A., & **Hardison, D. M.** (2005). The role of gestures and facial cues in second language listening comprehension. *Language Learning*, *55(4)*, 661–699.

Sutarsyah, C., **Nation, I. S. P.**, & **Kennedy, G.** (1994). How useful is EAP vocabulary for ESP? A corpus based study. *RELC Journal*, *25(2)*, 34–50.

Swain, M. (1985). Communicative competence: some roles of comprehensible input and comprehensible output in its development. In S. Gass & C. Madden (Eds.), *Input in second language acquisition* (pp. 235–253). Rowley, MA: Newbury House.

Swain, M., & **Lapkin, S.** (1998). Interaction and second language learning: two adolescent French immersion students working together. *Modern Language Journal*, *82(3)*, 320–337.

Swanborn, M. S. L., & **de Glopper, K.** (1999). Incidental word learning while reading: a meta-analysis. *Review of Educational Research*, *69(3)*, 261–285.

Swenson, E., & **West, M. P.** (1934). *On the counting of new words in textbooks for teaching foreign languages.* Toronto: University of Toronto Press.

Taylor, A. M. (2010). Glossing is sometimes a distraction: comments on Cheng and Good (2009). *Reading in a Foreign Language*, *22(2)*, 353–354.

Templin, M. (1957). Certain language skills in children: their development and interrelationships. *Institute of Child Welfare Monograph*, *No. 26*. Minneapolis: University of Minnesota.

Thorndike, E. L. (1908). Memory for paired associates. *Psychological Review*, *15(2)*, 122–138.

Thorndike, E. L., & **Lorge, I.** (1944). *The teacher's word book of 30,000 words.* New York: Teachers College, Columbia University.

Tinkham, T. (1989). Rote learning, attitudes, and abilities: a comparison of Japanese and American students. *TESOL Quarterly*, *23(4)*, 695–698.

Tinkham, T. (1993). The effect of semantic clustering on the learning of second language vocabulary. *System*, *21(3)*, 371–380.

Tinkham, T. (1997). The effects of semantic and thematic clustering on the learning of second language vocabulary. *Second Language Research*, *13(2)*, 138–163.

Tran, T. N. Y. (2012). The effects of a speed reading course and speed transfer to other types of texts. *RELC Journal*, *43(1)*, 23–37.

Uden, J., **Schmitt, D.**, & **Schmitt, N.** (2014). Jumping from the highest graded readers to ungraded novels: four case studies. *Reading in a Foreign Language, 26(1)*, 1–28.

United States Bureau of Labor (2006). American time use survey summary. Washington, D.C.: Author. http://www.bls.gov/news.release/atus.nr0.htm. Retrieved 21 October 2007.

Valipouri, L., & **Nassaji, H.** (2013). A corpus-based study of academic vocabulary in chemistry research articles. *Journal of English for Academic Purposes, 12(4)*, 248–263.

van Daalen-Kapteijns, M. M., & **Elshout-Mohr, M.** (1981). The acquisition of word meanings as a cognitive learning process. *Journal of Verbal Learning and Verbal Behavior, 20(4)*, 386–399.

van Daalen-Kapteijns, M., **Elshout-Mohr, M.**, & **de Glopper, K.** (2001). Deriving the meaning of unknown words from multiple contexts. *Language Learning, 51(1)*, 145–181.

van Zeeland, H., & **Schmitt, N.** (2013). Lexical coverage in L1 and L2 listening comprehension: the same or different from reading comprehension? *Applied Linguistics, 34(4)*, 457–479.

Verspoor, M., & **Lowie, W.** (2003). Making sense of polysemous words. *Language Learning, 53(3)*, 547–586.

Vidal, K. (2003). Academic listening: a source of vocabulary acquisition? *Applied Linguistics, 24(1)*, 56–89.

Vidal, K. (2011). A comparison of the effects of reading and listening on incidental vocabulary acquisition. *Language Learning, 61(1)*, 219–258.

Vongpumivitch, V., **Huang, J.**, & **Chang, Y. C.** (2009). Frequency analysis of the words in the Academic Word List (AWL) and non-AWL content words in applied linguistics research papers. *English for Specific Purposes, 28(1)*, 33–41.

Walters, J. (2006). Methods of teaching inferring meaning from context. *RELC Journal, 37(2)*, 176–190.

Wang, J., **Liang, S. L.**, & **Ge, G. C.** (2008). Establishment of a medical academic word list. *English for Specific Purposes, 27(4)*, 442–458.

Wang, M-T. K., & **Nation, I. S. P.** (2004). Word meaning in academic English: homography in the academic word list. *Applied Linguistics, 25(3)*, 291–314.

Ward, J. (2009). A basic engineering English word list for less proficient foundation engineering undergraduates. *English for Specific Purposes, 28(3)*, 170–182.

Waring, R. (1997a). A study of receptive and productive learning from word cards. *Studies in Foreign Languages and Literature (Notre Dame Seishin University, Okayama)*, *21(1)*, 94–114.

Waring, R. (1997b). The negative effects of learning words in semantic sets: a replication. *System*, *25(2)*, 261–274.

Waring, R. (2000). *The 'why' and 'how' of using graded readers*. Tokyo: Oxford University Press.

Waring, R., & **Takaki, M.** (2003). At what rate do learners learn and retain new vocabulary from reading a graded reader? Reading in a Foreign Language, 15(2), 130–163.

Watanabe, Y. (1997). Input, intake, and retention: effects of increased processing on incidental learning of foreign vocabulary. *Studies in Second Language Acquisition*, *19(3)*, 287–307.

Webb, S. (2002). Investigating the effects of learning tasks on vocabulary knowledge. Unpublished PhD thesis, Victoria University of Wellington, New Zealand.

Webb, S. (2007a). The effects of repetition on vocabulary knowledge. *Applied Linguistics*, *28(1)*, 46–65.

Webb, S. (2007b). The effects of synonymy on second language vocabulary learning. *Reading in a Foreign Language*, *19(2)*, 120–136.

Webb, S. (2008a). Receptive and productive vocabulary size. *Studies in Second Language Acquisition, 30(1)*, 79–95.

Webb, S. (2008b). The effects of context on incidental vocabulary learning. *Reading in a Foreign Language*, *20(2)*, 232–245.

Webb, S., & **Nation, I. S. P.** (2008). Evaluating the vocabulary load of written text. *TESOLANZ Journal*, *16*, 1–10.

Webb, S. (2009a). The effects of receptive and productive learning of word pairs on vocabulary knowledge. *RELC Journal, 40(3)*, 360–376.

Webb, S. (2009b). The effects of pre-learning vocabulary on reading comprehension and writing. *Canadian Modern Language Review, 65(3)*, 441–470.

Webb, S., & **Rodgers, M. P. H.** (2009a). Vocabulary demands of television programs. *Language Learning, 59(2)*, 335–366.

Webb, S., & **Rodgers, M. P. H.** (2009b). The lexical coverage of movies. *Applied Linguistics, 30(3)*, 407–427.

Webb, S. (2010a). A corpus driven study of the potential for vocabulary learning through watching movies. *International Journal of Corpus Linguistics, 15(4)*, 497–519.

Webb, S. (2010b). Using glossaries to increase the lexical coverage of television programs. *Reading in a Foreign Language, 22(1)*, 201–221.

Webb, S. A., & **Chang, A. C.-S.** (2012a). Second language vocabulary growth. *RELC Journal, 43(1)*, 113–126.

Webb, S., & **Chang, A. C.-S.** (2012b). Vocabulary learning through assisted and unassisted repeated reading. *Canadian Modern Language Review, 68(3)*, 1–24.

Webb, S. (2013). Depth of vocabulary knowledge. In C. Chappelle (Ed.), *Encyclopedia of applied linguistics* (pp. 1656–1663). Oxford, UK: Wiley-Blackwell.

Webb, S., & **Boers, F.** (2013) Do textual enhancement techniques increase incidental learning of collocation? Paper presented at Vocab@Vic conference, Wellington, New Zealand.

Webb, S., & **Macalister, J.** (2013). Is text written for children appropriate for L2 extensive reading? *TESOL Quarterly, 47(2)*, 300–322.

Webb, S., **Newton, J.**, & **Chang, A. C.-S.** (2013). Incidental learning of collocation. *Language Learning, 63(1)*, 91–120.

Webb, S. (2015). Extensive viewing: language learning through watching television. In D. Nunan & J. C. Richards (Eds.), *Language learning beyond the classroom* (pp. 159–168). New York, NY: Routledge.

Webb, S., & **Chang, A. C.-S.** (2015a). Second language vocabulary learning through extensive reading: how does frequency and distribution of occurrence affect learning? *Language Teaching Research, 19(6)*, 667–686.

Webb, S., & **Chang, A. C.-S.** (2015b). How does prior word knowledge affect vocabulary learning progress in an extensive reading program? *Studies in Second Language Acquisition, 37(4)*, 651–675.

Webb, S., & **Paribakht, T. S.** (2015). What is the relationship between the lexical profile of test items and performance on a standardized English proficiency test? *English for Specific Purposes, 38(1)*, 34–43.

Webb, S., & **Chang, A. C.-S.** (under review). How does mode of input affect the learning of multiword combinations?

Webb, S., **Sasao, Y.**, & **Ballance, O.** (2017). The updated Vocabulary Levels Test: Developing and validating two new forms of the VLT. *International Journal of Applied Linguistics, 168(1)*.

Webb, W. B. (1962). The effects of prolonged learning on learning. *Journal of Verbal Learning and Verbal Behavior, 1*, 173–182.

Wei, Z. (2015). Does teaching mnemonics for vocabulary learning make a difference? Putting the keyword method and the word part technique to the test. *Language Teaching Research, 19(1)*, 43–69.

Wei, Z., & **Nation, I. S. P.** (2013). The word part technique: a very useful vocabulary teaching technique. *Modern English Teacher, 22(1)*, 12–16.

West, M. (1953). *A general service list of English words*. London: Longman, Green & Co.

White, T. G., **Power, M. A.**, & **White, S.** (1989). Morphological analysis: implications for teaching and understanding vocabulary growth. *Reading Research Quarterly, 24*, 283–304.

Winke, P., **Gass, S.**, & **Sydorenko, T.** (2010). The effects of captioning videos used for foreign language listening activities. *Language Learning & Technology, 14(1)*, 65–86.

Wissman, K. T., **Rawson, K. A.**, & **Pyc, M. A.** (2012). How and when do students use flashcards? *Memory, 20(6)*, 568–579.

Wray, A. (2002). *Formulaic language and the lexicon*. Cambridge: Cambridge University Press.

Xue, G., & **Nation, I. S. P.** (1984). A university word list. *Language Learning and Communication, 3(2)*, 215–229.

Yang, M. N. (2015). A nursing academic word list. *English for Specific Purposes, 37*, 27–38.

Zhou, A. A. (2009). What adult ESL learners say about improving grammar and vocabulary in their writing for academic purposes. *Language Awareness, 18(1)*, 31–46.

Zipf, G. (1949). *Human behavior and the principle of least effort: an introduction to human ecology*. New York: Hafner.

INDEX

Page numbers annotated with 'g,' 't' and 'f' refer to glossary entries, tables, and figures respectively.